STOLEN TREASURE

*The Hunt for the
World's Lost Masterpieces*

KONSTANTIN AKINSHA
& GRIGORII KOZLOV
with
SYLVIA HOCHFIELD

Weidenfeld & Nicolson
LONDON

First published in Great Britain in 1995 by
Weidenfeld & Nicolson

The Orion Publishing Group Ltd
Orion House
5 Upper Saint Martin's Lane
London WC2H 9EA

A catalogue record for this book is available
from the British Library

ISBN 0 297 81428 1

Typeset by Selwood Systems, Midsomer Norton
Printed in Great Britain by Butler & Tanner Ltd, Frome and London

CONTENTS

HOSTAGES OF THE COLD WAR

REVELATIONS

ILLUSTRATIONS

Irina Antonova taking part in the unloading of trophy artworks on the steps of the Pushkin Museum, 1945 (Akinsha–Kozlov Archive)
Trucks arriving at the Pushkin Museum, 1945 (Akinsha–Kozlov Archive)
Depository of books in Ransbach mine, Merkers, 1945 (Klaus Goldmann)
Depository of books in Uzkoe church, Moscow, 1992 (Klaus Goldmann)
Master of the Prodigal Son, *Susanne and the Elders* (Akinsha–Kozlov Archive)

Between pp 168 and 169
A model of the Palace of the Soviets (Alex Lachmann)
Segei Merkurov, Kliment Voroshilov and Boris Vipper examining the trophy art works at the Pushkin Museum (Akinsha–Kozlov Archive)
Special depository, Pushkin Museum, November 1949 (Pavel Knishevsky)
Relief by Andrea de la Robia in the special depository of the Hermitage (Akinsha-Kozlov Archive)
Donatello, *Madonna with Child and Four Cherubs*, damaged by fire, the Hermitage, 1957 (Akinsha–Kozlov Archive)
Soviet leaders at the May Day military parade, late 1940s (ITAR–TASS)
Alexander Poskrebishev, Stalin's secretary, 1940s (ITAR–TASS)
Stalin's kitsch (Jamey Gambrell)
Pavin Korin copying the Sistine Madonna in the Pushkin Museum, Moscow, 1955 (Archive Staatliche Kunstsammlungen Dresden)
Nellandian's painting of Lenin admiring the Sistine Madonna (Jamey Gambrell)
Kukrinski's cartoon, *Return of the Dresden Gallery*, 1955 (Yuri Albert)
A propaganda drawing by the East German artist Hermann Kohlmann, *Painting is saved* (Archive Staatliche Kunstsammlungen Dresden)

Between pages 232 and 233
Trinity Monastery in Sergiev Posad (Viktor Baldin)
Joseph Stalin's death mask, made by Sergei Merkurov (Edouard Zhigailov)
The authors with the Bremen drawings, March 1993 (Alexander Kholopov)
Albrecht Dürer, *Landscape with a Castle Near a River* (Akinsha–Kozlov Archive)
Henri de Toulouse-Lautrec, *La Goulu* (Akinsha–Kozlov Archive)
Adrian von Ostade, *Tavern Scene* (Akinsha–Kozlov Archive)
Hans Baldung Grean, *Two Heads* (Akinsha–Kozlov Archive)
Jacob Jordaens, *King David* (Akinsha–Kozlov Archive)
A shipping document for the Trojan Gold (Akinsha–Kozlov Archive)
Manet, *Portrait of Rosetta Mauri* (Akinsha–Kozlov Archive)
Wilhelm Schirmer landscapes, Academy of Sciences sanatorium, Mozzhinka (Photo by Konstantin Gararin; Akinsha–Kozlov Archive)
Klaus Goldmann examining the Trojan Gold, Pushkin Museum, 26 October 1994 (Bildarchiv Preussischer Kulturbesitz)
Daumier, *Revolt* (Akinsha–Kozlov Archive)

PRINCIPAL CHARACTERS

ABAKUMOV, VIKTOR   General; head of SMERSH ('Death to Spies'); head of Ministry of State Security (MGB). He took part in the plot against Marshal Zhukov, was arrested in 1951 by his arch competitor, NKVD head Lavrenty Beria, and was tried for treason and executed in 1954.

ALEXANDROV, GEORGY   Head of the Department of Propaganda and Agitation of the CC CP USSR during the 1940s. As minister of culture, 1954–55, he most likely initiated the return of the Dresden Gallery to the GDR. Too popular for Krushchev and too liberal for the old guard in the Kremlin, he was accused of immorality in 1955 and expelled from Moscow.

ALEXEYEV, BORIS   Major in the trophy brigade active in Dresden, Leipzig, Berlin, and Gotha; head of Department of Sculpture, Department of Visual Arts, Arts Committee of the CPC USSR; later representative of the Arts Committee in Thuringia and Saxony. A porcelain expert, he was a curator at the Kuskovo Museum in Moscow before the war. He selected for removal porcelain objects from Dresden and paintings from the Museum of Fine Arts in Leipzig.

ANTIPENKO, NIKOLAI   Lieutenant general; head of the Home Front of the First Belorussian Front. He helped Belokopitov get Marshal Zhukov's order to remove artworks from the Zoo tower.

ANTONOVA, IRINA   Director, Pushkin Museum. As a young staff member, she helped unload and inventory the Trojan gold and the Dresden Gallery.

BELOKOPITOV, ANDREI   Lieutenant colonel/colonel; head of the trophy brigade active in Meseritz and Berlin. His brigade discovered the collection of the Kaiser Friedrich Museum in Posen stored in an underground shelter near Hohenwalde, the first important depository in German territory to be cleaned out by the Arts Committee brigades. Later he removed artworks from the Zoo tower in Berlin and sent the Trojan gold and paintings from German private collections to Moscow. In civilian life manager of the Moscow Art Theatre (MKhAT).

BERIA, LAVRENTY   Chief of state security (NKVD). One of Stalin's most trusted henchmen, he was executed soon after the dictator's death in 1953.

BERZARIN, NIKOLAI   Colonel general; commander of the Fifth Shock Army; military commandant of Berlin. He took an active part in protecting art valuables. He died in a traffic accident in 1945.

BLAVATSKY, VLADIMIR   Prominent art historian and archaeologist; professor at Moscow State University; lieutenant colonel in the trophy brigade active in Berlin and Dresden. He selected sculptures and antiquities from the New Mint in Berlin and sculptures from Dresden for removal to the USSR. In 1946 he led the excavation of the burned Friedrichshain flak tower.

BOKOV, FYODOR   Lieutenant general; member of the Military Council of the Fifth Shock Army; member of the Military Council of the Soviet Military Administration in Germany. He was responsible for the activity of the trophy brigades in the military administration.

CHEGODAYEV, ANDREI   Major in the trophy brigade active in Silesia. He removed tens of thousands of art books, which are still in the Pushkin Museum's library. He was the first curator of the museum's Dresden Gallery holdings. In October 1945 he was a member of the commission of the CC CP USSR that investigated charges of corruption in the trophy brigades in occupied Germany.

CHURAKOV, STEPAN   Captain/major in the trophy brigade active in Dresden and Leipzig. He selected and packed paintings and was in charge of special train No. 176/1760 that delivered the best works from the museums of Leipzig and Gotha to Moscow. In civilian life restorer.

DENISOV, LEONTY   Colonel; head of the Arts Committee brigade on the Second Belorussian Front. He sent art works from Danzig and the famous Marienburg coin collection to Moscow. In civilian life deputy head, Department of Visual Arts, Arts Committee of the CPC USSR.

DRUZHININ, SERAFIM   Major in the trophy brigade active in Berlin. He was responsible for searching for art valuables in the city and on Museum Island in particular, and packed the Trojan gold and other valuables found in the Zoo tower. He was in charge of the first special train, No. 176/2284, in which the Pergamum Altar, Degas' *Place de la Concorde*, and other masterpieces were sent to Moscow. In civilian life curator at the Tretyakov Gallery.

FILIPPOV, BORIS   Lieutenant colonel; head of Arts Committee brigade of the First Ukrainian Front, active in Silesia. In civilian life director of the Moscow Drama Theatre.

GRABAR, IGOR   Painter, architect, and art historian. He was one of the most prominent cultural figures in the Soviet Union. He drew up the plan to compensate Soviet museums for their losses with 'equivalent' works of art from enemy countries and headed the Bureau of Experts of the Extraordinary Commission, 1943–45, that composed the list of art works to be removed.

GRIGOROV, SERGEI   Major in the trophy brigade active in Silesia and Dresden. He was the main expert selecting paintings for removal from the Dresden Gallery. In civilian life chief secretary, Commission on the Registration and Preservation of Monuments.

GUBER, ANDREI   Chief curator of the Pushkin Museum after the war. He helped organize the museum's special depositories. In 1957 he was an author of the plan for the mutual return of art valuables by the USSR and GDR, but later he protested the one-sided return of art trophies.

IVANOV-CHURONOV, MIKHAIL   Major in the trophy brigade active in Dresden and Berlin. He helped pack the Dresden treasures, then investigated the Friedrichshain tower with Blavatsky. In civilian life restorer at the Tretyakov Gallery.

KAPTSOV, BORIS   Major in the trophy brigade active in Berlin. He helped remove art works from Museum Island and was in charge of special train No. 176/1758 from Berlin to Leningrad. In civilian life head of the Design Workshop, Tretyakov Gallery.

KHARKO, LEV   Major in the trophy brigade active in Danzig. He found art treasures in the bomb shelter of the city armoury and the famous Marienberg coin collection in the vault of a ruined bank. In civilian life curator at the Pushkin Museum.

KHRAPCHENKO, MIKHAIL   Head of Arts Committee of the CPC USSR. He was responsible for carrying out Stalin's order to remove art valuables from Germany. He supported the idea of creating a museum of world art in Moscow after the war.

KLIMOV, VASILY   First lieutenant in the trophy brigade active in Berlin. He took part in the removal of art works from Museum Island and the New Mint and was in charge of special train No. 176/1759 from Berlin to Moscow. In civilian life curator at the Tretyakov Gallery.

KONEV, IVAN   Marshal; commander of the First Ukrainian Front. He took an active part in deciding the fate of the Dresden Gallery when he telegraphed Stalin about the discovery of the collection.

KONSTANTINOV, ANDREI   Deputy head, Arts Committee of the CPC USSR. He was responsible for the activity of the Arts Committee trophy brigades. In May 1945 he was head of the Arts Committee group sent to Berlin to decide the fate of the art treasures of Germany.

KUCHUMOV, ANATOLY   Before the war, curator of the Palaces of Tsarskoe Selo; after the war, director of the Central Repository of Museum Valuables of the Palaces on the outskirts of Leningrad. In 1946 he was sent to Königsberg to investigate the fate of the Amber Room and decided it had not been destroyed in the castle fire. In 1947 he found numerous art works from Soviet collections in Berlin and sent them back to the USSR.

LAZAREV, VIKTOR   Prominent art historian; professor at Moscow State University. In 1943 he was one of the authors of the plan to compensate Soviet museums for their losses with 'equivalent' works of art from enemy countries. In Berlin he selected paintings for removal to the USSR. He tried to limit the number of art works removed, so that German museums would not be destroyed.

LUDSHUVEIT, YEVGENY   First lieutenant; representative of the

Trophy Department of the 47th Army. He was responsible for protecting and later removing the art works from the Potsdam palaces.

MANEVSKY, ALEXEI   Lieutenant colonel in the trophy brigade active in Berlin and Saxony. His mission was to collect books, archaeological and historical materials, and scientific collections, but he removed art works as well. In civilian life head of Department of Museums, Committee on Cultural Educational Institutions of the CPC Russian Federation; director of Research Institute of Museum and Regional Studies. He was fired during the campaign against 'cosmopolitanism' in the late 1940s because of his Czech origin and died soon after.

MERKUROV, SERGEI   Director of the Pushkin Museum during and after the war. In 1944 he proposed a plan to establish a museum of world art in Moscow based on trophy artworks. A well-known sculptor, he specialized in gigantic statues of Lenin and Stalin and made the death masks of prominent officials.

MIKHAILOV, NIKOLAI   Minister of culture, 1955–60. He took an active part in preparing the return of the Dresden Gallery. In 1957 he was appointed head of the commission that decided the fate of trophy valuables, and in 1958–59 he was in charge of the return of art works to East Germany.

NOVIKOV, FYODOR   Major in the trophy brigade active in Berlin and Saxony. He worked on Museum Island in Berlin, removed Dessau art works from the Solvayhall mine near Bernburg, and was in charge of special train No. 176/8042 from Berlin to Leningrad. In civilian life director of the Second Travelling Theatre.

ORBELI, JOSEF   Director of the Hermitage Museum during and after the war. He organized the unloading and sorting of trophy art works received from Germany. In 1946 he testified at the Nuremberg Trials about the German destruction of Soviet museums.

PIOTROVSKY, MIKHAIL   Director of the Hermitage Museum.

PONOMAREV, NIKOLAI   First lieutenant in the trophy brigade active in Dresden. In civilian life a student at the Moscow Art Institute. He later became head of the USSR Union of Artists.

RABINOVICH, LEONID   Second lieutenant of the 164th Trophy Battalion of the Fifth Guard Army. He was responsible for protecting the

Dresden Gallery paintings until an Arts Committee trophy brigade arrived from Moscow. In the 1950s he created the myth of the 'rescue' of the Dresden Gallery, used in Soviet and East German propaganda.

ROTOTAYEV, ALEXANDER   Colonel; head of the trophy brigade active in Dresden; after the war deputy head of the Arts Committee of the CPC USSR. He competed with other brigade members to be named 'rescuer' of the Dresden collection.

SABSAI, YULI   Major in the trophy brigade active in Berlin. In civilian life official, Arts Committee of the CPC USSR.

SABUROV, MAXIM   During the early years of the war head of Gosplan, the national planning board that ran the economy of the USSR. As a representative of the secret Special Commission on Germany, his responsibility was to remove material valuables from the occupied country. After the war he was again appointed head of Gosplan, then became deputy head CPC and a member of the country's ruling body, the Presidium of the CP CC.

SIDOROV, SERGEI   Major/lieutenant colonel in the trophy brigade active in Meseritz and Berlin. He was in charge of the first special train that delivered trophy art works to Moscow, from Meseritz (now Poland), in April 1945, and of special train No. 178/4090–91 from Berlin to Leningrad. In civilian life chief inspector, Department of Visual Arts, Arts Committee of the CPC USSR.

SOKOLOVA, NATALIA   Major in Filippov's trophy brigade active in Silesia. She decided to look for the Dresden Gallery collection and became the first Arts Committee expert to see the Sistine Madonna after its discovery. She selected Pillnitz castle as a collecting point for Dresden art works. In civilian life curator of the Museum of New Western Painting, Moscow.

TELEGIN, KONSTANTIN   Lieutenant general; member of the Military Council of the First Belorussian Front; member of the Military Council of the Group of Soviet Occupation Forces in Germany. He gave orders to remove artworks from Leipzig and other cities. After the war he was arrested by Stalin's order in connection with the plot against Marshal Zhukov, looting being one of the accusations against him. He was released from the gulag after Stalin's death.

TSIRLIN, ILYA   First lieutenant in the trophy brigade active in Königsberg. He took part in the search for the Amber Room. In civilian life a postgraduate student at the Institure of Art, he later became one of the first art critics active in the cultural underground. He was accused of homosexuality and died in mysterious circumstances at the beginning of the 1960s.

VIPPER, BORIS   Deputy director of the Pushkin Museum during and after the war. He was a member of the Arts Committee subcommittee responsible for receiving and distributing trophy valuables.

VOLODIN, MIKHAIL   First lieutenant in the trophy brigade active in Dresden. In civilian life a student at the Moscow Art Institute. After the war, he sent numerous letters to state agencies claiming that the brigade had 'rescued' the Dresden Gallery collection.

VOLOSHIN, ALEXANDER   Major/lieutenant colonel in the trophy brigade active in Berlin and Leipzig. He found the paintings of the Leipzig Museum of Fine Arts, served in the Arts Committee brigade in Berlin from May 1945 to August 1946. After his return to Moscow, he was fired from the brigade because of the scandal connected with the contraband found in the same plane as the Trojan gold. In civilian life circus director.

ZAMOSHKIN, ALEXANDER   Representative of the Arts Committee in Berlin. He removed works of art from Museum Island and the New Mint and sent trains loaded with trophies to the Soviet Union in wintertime. Director of the Tretyakov Gallery during the war, he later became director of the Pushkin Museum and took part in preparing the exhibition of art works returned to the GDR in 1958–59.

ZERNOV, PYOTR   Major general; representative of the Special Committee on Germany in Berlin. He coordinated the activities of the trophy brigades of all government departments in Berlin, including the Arts Committee brigades.

ZHUKOV, GEORGY   Marshal; deputy to the Supreme Commander of the Red Army; commander of the First Belorussian Front; chief commander of Soviet Occupation Forces in Germany; head of Soviet Military Administration in Germany. He gave Belokopitov the order to remove the Pergamum Altar and other art valuables from the Zoo tower within forty-eight hours. Later he ordered the removal of works of art from Museum Island and the New Mint. His own collection of trophy art works and other booty was confiscated when Stalin, jealous of his popularity, turned against him. He was exiled to the Urals until Khrushchev brought him back to become defence minister, but he displayed too much independence and was dismissed.

ZORIN, LEONID   Major general; head of Department of Reparations and Supplies, Soviet Military Administration in Germany. He was in charge of the restitution of art works looted from Soviet museums by the Germans. In 1948 he was responsible for the removal of the Otto Krebs Collection and its transport to the Hermitage.

ACKNOWLEDGEMENTS

We would like first of all to thank Milton Esterow, editor and publisher of *ARTnews* magazine, without whom the story of art trophies hidden in the vaults of Soviet museums would have remained untold. His friendship and support during the years of preparing this book made him much more than a publisher to us. Our thanks go also to the staff of *ARTnews*, where our articles dedicated to the trophy problem have appeared since 1991.

We are grateful to our teachers – Dmitry Sarabianov and Alexander Morozov of Moscow State University and the late Alexander Kamensky – for their support at a critical moment. Dr Morozov also gave us much valuable advice throughout the writing of this book.

To Dr Rudolf Blaum, head of the Bremen Kunstverein, and Dr Peter Hasskamp, chairman of the Management Board of the Bremen Landesbank, we owe the research grant that allowed us to work in German archives and visit the places described in the book. Our special gratitude goes to Dr Wolfgang Eichwede, director of the Research Centre for Eastern Europe of Bremen University for his friendship and encouragement, and for the free access he gave us to the Centre's rich collection of documents on Soviet museum losses during the Second World War. Dr Werner Schmidt, general director of the Dresden State Museums, gave us access to archives and made it possible for us to tour the fortress and castles in the area of Dresden where the museums' treasures were hidden during the Second World War.

We could not have written so complete an account of the trophy problem without the help of Dr Klaus Goldmann, chief curator of the Museum for Pre- and Early History in Berlin. An enthusiast who has dedicated his life to finding the art treasures that disappeared during the war, Dr Goldmann provided us with important documents from his private archive and shared with us his incomparable knowledge of the subject. Professor Dr Armin Jahne, of Humboldt University in Berlin, also gave us valuable assistance.

Igor Torbakov, of the *Christian Science Monitor* bureau in Moscow, and Alexey Sobchenko, of Radio Liberty in Munich, helped us monitor the numerous publications on the restitution problem in the Russian and international press. Dr Pavel Knishevsky used his unrivalled knowledge of Russian archival collections on our behalf.

The late Bernard V. Bothmer, chairman emeritus of the Department of Egyptian and Classical Art at the Brooklyn Museum, shared with us his memories of prewar German collections and on one notable occasion acted as a messenger in a situation that was not without peril.

We are deeply grateful to Tete and Astrid Böttger, who with awesome generosity turned over their country house to us for nine months while we worked on this book. The friendship and support of Caroline Moorehead, Suzanne Schutz, and Ginger Henry-Künzel helped make it a reality.

We would like to express our gratitude to several Russian citizens whose names cannot be mentioned.

INTRODUCTION

In 1920, the Russian economist and writer Alexander Chayanov published, under the pseudonym Ivan Kremnev, a utopian novel, a vision of the future Russia entitled *My Brother Alexei's Journey to the Land of the Peasant Utopia*. Among other events, he described a war with Germany:

> On 7 September three German armies escorted by clouds of aeroplanes invaded the Russian Peasants' Republic ... Two days later the invasion was halted. The Berlin government surrendered and said that it was ready to pay a contribution in any form. The Council of People's Commissars chose a few dozen canvases by Botticelli, Domenichino, Titian, Holbein, the Pergamum Altar, and a thousand Chinese prints of the Tang dynasty.

Chayanov was wrong about the date, the duration, and the difficulty of the actual war with Germany, which began twenty-one years after his book appeared. Indeed, his only accurate prediction was about one of the German 'contributions'. At the end of the war, in 1945, the huge Pergamum Altar, built in the second century BC, was transported to the Soviet Union from Berlin. Reality was in fact more extravagant than Chayanov's fantasy: not just a few dozen canvases but more than two and a half million art objects, books and archival documents were confiscated from the defeated Germans. It was the most prodigious secret removal of looted cultural property in human history, carefully organized and carried out by the Red Army and the Soviet military administration. Museum collections and the property of German citizens were ransacked and hauled back as war booty, along with objects that had been 'bought' by the Nazis in France and the Netherlands, seized in Poland, or confiscated by Eichmann from Hungarian Jews bound for the gas chambers.

The Soviet government had been planning since 1943 to strip the conquered enemy of all kinds of property in compensation for its own terrible losses. Works of art were to be collected by special trophy brigades made up of art historians, museum officials, artists and restorers. They were given officers' uniforms and sent to Germany to find objects of cultural value – museum and library collections, musical instruments and theatrical equipment, printing presses and film projectors – and send them back to the USSR. The trophy brigades were unlike the American army's Monuments, Fine Arts & Archives group, whose mission was to preserve monuments and works of art from theft and destruction. The MFAA officers shored up bombed churches and palaces, put vandalized collections in order, and tracked down art looted or hidden by Germans. They brought together hundreds of thousands of works of art in collecting points, cared for them, and ultimately returned them to German museums or their country of origin. When the United States government decided to bring 200 paintings from the Berlin museums to Washington to be kept in 'protective custody' in the basement of the National Gallery of Art, MFAA officers protested against the removal as 'neither morally tenable nor trustworthy'. Their protest was successful: the paintings were returned to Berlin. Soviet trophy brigade members, in contrast, never protested against the policies of their government. Only one person, the eminent art historian Viktor Lazarev, tried to limit the extent of the looting, but no one paid any attention.

The Soviet trophy brigades justified their activity with 'An eye for an eye': the ruined palaces of Peterhof and Tsarskoe Selo, the blasted churches of Novgorod and Pskov, the devastated cities and villages of Ukraine and Belorussia were in their minds. Museums and libraries in the territory occupied by the Germans had been destroyed. Thousands of paintings, icons, and objects of applied art from the museums of Kiev and millions of books from its libraries had been sent to Germany. The picture gallery in Kharkov was looted and burned. Minsk was totally denuded of its rich and valuable collections.

The Nazis despised Slavic culture and attacked it with special brutality. When German troops first entered the USSR they were welcomed in many areas as liberators by a population terrorized by Stalin's tyranny, but disillusionment was swift. The Germans considered the Slavs fit only to toil for the Reich. Three and a half million Soviet prisoners of war died in German prison camps. Millions of Soviet citizens were driven into forced labour, tortured in concentration camps, massacred in cold blood, or starved to death.

The Jewish population of Ukraine, Lithuania, and other occupied territories, was eradicated.

The looting of conquered enemies is hardly a new phenomenon. The Romans flaunted their prisoners and their captured treasure through the streets of the capital. Inspired by their example, Napoleon did much the same over 2,000 years later, parading the bronze horses of Saint Mark's through the streets of Paris. All of the Old World's great museums were enriched by plunder. But at the end of the nineteenth century, the idea developed that cultural monuments had to be shielded from military conflict. This concept was embodied in the Hague Conventions of 1899 and 1907, which included articles designed to protect cultural institutions, historical monuments, and works of art from 'premeditated seizure, destruction, or damage'. Both the German Reich and the Russian Empire signed these conventions.

But idea and reality diverged. During the First World War, the German army destroyed Belgian churches and libraries. The victorious Allies included a paragraph in the Versailles peace treaty giving works of art and historic objects from German museums to Belgium and other damaged countries. A few months after the beginning of the Second World War, the Soviet government adopted the Hague Convention that the czarist government had signed in 1907. Nevertheless, both Nazi Germany and the Soviet Union methodically robbed museums and cultural institutions in occupied territories. Their plunder of cultural objects was as unprecedentedly thorough as the violence against human beings.

As early as 1943, Soviet cultural officials had discussed the need to establish a supermuseum in Moscow filled with trophies – not so different from Hitler's project for a grand Führer Museum in Linz. The Soviet pillaging of European art was less efficient than that of the Nazis, however. There was even a touch of absurdity about the enterprise. The Russian émigré writer Sergei Dovlatov wrote in his diary about a high-ranking Soviet cultural official who was sent to occupied Germany as a political commissar. There he 'collected' porcelains, bronzes and wristwatches, but the real object of his desire was a good German typewriter. Finally, in a ruined office, he found a shiny new one. It was very heavy, but the ecstatic commissar carried it across half of Europe, thinking that in Moscow he could have the German characters replaced with Cyrillic ones. When he took the typewriter to a Soviet repair shop and asked for the keys to be changed, however, the mechanic answered that this was impossible because the looted typewriter had Hebrew characters, which printed from right to left.

The pointless theft of the typewriter is analogous to that of the works of art that became Soviet 'prisoners of war'. The paintings, sculptures, *objets d'art*, books, and archives that was transported to the Soviet Union never found their way to a supermuseum where they could be exhibited or made available to scholars. About a million paintings, drawings, books and archival documents were hidden, and are still hidden today. The Trojan gold excavated by Heinrich Schliemann, masterpieces by El Greco and Daumier, Degas and van Gogh, drawings by Dürer and manuscripts by Goethe were missing from world culture for half a century. They were as inaccessible to the Soviet public as to everyone else. Many were damaged or destroyed.

The looting of Germany, which took place against a background of rising tensions between the Soviet Union and the Allies, was part of the prologue to the cold war. The fate of the trophies mirrors the strange turns of Soviet history in the last half-century, from Stalin's postwar foreign policy and Khrushchev's aborted reforms through the stagnation of the Brezhnev era to the fever of post-perestroika Russia. The story is not over yet. Today, when nationalistic ideas have become more and more influential in Russian life, even the trophy works of art whose existence has been acknowledged are being turned into hostages of politics.

The trophy brigades tried hard to conceal their activities from the Western Allies. The atmosphere of secrecy was profound and sometimes surrealistic – even information about the losses of Soviet museums was hidden. For decades, the people who knew about the existence of the special depositories filled with looted art from Germany were afraid to speak about them. Even at the beginning of the perestroika period, an article devoted to the subject was censored so heavily it became meaningless. At the same time, rumours circulated in the art community about the stores of hidden art. In Russia, Mme de Staël quipped, everything is a mystery but nothing is secret.

We began our joint research into the problem of trophy art eight years ago. We interviewed many participants in the events in Germany; worked in the archives of Russia, Ukraine and Germany; read American documents in the archives of *ARTnews* magazine and in private archives. We also have our own archive. But we found the most sensational information about the political background of Soviet occupation policy in defeated Germany and about the activity of the trophy brigades in accessible files in the central Moscow archives. The notoriously inefficient Soviet bureaucracy never classified a great number of documents containing detailed information about the secret depositories. Even though responsible cultural officials still believe that the key to the mystery is hidden in some secret place, exactly the opposite is true.

In 1991 we published our first article about the problem of trophy art in *ARTnews*. The result was to make the fate of the looted works of art a subject of international discussion. We have continued to research the history of the operation, and in this book we have tried to tell the story of our own experience as well as to reveal the trophy saga. Since the publication of that first article, the position of Soviet and later Russian cultural officials has changed frequently. In the beginning they denied the existence of secret depositories. Now they have revealed the location of such looted treasures as the Trojan gold and the Koenigs Collection of old master drawings from Rotterdam. The Hermitage has exhibited looted drawings from the Bremen Kunsthalle and, recently, Impressionist and Post-Impressionist canvases from private German collections. The Pushkin Museum, too, has shown trophy paintings and has promised to exhibit the Trojan gold.

The question of what to do with war loot, which had become a subject of little interest outside academic circles, is once again hotly debated. The revelation of the secret depositories has triggered the biggest treasure hunt since the end of the war, with the heirs to sequestered collections, museums, auction houses, and governments preparing their claims. Early in 1995, a conference in New York called 'The Spoils of War' was attended by representatives of the Russian and German governments and experts on restitution from all over the world. But if information about the location of works of art removed from world culture for so many years has finally become known, the story of their sad odyssey from West to East remains untold. This book is an attempt to reconstruct it.

May 1995

THE MYSTERIES
OF THE GOLD AND
THE AMBER

A DISCOVERY IN THE
BASEMENT

One day in September 1987, Grigorii Kozlov, who had recently become the curator of the new Museum of Private Collections in Moscow, a branch of the Pushkin Museum, was asked by a colleague to make photocopies of some papers. In 1987 this was still a formidable task. Copying machines were rare in the Soviet Union, and there were none in the Pushkin Museum. But Kozlov had worked in the Ministry of Culture and had friends there, and he thought he could use his connections to get access to a copier.

Kozlov walked across Gogolevsky Boulevard and turned into the Arbat on a warm, sunny day at the height of an Indian summer. The ministry was housed in a huge and imposing nineteenth-century mansion opposite the Vakhtangov Theatre. Officials joked that it had been a brothel before the Revolution and, they hinted ironically, it still was. After the Revolution the prostitutes had been evicted and the building was turned into communal apartments. Then, in the mid-1970s, the Ministry of Culture was moved there from a smaller and less stately building, and the interior was completely renovated. There was a concert hall, a buffet restaurant, and offices and conference rooms opening off long, intimidating corridors whose parquet floors were covered with wide strips of the red carpet that was traditional for Soviet officialdom.

When Kozlov reached the fourth floor, where the Department of Visual Arts was located, he saw with astonishment that piles of papers and books were strewn about in complete disorder. At first he thought there had been an accident of some sort. Then he saw a former colleague, G., walking towards him with a heap of old documents in his arms.

'What's going on?' Kozlov asked him.

'We had a *subbotnik* yesterday,' G. answered.

A *subbotnik*, from the word *subbota*, Saturday, was a day of 'voluntary' labour. The custom was established by Lenin and transformed into a completely involuntary exercise. Kozlov's friend told him that the chief of the department of museums had decided to clean out old papers and other 'junk'. They had already thrown away tons of documents, he said, and then he told Kozlov to help him carry a batch to the basement, where they would be destroyed. Kozlov took part of the load and followed him.

The basement was the realm of the technical staff, and Kozlov had never been there before. They walked through narrow corridors where pipes ran in all directions below low ceilings and doors were sheathed in metal. Some of the doors were open, and they could see chauffeurs and electricians playing chess and dominoes in tiny rooms shrouded in clouds of tobacco smoke. Finally they stopped, and G. knocked on a door that was soon opened by a woman wearing a dirty white overall, a gauze mask and rubber gloves. She was carrying a long knife.

'Ach, they've brought more,' she said to someone inside. The room was dimly lit by a couple of unshaded light bulbs hanging from the ceiling, and the air was full of dust. Another woman similarly attired was standing at a big metal table heaped with bundles of old documents, cutting the strings and throwing the papers into a pile on the floor. At the other end of the room there was a shredding machine. The woman who had opened the door showed the men where to put their loads. In the dim light Kozlov noticed that a sheet of paper lying on the floor near his foot had the words 'State Pushkin Museum' at the top. He picked it up and began to read. G. was in a hurry, and left Kozlov alone with the two women.

'May I see the papers?' Kozlov asked them. 'Maybe I'll find something I need.'

'Certainly,' answered the older one. 'Take a knife and cut the strings. Your help is welcome.'

Kozlov was having trouble breathing in the dusty air, and he made a mask of his handkerchief. As he opened the bundles, he glanced quickly over each paper. On the sheet he had picked up from the floor, he noticed something that made his heart skip a beat. Near the name of the museum was written in red pencil the word 'restitution'. The word conjured up an event that he had until recently thought he knew all about: the Soviet Union's return to East Germany in 1955 of the masterpieces taken from the Dresden Gallery at the end of the Second World War. The 'rescue' of the Dresden Gallery was the major cultural event of the war as far as the Soviet Union was concerned, and its restitution ten years later was a milestone in relations between the two countries.

Like every Soviet schoolchild, Kozlov had learned the official story of the Red Army's discovery of the Dresden Gallery collection during the final days of the war. The contents of one of the world's great museums was said to have been found hidden in a flooded underground cave near the little village of Gross Cotta and had been saved from destruction by heroic Soviet forces. Raphael's beloved altarpiece known as the Sistine Madonna, along with 750 other treasures of world art had been brought to Moscow, hidden for ten years, and then magnanimously returned to the German Democratic Republic. This act of friendship was trumpeted in a massive propaganda campaign that contrasted the generosity of the Soviet Union with the greed of the American imperialist warmongers who had looted Germany and sold their plunder to private collectors.

While researching an exhibition devoted to the arts in wartime, Kozlov had picked up some information about the Dresden Gallery story that made him question the official version. He had been told by Nikolai Ponomarev, an important official of the Union of Artists who had taken part in the Dresden operations, that the pictures had been stored in reasonably well-equipped mine tunnels, not in the dark, flooded caves of the familiar story. The old restorer Praskovia Korina had filled in a few more pieces of the puzzle. Recalling how she and her husband, the famous painter and restorer Paul Korin, had worked on pictures from the Dresden Gallery in 1945, she flatly denied that the paintings had been seriously damaged by humidity. If they were right, then the legend of the rescue of the Dresden Gallery taught to all Soviet schoolchildren was nothing but propaganda.

There was much more to the story that remained secret or had been forgotten. Kozlov had read in old newspapers that there had been a second, quiet, return of hundreds of thousands of works of art to East German museums by the Khrushchev government in the late 1950s. But his attempts to find out how and why this immense number of works had come to the Soviet Union in the first place had led nowhere. The second return had never been transformed into a legend for popular consumption. Kozlov realized that it was easier to create a myth about the dramatic rescue of a single collection than to explain how a good half of German museum objects had ended up after the war in the Soviet Union.

A more urgent question had occurred to him: could there be works of art removed from Germany that were still hidden in secret storerooms in the Soviet Union – great and famous masterpieces that the world believed destroyed or lost?

Now, cutting the strings and sorting quickly through the brittle papers in the cellar of the Ministry of Culture, Kozlov hoped to find answers to some of his questions. He could see that the documents were important. After half an hour of digging in the dusty heaps, he found what he wanted: minutes of the Soviet–German negotiations for the return of the Dresden Gallery pictures and papers dealing with their exhibition in Moscow before they were sent back to Germany. Kozlov kept on sorting through the papers, hoping for more information. And then he turned up something that made him gasp. A handwritten document was titled 'List of the Most Important Works of Art Kept in the Special Depository of the Pushkin Museum'. Another was called 'Unique Objects from the "Large Trojan Treasure," Berlin, Völkerkundemuseum'. It was signed by Nora Eliasberg, acting chief curator of the Pushkin Museum, and dated 28 March 1957. Kozlov had in his hands evidence that the famous Trojan treasure excavated by Heinrich Schliemann in 1873, which had mysteriously disappeared from Berlin in 1945, had not been destroyed but had been hidden in the Soviet Union for over forty years.

SCHLIEMANN'S TREASURE

The 'Trojan treasure' listed in Nora Eliasberg's inventory was more than simply one of the greatest archaeological discoveries in history. From the moment Heinrich Schliemann announced to the world that he had found the treasure of King Priam of Troy, the ancient gold and silver objects had exerted a special hold over the popular imagination. Had Priam himself poured wine into this small gold goblet? Had Helen of Troy worn these diadems and adorned her fingers with the gold rings?

Schliemann was a rich German businessman and amateur archaeologist obsessed with proving that the Trojan War was a real event, not just a legend handed down by generations of bards to the blind Homer. He believed that Priam and Helen, Hector and Agamemnon were real people. The discovery of the golden hoard was his proof.[1]

Had Schliemann been a better archaeologist, he might never have found his treasure at all. He was digging in the right place – the hill of Hissarlik, on the northwestern coast of Anatolia – but he was so fiercely impatient to find something extraordinary that he dug right through the city that is probably Priam's Troy, which was destroyed in fire or earthquake about 1200 BC. He was looking for monumental ruins, and in April 1873 he thought he had found them: a tall double gateway, a long stone ramp, and the remains of a substantial building he was convinced was King Priam's palace. One hot morning a few weeks later he was digging in a wall near the gate when he suddenly noticed, at a depth of twenty-eight feet, a 'container or implement of copper of remarkable design'. The container was broken, and he could see that there was something made of gold behind it.

Schliemann cut into the wall with a large knife, ignoring the threat of a structural collapse. 'The sight of so many objects, every one of which was of inestimable value to archaeology, made me foolhardy,' he later wrote, 'and I never thought of any danger.' After transferring everything to the wooden hut where he stored his finds, he locked the door, covered the windows, and spread the treasures out on a table. The objects had been packed in a disorderly manner, one crammed inside another or bent to fit a small space. There was a large copper shield and a flat-bottomed cauldron, a silver goblet and three silver vases, a gold bottle and gold cups. There were silver knife blades and copper daggers and lance heads. At the bottom of the largest silver vase Schliemann found two elaborate diadems, a slender fillet, four intricately worked ear drops, fifty-six earrings, six bracelets, two small goblets, and 8,750 rings and buttons, most of them tiny. The gold had a rich reddish glow. One of the diadems was made of ninety chains of little rings, with delicate pendants shaped like leaves and flowers, and long tassels hanging down the sides. 'In my imagination,' Schliemann wrote, 'I saw the fair Helen, and during this moment of overwhelming emotion I conjured up the picture of a Grecian queen on Trojan soil bedecked with jewels.'

Perhaps there was such a queen, but she was not Helen. 'King Priam's Treasure' and the other hoards Schliemann found were about 1,200 years older than Homer's Troy. But he had rediscovered a lost world and demonstrated that the city of the *Iliad* could plausibly be identified with the mound of Hissarlik.

Schliemann had no intention of letting the Turkish authorities know about his discovery. His permit obliged him to share his finds with the state, but he smuggled the treasure out of the country and into Greece, and in June he abruptly terminated his excavation at Hissarlik. From Athens, he wrote letters to all of Europe's learned societies announcing that he had made 'the greatest discovery of our age, the one which all men have been looking forward to', but while he was exulting in the treasure he was also hiding it, in stables, barns, and farmyards all over Greece, where it would be safe from Greek as well as Turkish authorities.

The next April, the furious Turks sued Schliemann in a Greek court for half the treasure. The trial dragged on for a year and ended in a victory for the German archaeologist. He was ordered to pay the Turks an indemnity of 10,000 gold francs. As a friendly gesture, he sent 50,000 gold francs to the Imperial Museum in Constantinople, along with some of the less important finds.

In 1881 Schliemann presented the treasure to the German nation, 'in perpetual possession and inalienable custody', and Berlin museum officials promised that it would be on view in the Völkerkundemuseum for all time. It remained there for sixty years, in a wing with Schliemann's name written in gold letters above the doors.

In 1937, as war became imminent, officials of the Berlin State Museums were told to safeguard their precious possessions, and all the exhibits of the Museum for Pre- and Early History, as the Völkerkundemuseum was now called, were packed up and trundled down to the basement.[2] Objects made of precious metals and those that were considered irreplaceable, including most of the objects from Troy, were packed into three crates. An inventory list was stuck into each crate and they were sealed. In January 1941 most of the museum's exhibits, including the three crates, were moved to the vault of the Prussian State Bank to protect them from air bombardment. Later that year they were moved again, to one of the new fortress-like anti-aircraft towers that Albert Speer's workshop had designed to protect the capital of the Reich. Two of these steel and concrete behemoths, which were considered impregnable, had been fitted out with rooms earmarked as repositories for Berlin's cultural treasures. The Museum for Pre- and Early History was assigned two rooms on the north side of the tower near the zoological garden – the Flakturm Zoo.

The Zoo tower, occupying almost an entire city block, was the largest of the Flakturms. From its roof, the Luftwaffe directed the defence of Berlin, firing off 128mm guns with a deafening boom. Ammunition was stored deep below ground and brought up in steel lifts. The museum's exhibits remained in the tower until 1945. By this time the surrounding area was reduced to rubble. The zoo was destroyed and most of the animals killed. A team of veterinarians chopped up the carcasses of the dead elephants to be processed into soap and bonemeal, and hungry Berliners were said to be cooking crocodile tails and sausage made of dead bears.

In February 1945 the directors of the Prussian State Museums were ordered to evacuate all their collections to an area west of the Elbe, which had been designated as an American and British occupation zone if there were to be a surrender. The Germans did not want their treasures to fall into Russian hands. But the museum directors thought it would be so dangerous to move the collections on roads, railways, or waterways subject to enemy bombing that they were unwilling to obey the order. Hitler himself was consulted, and in March a 'Führer's Order' was issued. The works of art were moved.

Marshal Zhukov, deputy supreme commander of the Red Army and leader of the assault on Berlin, launched the final battle for the capital on 16 April 1945. By this time, most of the art treasures had left the city, headed for several salt mines. Many ended up in Merkers, where they were found by General Patton's Third Army. Several thousand crates filled with works of art and archaeological objects, including fifty from the Museum for Pre- and Early History, were discovered in Grasleben by the American First Army. But the three crates containing the Trojan gold had a different fate.

Dr Wilhelm Unverzagt, director of the Museum for Pre- and Early History and a loyal Nazi, had obeyed Hitler's order to transport his collection out of the city – except for the three precious crates. He did not want them to leave Berlin, and as the Red Army attacked the Zoo tower he remained with the crates, sleeping on top of them at night. The din of battle was made more horrible by the groans of the wounded from the hospital that had been set up in a nearby room. Corpses and amputated limbs piled up. Terrified civilians who had fled the bombardment were crammed in so tightly that they could hardly move. The city was in flames.

The devoted Unverzagt remained in the tower after everyone else had fled. On 1 May, the day after Hitler's suicide, it was surrendered to the Russians. They swarmed in, clattering up and down the staircases looking for loot. Unverzagt stood his ground until a senior officer appeared. He told him about the treasure packed in the crates and asked for his help. The officer posted guards at the door of the room. A few days later, Colonel General Berzarin, the Soviet commander of the city, came to inspect the tower and assured Unverzagt that the crates would be taken to a safe place. At the end of May, the three crates containing the Trojan gold were loaded onto a Studebaker truck. Unverzagt never saw them again.

The fate of Priam's gold was one of the great mysteries of the Second World War. Scholars had been attempting to track it down for over four decades by the time Grigorii Kozlov picked up the piece of paper on the basement floor that indicated that the treasure was locked away somewhere in Moscow's Pushkin Museum, an MIA from yet another siege and the sacking of a great city. The document that pointed the way to the gold was part of a huge puzzle that was about to be unravelled, a puzzle that involved a vast hoard of stolen things.

THE AMBER ROOM

If the Trojan gold became a symbol of the cultural treasures lost by the Germans, the Amber Room from the Catherine Palace in Tsarskoe Selo played the same role for the Russians. It was a unique masterpiece and the Russians have been reluctant to accept that it is gone for ever. Although they possess abundant evidence that it was destroyed, they have continued to search for it. The Amber Room seems to exert a strong force over the minds of treasure hunters.

The Amber Room was made in Germany. It came to Russia because a Prussian king was a penny-pincher. The idea of using amber for interior decoration belonged to Andreas Schluter, the court architect of King Frederick I of Prussia. Traditionally, amber was used for jewellery or small boxes, but the king had a large collection of the material, and Schluter thought a room panelled entirely in amber, with a mirror set in a carved amber frame on each wall, would be spectacular. German master craftsmen spent twelve years carving the material, but the room was unfinished when Frederick died in 1713. His successor, Frederick William I, did not want to spend any more money on his father's expensive caprice, and the unfinished decorations were packed and stored.

In 1716 the king presented the room to Peter the Great of Russia. According to legend, the Russian emperor expressed his gratitude to the Prussian king, whose only passion was for tall soldiers, by sending him fifty-five guardsmen, every one of them over six feet tall. The unfinished decorations were shipped to Russia and forgotten for more than thirty years until Peter's daughter, the Empress Elizabeth, decided to complete Schluter's vision. She ordered Bartolomeo Francesco Rastrelli, the court architect, to install the panels in the Winter Palace in St Petersburg. When Frederick the Great, who had succeeded Frederick William as king of Prussia, heard that the Russian empress was unhappy because the fourth mirror frame had not been completed by the German masters, he decided to surprise her and ordered the last frame to be made in Königsberg.

The empress was delighted with her 'Precious Box' made of amber. It was in this small but opulent room that she met foreign ambassadors, impressing them with the luxury of her residence. A few years later she had the room moved to her new summer palace at Tsarskoe Selo, outside the city. It was installed in a much larger space, so mirrored pilasters with gilt bronze candelabra were made to fit between the panels. Above them were Florentine mosaics made of multicoloured jasper framed in amber. A carved and gilded wood frieze ran around the room. It took German craftsmen another fifteen years to make eight additional panels, overdoor decorations and a corner table, all of amber. When the work was finished, in 1770, the room was a dazzling sight. It was illuminated by 565 candles whose light was reflected in the warm gold surface of the amber and sparkled in the mirrors, gilt, and mosaics. The Amber Room was famous all over Europe and was visited by every traveller to Russia. Théophile Gautier composed a rhapsodic description of it. For almost 200 years it was the jewel of the Catherine Palace.

On 22 June 1941, the day German troops overran the Soviet Union, officials of the Catherine Palace, which had become a museum, tried to remove one of the amber panels from the wall. It crumbled in their hands. They decided to leave the room where it was, and covered the panels with paper and cloth for protection. On 17 September Nazi troops took Tsarskoe Selo. The museum officials had all fled, leaving the palace to the mercy of fate. Tsarskoe Selo was near the front. The vanguard units of the German army were stationed in the palace, which was shelled by Soviet artillery. In November, by order of the German commanders, Captain Solms-Laubach and Captain Poeng-sen, the officers of a special so-called art protection unit of Army Group North, supervised the dismantling of the Amber Room and removed it to Königsberg. The German officers and seven soldiers accomplished in thirty-six hours what the Soviet museum officials had been unable to manage.

In 1942 the Germans installed the Amber Room in Königsberg Castle. It survived the fire that began after the Allied bombardment of the city in August 1944 with minimum damage; only the mirrored pilasters and some small panels were destroyed. The last German document connected with the Amber Room is dated 12 January 1945. At that time the room was being packed up again because officials had decided to evacuate it to Saxony.

What happened after that day remains a mystery. On 15 January Königsberg was surrounded by Soviet troops, and on 10 April the city was stormed and almost completely destroyed.

In May a Soviet commission led by Professor Alexander Brusov began to investigate the fate of the Amber Room. Their main inform-ant was Dr Alfred Rohde, director of the Königsberg art collections. He was a fanatic lover of amber, and it was thanks to his initiative that the room had been sent to Königsberg. Rohde told Brusov that the crates filled with amber panels were still in the castle on 5 April, when he left the building. But when the castle burned, the crates burned too. Rohde showed Brusov the room where he had left the crates, and Brusov saw for himself the charred fragments. He picked up bits of gilded wood decoration and copper hinges that he believed had belonged to the doors. He ended the search and informed Moscow that the famous room had been destroyed.

That would have been the end of it, and the Amber Room might not have disturbed the imaginations of art historians and treasure hunters, if Anatoly Kuchumov, a curator of the czarist palaces outside Leningrad, had not come to Königsberg in March 1946. Sifting through the debris in the great hall of the castle where Rohde had showed Brusov the remains of the Amber Room, he found three of the mosaics, which crumbled when he touched them. But he did not find any remains of amber, and he decided that, although the other elements of the room might have burned up, the amber panels had not. He ordered a new search.

This time it was not art historians but secret police from the MGB, the Ministry of State Security, who looked for the lost treasure. Rohde could not be found; he had mysteriously disappeared. The police decided that he had been lying, and Brusov was called back from Moscow and accused of criminal negligence because he had trusted Rohde and been tricked by him. After his treatment at the hands of the MGB he returned to Moscow and had a heart attack. But the secret police were no more successful than he had been.

Still dissatisfied with the results of the searches, the Ministry of Culture of the Russian Federation organized a 'geological–archae-ological expedition' in Kaliningrad, as Königsberg was now called. The neutral term was camouflage for a secret operation: yet another attempt to find the Amber Room. The expedition worked for almost thirty years, but all its documents were classified and the names of people involved were changed in the few articles the Soviet press was allowed to publish on the subject.

Rumours and fairytales inevitably flourished on the subject. According to one story, a group of SS men had forced Russian prisoners to hide the Amber Room and then shot them so they could never reveal where it was. There were rumours about an underground passage from Kaliningrad to Berlin. After the suicide of George Stein, a German researcher into the fate of the room, who was mentally unstable, journalists remembered the disappearance of Rohde and began to write about the 'curse of the Amber Room'.

Until 1984 the Russian expedition looked for the treasure in various places in Kaliningrad and in nearby castles and country estates. Finally the Russian Ministry of Culture decided that further search was useless and ended the operation.

With the coming of perestroika, the closed city of Kaliningrad became accessible, and foreigners – mostly Germans – continued the search. Many believe that Rohde hid the Amber Room in a secret place in the city or nearby and then tricked the Russians into thinking it had been destroyed. But their efforts to find the secret shelter have also failed.

Another version of the story holds that the room was evacuated from Kaliningrad to Danzig, where it was loaded on board the *Wilhelm Gustloff*, bound for Hamburg. The boat left the harbour on 30 January 1945, with 8,000 civilians, 1,500 submarine trainees, and a valuable cargo on board. A few hours later it was torpedoed by a Soviet submarine. Only 950 people were saved. The rest perished in what was the greatest sea disaster of all time. There were five times as many victims as on the *Titanic*. If the amber were indeed on the *Wilhelm Gustloff* it returned to its source at the bottom of the Baltic Sea.[1]

Two other versions of the Amber Room's fate are based on the belief that it was evacuated to central Germany. One might call them the 'English version' and the 'American version'. According to the former, half the crates containing the Amber Room decorations were evacuated by rail, together with the library and the amber collection of Königsberg University. All these valuables were hidden by the Nazis in a mine near Göttingen, together with a supply of ammunition. When British troops occupied the area, they exploded the mine, believing that it contained only ammunition.[2] The 'American version' holds that the room was sent to Thuringia and stored either in the Grasleben mine or in Merkers. There it was found by the Americans and taken to the United States, where it presumably remains.

Finally, there is what we might call the 'Moscow version'. Elena Storozhenko, who led the Russian Ministry of Culture expedition for many years, says she does not exclude the possibility that the Amber Room survived, in Germany or America or even in Moscow. Considering how carelessly many valuables were treated at the end of the war, 'It's not so fantastic,' she says. 'Many of the objects sent by Brusov may be stored still unpacked today in various depositories. Who knows what is stored where? And remember that many valuables were removed by military officials as private trophies. Anything is possible.'[3]

THE LOOTING
OF GERMANY

MOSCOW

How Much Is a Rembrandt Worth?

At the end of the last winter of the Second World War, like many of his colleagues in Moscow's academic institutions, Professor Vladimir Bogdanov was asked to compile a list of objects in German museums that he thought were exceptionally valuable. The order to do this came from a powerful group: the Extraordinary State Commission on the Registration and Investigation of the Crimes of the German-Fascist Occupiers and Their Accomplices and the Damage Done by Them to the Citizens, Collective Farms, Public Organizations, State Enterprises, and Institutions of the USSR.

This awkwardly titled commission was established in November 1942 to deal with problems connected with the Nazi occupation, from investigating the horrors of the concentration camps liberated by the Red Army to estimating the value of the art looted from Soviet museums. Late in 1945 the commission would have more sinister duties: it sent thousands of Soviet citizens – former prisoners of war and other 'traitors' – to the gulag.[1]

The head of the Extraordinary Commission was Nikolai Shvernik, who had made his career as a merciless political commissar during the civil war. After Lenin's death in 1924 he supported Stalin in his challenge to the old guard of the Party. Stalin made him Party secretary in Leningrad, the stronghold of the opposition, and Shvernik did so well in purging his boss's enemies that in 1926 he was appointed secretary of the Communist Party Central Committee. His main occupation during the war was the Extraordinary Commission.

Bogdanov, a professor at Moscow State University and head of the museology department at the Institute of Museology and Regional Studies, had visited Germany before the war and was familiar with German museum collections. He refreshed his memory with the help of museum catalogues, research monographs and turn-of-the-century Baedeker guidebooks. His list of things that had exceptional value for ethnographical and ethnological research included twenty-nine objects and collections from the museums of Berlin, Frankfurt, Nuremberg and Bremen. Bogdanov's list was remarkably detailed, including not only short descriptions of the desired collections and their locations but even the rooms or galleries in which they could be found. In some cases he explained why those collections were valuable to the USSR. No. 13 on his list was 'Trojan Ethnological Collections excavated by Schliemann 1871–82'. The short commentary said: 'Have extreme value for research of history of South Russia and ethnic origins of Slavic population'.[2]

Bogdanov was not the only one who remembered the so-called Diadem of Helen of Troy and the other dazzling gold and silver objects he had seen in Berlin. Another expert mentioned the same treasures and gave a more detailed commentary:

> The collection has great value for the study of the antiquities of the USSR. Russian scholars have established not only a certain similarity between it and some categories of objects of South Russian origin, but have discovered the existence of some types of objects in the central regions of the Union that are close to the Trojan one.

Then the expert added: 'We must remember that Schliemann first offered his collection to the Russian Government.'[3] He withdrew the offer when the government refused to put the gold in the Hermitage, the czar's private collection.

Professor Bogdanov and his academic colleagues had been given their research assignments as the result of an idea hatched by Igor Grabar, one of the most prominent men in the cultural life of the Soviet Union. In the spring of 1943 Grabar wrote a letter to Shvernik proposing that Soviet museums damaged by the Nazis should receive compensation after the war in the form of works of art equivalent to their losses from enemy collections. Shvernik liked the idea immediately.

Grabar was a painter, architect and art historian who had been famous since before the Revolution. He had been a member of the World of Art group, whose romantic winter landscapes in a style heavily influenced by French Impressionism became emblems of the Russian Silver Age. Grabar was popular in Germany as well as in Russia, thanks to Diaghilev's 1906 exhibition of Russian art in Paris and Berlin. The exhibition was so successful that even Kaiser Wilhelm II visited it. Grabar, who spoke excellent German, was his guide and later remembered that the Kaiser's bad taste and ignorance of art had made a very unfavourable impression on him.

Grabar was also an extremely influential art historian and an Academician, a member of the prestigious Academy of Sciences. The thirteen-volume *History of Russian Art* he co-edited and partly wrote played a major role in the rediscovery of Russian eighteenth-century painting and architecture. Unlike many of his friends, Grabar did not emigrate after the Revolution. On the contrary, he demonstrated his loyalty to the new regime and very soon received a high position in the Soviet cultural hierarchy. In the 1930s he reached the acme of his career when his book about Ilya Repin, his former teacher and aesthetic rival, was honoured with a Stalin Prize, the highest award of the Soviet state.

Grabar continued to paint, but he gave up his famous Impressionist style for the traditional Realism favoured by the regime. His huge canvas depicting Lenin reading a telegram as it spools out of a teletype machine became the classic example of state-approved official art. In 1933 he painted a portrait of a young girl that was reproduced all over the country. The girl's name was Svetlana and she was Stalin's daughter – a fact never mentioned but known to everyone. Before the Revolution, an enemy had coined a nickname for Grabar, Ugor Obmanuilovich Grobar, a play on words based on his three names and roughly translatable as 'Eel Humbugovich Coffin'. Grabar had the slipperiness of an eel. He was one of those who have the gift of being in favour in every regime and are very difficult to catch.[4]

The recommendation of so influential a figure was received with respect. When Grabar learned that his idea interested high-ranking officials, he sent a more detailed plan to Shvernik.

Because the matter of collecting equivalents in certain cases in compensation for artworks removed or destroyed by the GFO [German-Fascist occupants] was settled positively by the ESC [Extraordinary State Commission] of the CPC [Council of People's Commissars] of the USSR, I think it is a timely measure to establish now a special division of ESC to make up lists of objects in the museum collections of Germany, Austria, Italy, Hungary, Romania, and Finland that could be named as eventual equivalents. Business trips abroad would not be necessary for the conduct of this work because complete sets of the catalogues of all European museums are in the libraries of some Soviet art historians, and their own notes contain complete information about these museums.

Grabar suggested that a troika of experts – on painting, sculpture, and applied arts – be appointed as a special division of the Extraordinary Commission. He named the three people he considered best qualified: Viktor Lazarev, former curator of paintings at the Pushkin Museum; Sergei Troinitsky, former director of the Hermitage; and 'the author of this letter', namely himself. 'Such a troika,' he concluded, 'has the ability to accomplish this task in a short time.'[5] Shvernik approved. He noted on the letter, 'Igor Grabar's proposition deserves attention. We must remember to use the persons mentioned for work in the expert commissions', and sent it on to the Politburo.[6] Vladimir Makarov, head of the culture department of the Extraordinary State Commission, also liked Grabar's proposal. He sent Shvernik a detailed report, analysing the tasks of the future board and proposing to name it the Bureau of Experts. Grabar's brainchild – an expert committee to select works of art belonging to European museums that could be taken to the USSR after the war – became a reality.[7]

Actually describing or evaluating Soviet cultural losses – the damage to property and the works of art for which European equivalents were to be found – was not an easy matter at this point. Novgorod, Pskov, the palaces outside Leningrad, Kiev and Minsk were still occupied by the Germans. Grabar and his commission had some information about the situation in the occupied territories, but it was incomplete and inaccurate. In the days of hysteria and confusion that followed the invasion by the Germans, the evacuation of museum collections had not been a major concern and was sometimes carried out incompetently. When German troops were on the threshold of Kiev, local officials ordered museum directors to give priority to evacuating objects made of nonferrous metals because of their industrial value. As a result, nineteenth-century bronze candlesticks of little art historical significance were saved, while Renaissance paintings were left in the occupied city. In other cases, the evacuation of museum treasures was prevented by military and Party officials who wanted to demonstrate to the public that the situation was not so desperate as it seemed. When the collections of Peterhof, Peter the Great's palace outside Leningrad, were packed into crates and ready for transportation, officers of the NKVD (the predecessor of the KGB) stopped the evacuation by accusing museum workers of defeatism and asking them if they thought the courageous Red Army would surrender Peterhof to the enemy. Thus, numerous museum collections were left in the territory occupied by the German army.

By the end of 1941 Ukraine and Belorussia were occupied. In the Russian Federation the cities of Novgorod and Pskov, both major historical landmarks, had been battlegrounds before they were taken by the enemy. Leningrad was never captured, but the great czarist palaces outside the city were occupied, pillaged, and destroyed during the bombardments and artillery duels. Some of the worst damage was due to a special order issued by Stalin in November 1941, commanding the Red Army to 'destroy and burn out all populated areas behind the German lines situated at a distance of 40–60 kilometres behind the front line and to a distance of 20–30 kilometres on the right and left sides of the roads.'[8] (Anatoly Kuchumov, who was a curator of the Tsarskoe Selo museums outside Leningrad, stated in an interview in 1993 that the Catherine Palace was burned not by the Nazis but by Soviet air force bombardment.[9] Soviet cities and villages occupied by the Nazis were treated by Red Army commanders as enemy territory.)

From the first days of the war, the Nazis prepared to strip Soviet museums. As early as the summer of 1941, Hans Posse, who was entrusted by Hitler with acquiring a collection for the grandiose museum the Führer planned to build in his native city of Linz, Austria, chose Nils von Holst, an expert on the Leningrad collections, to select objects for the museum. In October, Alfred Rosenberg, head of the Einsatzstab-Reichsleiter Rosenberg (ERR), whose mission was to gather material and property that illustrated German superiority in creative expression, wrote to Hitler, asking him to place von Holst under the command of the ERR, because it was responsible for the transport of objects to the Reich. Another competitor after spoils was Reichsmarschall Hermann Goering, who sent a special group to Leningrad led by state secretary Kaj Mühlmann, who had been the commissioner for confiscation of art treasures in Poland.

Minsk, the capital of Belorussia, fell to the Nazis on the seventh day of the war. Most of its art objects were confiscated, but Mühlmann, Himmler, and other interested parties had time to capture some of the spoils. After the invasion, Minsk was so totally denuded of its treasures that Wilhelm Kube, commissioner general for Belorussia, wrote to Rosenberg:

Minsk possessed rich and valuable collections of paintings and art objects, which were almost completely removed from the city. According to the orders of ... Himmler, the SS sent numerous pictures to Germany ... These were treasures worth millions, which the general regions of Belorussia lost. The pictures should have been sent to Linz and Königsberg [East Prussia].[10]

In Kiev the special troops confiscated and sent to Germany thousands of paintings, icons and objects of applied art from the city's museums and plundered millions of books from its libraries. Hundreds of pictures were stolen from the Kharkov and the Smolensk museums. Since most of these collections were incompletely catalogued, and lists of stolen objects were not compiled at the time, it is still difficult to know precisely what was taken, but the objects included icons, European paintings and drawings, nineteenth-century Russian art, and objects of applied art.[11]

In spite of the difficulty in establishing exactly what the Soviet Union had lost, Grabar's Bureau of Experts met frequently in 1943, in the nineteenth-century building on Pushkin Street in the centre of Moscow that housed the Commission on the Preservation and Registration of Monuments, also headed by Grabar.[12] On 22 October they held a particularly important meeting, to discuss the problem of paying for the research necessary to compose the lists of equivalents. Grabar told the others:

We need equivalents in all fields. All this must be divided among people who know German and West European museums. It seems that the question will be raised about Germany and Austria, but we still think that Romania, Hungary, and Finland are included. We did a lot of work finding equivalents in various museums, and it is very sad that most of it concerned Italy.

Talking about Germany and Austria, I think that in any case we must not make claims to those exhibits of German museums that are national monuments of Germany. It is not as important for us to receive German works of art as to receive those objects they had time to gather around the world. They had time to collect a lot of French, Italian, and Spanish valuables.[13]

Then Grabar began to speculate about how to select works of art for removal: 'If in a museum there is only one painting by Holbein and in another museum there are twelve of them, it clearly does not make sense to take one picture ... but the removal of one painting from twelve cannot create a trauma. I think we must keep in mind all these specific aspects of a political character.'[14]

Another question involved masterpieces. Would the Soviets take the best works of art without hesitation? Grabar repeated that it was senseless to remove secondary works, and asked his colleagues to prepare proposals concerning what kind of pieces were necessary to enrich Soviet museums, directing them to pay special attention to artists who were not represented or were represented badly in the country's collections.

After his speech, the members of the Bureau discussed the problem of ruined or damaged museums and architectural monuments in the occupied territories. Some things were not clear. What compensation could there be, for example, for a ruined architectural monument? Sergei Tolstov, director of the Institute of Material Culture, wanted Slavic archaeological objects.[15] Viktor Lazarev could not understand why it was not possible to take compensation in materials that would be needed to rebuild the country's damaged economy. They began to argue but were interrupted by Grabar, who reminded them that making such decisions was not their responsibility. 'We cannot dictate to the state; the state knows better,' he said.[16]

At this moment Boris Iofan, who had been silent so far, decided to express his opinion. Iofan was one of the most famous Soviet architects. In 1933 he won an international competition to design the Palace of Soviets, the ultimate symbol of Soviet power. The gigantean structure was to be built on the site of the Cathedral of Christ the Saviour, on the bank of the Moscow river not far from the Kremlin. The competition was a sham since it was known from the beginning that Iofan's project had been personally approved by Stalin and therefore would certainly win. But foreign architects, including Le Corbusier and the *emigré* Naum Gabo, were invited to participate, to show the world once more that Soviet practitioners were more talented and original than their Western competitors.

The cathedral was blown up. Construction of the Palace of Soviets began, but the ambitious project of an immense skyscraper topped by a colossal statue of Lenin was never realized. The war intervened. The enormous carcass made of special high-quality steel produced for the base of the building was chopped to pieces and melted to produce tanks. The excavation later became the site of the world's largest outdoor swimming pool.

Iofan was invited to the meeting because it was dealing with damage to architectural monuments. In the middle of the discussion he unexpectedly returned to the Italian question. 'Perhaps from a country like Italy we might receive nothing but works of art,' he said hopefully. Grabar interrupted him angrily: 'Forget about Italy. It is our ally and fights against [the Germans].'[17]

Iofan kept returning to the Italian question because he was familiar with the country. He had emigrated to Italy in 1914 and lived there for ten years, joining the Italian Communist Party in 1921, the year it was established. He was even involved in sabotage. When the Fascists held a congress in Rome, Iofan, who had worked as an engineer on the construction of the Tivoli power station, shut off the power, leaving the capital – and the congress – without electricity.[18]

But the biggest problem was still to establish Soviet losses so that a legal ground could be provided for so-called equivalents. Various cultural institutions were ordered to prepare damage evaluations, including even experts from blockaded Leningrad.

Grabar was honest about Soviet museum losses: 'There are no more museum exhibits,' he confessed. 'Perhaps there are no inventories, and if they exist, one must select only certain bits of information ... because in most cases unqualified staff were sitting in the museums and no serious research took place. We must think seriously how in this situation we can compile price lists as good as those made up by the Extraordinary State Commission in the case of collective farms.'[19] But the value of looted works of art was more difficult to estimate than destroyed agricultural and industrial facilities.

Lazarev thought it was impossible. 'What are the losses of the provincial museums?' he asked. 'The level of provincial museum officials was not very high and if Rembrandt is mentioned in the inventory book, that does not prove it is really a Rembrandt ... *Izvestia* once published that the Germans had removed from one little town works by artists as famous as Rubens or Rembrandt, but it seems that these works were copies misattributed by the local experts.'[20]

Despite these doubts, Grabar thought that compiling an inventory of looted works of art and price lists was essential. Looking for a good example, he mentioned the town of Istra, not far from Moscow. The city was plundered by the Nazis and many objects disappeared from the local museum. Experts from the Historical Museum in Moscow who tried to assess the damage asked art historians who had visited Istra before the war to create a list of the most valuable objects from memory.[21]

In December the subject was discussed again. Nikolai Belekhov, head and chief architect of the State Inspectorate on the Preservation of Monuments in Leningrad, gave a speech on estimating losses. He had come to Moscow especially for the meeting, having made his way through territory controlled by Soviet troops, a narrow corridor that was under constant German fire. His proposal concerning how to assign a value to lost works of art provoked sharp protests. Belekhov proposed that the total value of a work comprised such components as 'the price of a canvas, a stretcher, and the work of an artist' and 'the quantity of socially useful time needed for re-creation of a similar piece'.[22] To these segments of total value he recommended adding a special coefficient, or additional price, for the type of painting: genre painting cost more than portraiture, which was more expensive than still life, and so forth. He believed that the price had to be increased if the lost work had high national or even political value. As an example, Belekhov chose the famous painting by Ilya Repin, *Zaporozhian Cossacks Write a Letter to the Turkish Sultan*. This masterpiece of Russian Realism had been evacuated to Novosibirsk and was perfectly safe, but Belekhov chose it because of its national value and political correctness. When everything from the price of the stretcher to the political and propaganda value had been estimated, Belekhov stated that if such a work were lost, compensation of $1,425,500 must be paid.[23]

In the complete silence that followed Belekhov's words, Grabar asked, 'Do you think it is possible to re-create a painting by Rembrandt?'[24]

There was further discussion. Both Grabar and Lazarev thought that the only way to value looted works of art was according to real market prices. But Soviet art historians had been isolated from the international art world for many years, and the members of the commission had only the vaguest knowledge of prices on the Western art market. Drawing on his pre-Revolutionary experience and observations made during his rare trips abroad after 1917, Grabar attempted to explain that the prices of Russian art on the international market could not be as high as Belekhov believed. His arguments only provoked more emotional declarations. 'The market for our works of art is different from the market for five-sixths of the world ...' Belekhov insisted. 'We must make the prices for the entire world. An American millionaire would buy a portrait painted by Repin for 125,000 US dollars.'

Grabar interrupted him: 'He would never buy it.'

'Even if he wouldn't,' Belekhov answered, 'it makes no difference. We are not talking about the price but about the national value of Repin, of his *Burlaks*, his *Zaporozhian Cossacks*. It is our soul. These masterpieces have no valuation because they are priceless.'[25]

Grabar and Lazarev argued that they had to be more realistic. 'Because we are trying to find equivalents, our valuations must be as follows: for the damage we ask such and such price. We can increase this price by the additional value of our national treasures, but within realistic limits,'[26] Lazarev said. It was difficult to persuade Belekhov. He immediately accused Lazarev of trying to transform compensation into a banal trade: 'We are dealing with political values,' he asserted hotly. 'We must act according to our principal national interest. Let's take for example the Wanderers group. They have never been highly valued abroad. In terms of artistic skill their works are questionable, but as the manifestation of our cultural and political life they represent a period of great importance.'[27]

His opinion, based on a mixture of vulgarized Marxism and nationalism, was typical of the period, but the emotionalism of his accusations disturbed Grabar, who did not want a political scandal inside the commission. He interrupted Belekhov and invited Yuri Almazov, the deputy director of the Research Institute of Museology, to express his opinion on the issue. Almazov proposed a price list for appraising the value of lost works according to which a fourteenth-century icon cost about $250,000 and a canvas painted by a member of the Wanderers group cost no more than $125,000. Appraisal criteria included the importance of the artist, the quality of the piece, and the presence or absence of a signature. Ivan Kryzhin, director of the Research Institute, explained that the price list prepared by the institute was based on prices on the Russian art market in 1913, recalculated in Soviet rubles of 1927 (when the ruble had been briefly convertible, at a good rate of exchange). The recalculation surprised no one; they knew that Soviet officials would have regarded it as politically very incorrect to cite the market situation in czarist times.

Professor Viktor Shulgin, curator of the Museum of the Revolution, proposed to compare Russian and European artists by their importance. 'Repin for us is as important as, for example, Matisse for France,'[28] he said. Inspired by this idea, the other members of the commission tried to find more suitable Western analogies to the famous Russian Realist. Lazarev named the German artist Adolf Menzel. 'It is possible to get 50,000 marks for Menzel,' he said.[29]

Grabar asked them all to be more realistic. 'When we are trying to name an equivalent, there is no place for fantasy ... Even now we can give the correct market price of the Sistine Madonna,'[30] which, he reiterated, was impossible for Russian art. He was very disappointed with the discussion. Coming up with valuations was a serious matter, since Foreign Minister Molotov would need the information for future negotiations with the Allies on compensation for Soviet museum losses. Grabar was looking ahead.

MOSCOW

Plans for a Supermuseum

Placing a value on stolen and destroyed works of art was a big problem, although it was clear that 'equivalents' would come in the form of art treasures from enemy museums. It was more difficult to establish 'equivalents' for destroyed or damaged architectural monuments. In Novgorod the Germans had torn down the twelfth-century Church of the Saviour at Nereditsa as well as other ancient monuments. Ancient Pskov, too, suffered greatly. The czarist palaces outside Leningrad were devastated. The churches, monasteries and palaces of Chernigov, Istra, Kalinin, Mozhaisk, and Smolensk had been shelled and burned.

To deal with this question, Grabar called a meeting of the most prominent architects and architectural historians in the country. A few days before the meeting, on 14 January 1944, the battle for the liberation of Leningrad from the blockade began. In the area of Peterhof an artillery duel was in progress, Pavlovsk and Gatchina were burning. But the participants in the meeting did not know, because news about the destruction had not yet reached Moscow.

The stars of Stalinist architecture were in attendance: Alexei Shchusev, designer of the most important shrine in the country, the Lenin Mausoleum; Vladimir Gelfreikh, designer of the Lenin Library; and of course Boris Iofan, architect in chief of the ill-fated Palace of Soviets. Historians and restorers were also invited. Among them were people who had fought for the preservation of historical monuments and detested their more prominent colleagues, who sometimes supported the state in its ruthless destruction of old buildings. Now they were all united by a common goal.

Everybody present at the meeting knew that the Soviet authorities had been responsible for more destruction in the cities of Russia, Ukraine, and Belorussia than the German army. In Moscow alone dozens of churches and monasteries had been destroyed, including Kazan Cathedral on Red Square, built in 1625 to commemorate the liberation of Moscow from the Poles, and the gargantuan cathedral of Christ the Saviour, built in 1883 to commemorate the Russian victory over Napoleon. If the Kremlin had been bombed by the Luftwaffe, the damage might not have been as terrible as the result of all Stalin's 'reconstructions'. The Ascension Nunnery, burial place of Russian czarinas, and the cathedral of the Chudov Monastery, one of the oldest buildings in Moscow, were destroyed, along with the famous Red Threshold, the place of coronation ceremonies.

The destruction had taken place all over the country. Thousands of churches in villages and small towns were blown up or turned into stables, warehouses or, at best, clubs. Countless country estates were burned out, robbed, or transformed into prisons or dachas for high-ranking party apparatchiks.

Two of those who attended the January meeting had undergone very sad experiences. As the architect in charge of the cultural monuments of the Kremlin, Dmitry Sukhov had been forced to sign the documents for the destruction of churches, monasteries and palaces that he had spent his life preserving and restoring. When officials decided to destroy the Sukharev Tower because they thought it obstructed traffic, Sukhov and his pupils devised a plan to reorganize traffic and save the monument. Stalin responded angrily: 'The Sukharev Tower must be destroyed ... The architects are blind and hopeless.'[1]

Pyotr Baranovsky had been more successful and managed to save St Basil's Cathedral on Red Square. In 1933 it was designated for destruction by the all-powerful Lazar Kaganovich, commissar of transportation and head of the Moscow city council, because it blocked the route of the tank columns in military parades. Baranovsky was ordered to measure the cathedral before its destruction, but he threatened to commit suicide in Red Square if St Basil's was touched, and he sent a hysterical letter to Stalin. The cathedral was saved, but Baranovsky was arrested and spent some years in the gulag. While he was in prison the new head of the Moscow city council, Nikita Khrushchev, gave the order to destroy Kazan Cathedral, which Baranovsky had restored in 1930. Baranovsky was at the January 1944 meeting semi-officially, since former gulag prisoners had no right to be in Moscow, but a month later, thanks to the support of the powerful Grabar, he received permission to live in the capital.

The first question discussed that day was how the Germans could make restitution for the monuments they had destroyed. Grabar

proposed to follow the Americans' example. 'If the church at Nereditsa were in Germany, American millionaires would probably transport it to their country,' he said. 'They would not grudge the money.
Americans exported entire castles from Germany, France, Italy ...
The fact is that the easiest way to make restitution for the Church of
the Saviour at Nereditsa is to take and import something like Rheims
Cathedral.' But after a short exchange, participants in the discussion
agreed that the idea of transporting this monument of French Gothic
to the outskirts of Novgorod was unrealistic, and the plan to resettle
it on the site of the Church of the Saviour at Nereditsa was dropped.[2]

'It is impossible, and therefore we must be compensated by a few
Sistine Madonnas, etcetera,' Grabar summarized the debate.[3] Then
he made another proposal. The great marble altar of Zeus, from the
ancient Greek city of Pergamum, which occupied its own building
on Berlin's Museum Island, would do instead of Rheims Cathedral.
'Certainly we will remove the Pergamum Altar,' Grabar said, but he
wondered whether British and American experts would agree that its
value was equal to that of the twelfth-century Russian church.[4]

At the end of the meeting Grabar gave a short speech. He and
Lazarev, he said, had been drawing up a list of equivalents, on orders
from the Extraordinary State Commission. 'The greatest works of art
from the museums of Germany and its allies are being selected,' he
announced. 'The question that was raised only a short time ago ...
is, can we select anything in Italy, because it has become our ally. This
question is not our responsibility and it will be explained to us. But
all this work is taking place. It seems that in Moscow there will be a
museum whose equal never existed in the world.'[5]

Boris Iofan added: 'There are excellent Greek architectural objects
in German museums; at least there are objects of Oriental architecture,
which are so close to us; or paintings, which it is possible to take as
equivalents. It would be possible to establish ... a superb museum of
fine arts in our Moscow.'[6]

The idea of creating a supermuseum in Moscow after the war
seems to have become very popular among cultural officials. Grabar
and Iofan only touched on the possibility, but a representative of the
Research Institute of Museology, Topornin, gave the proposal shape.
Speaking at an earlier meeting organized by the institute to discuss
the problem of selecting equivalents, he postulated that in addition to
the compensation for its museum losses, the Soviet Union should

receive something extra, a 'penalty' imposed on the Germans that had to include cultural valuables. He sketched for his colleagues an ambitious plan to create two immense museums in Moscow after the end of the war: a museum of world history and a museum of the history of science and technology. The exhibits for these future institutions should be received as part of the 'penalty' imposed on enemy countries. Topornin's colleagues did not share his opinion that the undertaking was realistic, but he insisted that if a discipline such as world history existed, it would not be difficult to create a museum of world history.[7]

In March 1944 Sergei Merkurov, the director of the Pushkin Museum and a well-known sculptor who had been honoured with the title 'People's Artist of the USSR', made a proposal to Mikhail Khrapchenko, head of the Arts Committee of the Council of People's Commissars, one of the most powerful cultural figures in the country. Merkurov had an ambitious plan to establish a Museum of World Art in Moscow after the war. Khrapchenko liked the idea, and together they drew up a detailed letter to Vyacheslav Molotov, at that time the deputy head of the Council, second only to Stalin.[8] The letter said that the capital of the world's first proletarian state had no real museum of world art, whereas 'the capitals of the most important states have such museums'. Moscow, the centre of Soviet political and cultural life, and the spiritual capital not only of the USSR but of all progressive foreign countries, had the right to a museum in which the development of art and culture would be represented from antiquity to the present day.

Merkurov and Khrapchenko thought that the Museum of Modern Western Art and the Museum of Oriental Cultures could be united with the Pushkin Museum, which would be the heart of the future institution. It would not be difficult to amass a rich collection.

> The German-Fascist barbarians, who tried to annihilate Russian culture and destroyed many famous examples of Russian art, must be held responsible for all their crimes. The museums of the Axis countries are full of wonderful masterpieces, which must be given to the Soviet Union as compensation. All valuables received from the Axis countries must be concentrated in one place and can play the role of a perfect memorial dedicated to the glory of Russian arms.[9]

The place, of course, would be the Museum of World Art in Moscow.

Such a collection would require a much bigger building than the Pushkin Museum. Merkurov thought about the Palace of Soviets, which was to be built only fifty metres from the Pushkin Museum. He had been chosen to supply the colossal statue of Lenin, eighty metres high, that would crown the structure. His new idea was that the Pushkin Museum could be enlarged by the addition of wings and absorbed into the Palace of Soviets complex. As part of the most impressive manifestation of Communist grandeur, it would be a suitable home for the Museum of World Art.[10] In comparison to Merkurov's vision, Hitler's plan to build a huge museum in Linz seems like a provincial undertaking.

A decree of the State Committee of Defence was attached to the letter to Molotov. It asserted the necessity for the museum and gave it the exclusive right to receive works of art from the Axis countries sent as compensation. Lazar Kaganovich was made responsible for the realization of the project. But Merkurov and Khrapchenko did not forget the Soviet cities that had been damaged by Nazi occupation. They intended to establish a publishing company as a department of the new museum that would supply the unfortunate cities with high-quality colour reproductions of the works of art from Axis countries. And they promised to supply plaster copies of the sculptural master-pieces.[11]

The plan to create a supermuseum in the capital of the first proletarian state was inspired by new ideas that gained strength during the war. Before the war Stalin had begun making attempts to rethink Russian history from the nationalist rather than the Marxist view-point, and this tendency became even stronger as nationalistic feelings were encouraged by the Soviet government to unite the people against the aggressor. Soviet propaganda began to use images of Russian czars and military commanders whose very names had been prohibited during the 1920s. The glory of Imperial Russia was re-interpreted as presaging the splendour of the Soviet state. The last volume of Alexei Tolstoy's novel *Peter the Great* was written during the war, and its image of the czar-reformer defending the motherland against foreign enemies was a glorification of Stalin only slightly camouflaged by historical details.

New military decorations were introduced: the order of Field Marshal Kutuzov, the order of Generalissimo Suvorov, and even the order of Prince Alexander Nevsky. The old system of military ranks was restored in the army, and such symbols of the previous regime as shoulder boards were reinstated. The Orthodox Church which had been under permanent attack by the state during the 1920s and 1930s, was temporarily reprieved. Priests blessed military units departing for the front, and the patriarch of Moscow wrote leaflets that were released behind German lines. Painters, poets, and cinematographers glorified Russian saints and princes locked in battle with Mongol warriors or German knights. Two myths fed this propaganda machine: the ultranationalistic myth of Russian superiority and the Pan-Slavic myth of the family of Slavic peoples led by the Russian 'big brother'.

These ideas were reflected in the activity of Grabar and his colleagues. The experts all expressed a particular desire to enrich Soviet collections with objects belonging to the Russian or Slavic cultures. 'It is very important to nominate Slavic archaeological objects, which are exceptionally well represented in German collections, as equivalents,' said Sergei Tolstov.[12] Grabar dreamed about Germany's rich collections of Slavic manuscripts but was afraid that there would be many pretenders to them: 'Poles, Czechoslovaks, Serbs, etc.'[13]

Vladimir Bonch-Bruyevich, director of the Anti-Religious Museum in Leningrad, had no clear idea of what Grabar was doing, but his ideas tended in the same direction. He wrote to Stalin in February 1945 stating that all museums and archives from the aggressor countries and their satellites – Germany, Italy, Austria, Romania, Bulgaria and Finland – must be removed in their entirety. Most particularly, everything Russian or Slavic – manuscripts, portraits, correspondence, paintings, books, material objects – had to be confiscated, especially from Germany.[14]

The experts were puzzled by the low prices of Russian art on the international market, but it seemed to them that this incomprehensible anomaly would soon be corrected. Grabar even gave an inspiring speech in which he tried to justify the removal of the Pergamum Altar from Berlin:

> Try to valuate the Pergamum Altar and think, here is the Pergamum Altar and here is Nereditsa ... We will say ours is more valuable; they will say theirs is more valuable. I know West European circles perfectly well, how they will judge. It makes no difference how we estimate our Surikov; they don't care a straw for him there and wouldn't even trade one portrait by Louis Tocqué for Surikov. The West European consciousness doesn't

understand Russian art, just as it doesn't understand Russian literature.
Finally they understood that a writer like Tolstoy was unique, and they
will finally understand our art. In New York both children and adults
sing in the street, 'Why Is He Winking?' – there is such a fashion for us.
It will be something unbelievable.[15]

'Why Is He Winking?' was an extremely popular Russian song, but
Grabar was probably deluded in thinking it was so well known in
New York.

The experts who had been asked to compile lists of scientific
materials were particularly fervid in their expressions of patriotic
sentiment. In almost every case the word 'Russian' was written in
capital letters. The word 'foreign' was not used; they preferred 'alien'.
Their list repeatedly mentioned the need to import from Germany
all 'materials removed at different times from our country and in
many cases connected with the heroes and events of our history',
including materials 'connected with trade and cultural links' and
materials relating to 'the general history of culture ... that could be
used for replenishing damaged or destroyed collections'.[16] They tried
to include in their list almost every object in German collections that
had the slightest connection with Russia: minerals gathered in the
eighteenth century by German travellers and 'Russian meteors' –
meteors that had fallen on Russian territory. Even the amber collection in Königsberg was regarded as fair game because the amber
had come from 'the Russian Baltic states'.

Special attention was paid to the 'historical exhibits connected
with the creative work of Russian inventors, which must be returned
to the motherland'.[17] This amazing list magically transformed every
German scientist and traveller who had visited Russia in the last three
centuries into a Russian. Both the famous zoologist Peter Simon
Pallas and the entomologist Heinrich Friese were asserted to be
Russian scientists who by some mistake had finished their days in
Germany and donated their collections to German museums. In some
cases, when the Russian identity of the owner of a desired collection
was impossible to uphold, other justifications were found. The desir-
able collection of the Koenig Museum in Bonn really belonged to
Russia, the authors of the list wrote, because the founder of the
museum, Alexander Koenig, was 'one of the former owners of sugar
refineries in the Ukraine ... and the museum ... was founded on

money received from this venture'.[18] The list included ethnographic, archaeological, zoological, entomological, geological, botanical, and other collections.

Grabar had taken the Grand Tour in 1895 and had been impressed by Germany. In Berlin he 'liked almost everything – the unbelievable cleanliness of the streets . . . the traffic, the beer, the museums. I spent whole days in them.'[19] In the Dresden Gallery, the young painter was impressed by Rembrandt's *Portrait of a Man in a Hat with Pearls*, the works of Vermeer, and Velazquez's *Old Man*. In the Alte Pinakothek in Munich, Grabar was especially astonished by Titian's *The Crowning with Thorns* and by Jordaens' *The Satyr and the Peasant*. In Italy, he was dazzled by Velazquez's *Portrait of Pope Innocent X* in Rome and Bruegel's *The Blind Leading the Blind* in Naples. He did not forget these preferences of his youth: all of the paintings were later included in the list of equivalents prepared by the bureau.

The final version of the list covered five countries: Germany, Austria, Hungary, Romania, and Italy. Finland, for some reason, was forgotten.[20] The experts were not optimistic about receiving works of art from Italy, which had left the Axis camp, but they included a few masterpieces from Italian museums that they believed it might be possible to acquire after the war. From the Doges' Palace in Venice they chose ten paintings, including Tintoretto's *Portrait of Two Senators* and Tiepolo's *The Copper Serpent*. Only five paintings were marked down from the Uffizi in Florence: Botticelli's *Madonna with a Pomegranate*, Ghirlandaio's *Adoration of the Magi*, Piero di Cosimo's *Perseus and Andromeda*, and two Madonnas by Filippino Lippi. They added to the list Cavazzola's *Crowning with Thorns* from Verona, Velazquez's *Portrait of Innocent X* from the Doria Pamphili Gallery in Rome, and Bruegel's *The Blind Leading the Blind* from the National Gallery in Naples that had impressed Grabar so much before the war.

The list of Italian works of art was severely cut in the final version because of changed political realities, but there were hopes of receiving important works from Austria and Hungary. The experts chose thirty-five paintings from the Kunsthistorischesmuseum in Vienna, including six by Bruegel, four by Velazquez, three each by Tintoretto and Rubens, Hieronymus Bosch's *Christ Carrying the Cross*, and Giorgione's *Three Philosophers*.

From the Lichtenstein Gallery they selected works by Fouquet, Chardin and Rubens. Even the provincial city of Innsbruck was not overlooked; the experts included a work by Carel Fabritius from the Ferdinandeum.

The National Gallery in Budapest had fifty-two paintings worthy of gracing Soviet collections, according to the experts, by Velazquez, El Greco, Goya, Titian, Rembrandt and Vermeer. From Romania, which left the German camp in August 1944, they chose only one painting: El Greco's *Adoration of the Magi*, from the private collection of the king of Romania.

Naturally, however, they concentrated on the German museums. When the order had been given to compile the list, in 1943, the future of Germany was still unclear, and the experts decided to include all the German museums. They thought that even if the Red Army did not occupy the entire country, the Allies might allow the Soviets to collect compensation from their zones as well. They paid particular attention to the museums of Munich that Grabar loved so much. From the Alte Pinakothek, they listed 125 paintings as equivalents. Following Grabar's recommendation not to claim 'national monuments', they chose only four German paintings for future removal: Altdorfer's *Danube Landscape*, Elsheimer's *Rest on the Flight into Egypt*, Holbein's *Portrait of Sir Bryan Tuke*, and *St Bartholomew with St Agnes and St Cecilia* by the Master of the St Bartholomew Altarpiece. But their selection of non-German paintings was not so modest. The famous St Columba Altarpiece by Rogier van der Weyden, Botticelli's *Lamentation*, all three Madonnas by Raphael, Tintoretto's *Mars and Venus Surprised by Vulcan*, Titian's *Crowning with Thorns*, Tiepolo's *Adoration of the Magi*, Velazquez's *Young Spanish Nobleman*, Poussin's *Lamentation*, and five paintings by Goya were on the list. They particularly liked Rubens, selecting almost all of his canvases, even the immense *Fall of the Damned*, for export.

The Neue Pinakothek did not interest the Russians so much. Only fourteen works of art from that museum were considered important enough to be nominated as equivalents. Among them were German paintings – by Leibl, von Marées, Schuch – but no Nazarenes or Romantics. There was more enthusiasm for the French Impressionists: van Gogh's *Vase with Sunflowers* and *View of Arles*, Manet's *Breakfast in the Studio*, canvases by Renoir and Monet, and a sculpture by Maillol were proposed for removal.

During his first trip to Dresden Grabar had not been impressed by Raphael's Sistine Madonna, perhaps the most famous painting in the world at that time. In 1929, he went to Germany again, with an exhibition of Russian icons, and decided to go back to Dresden for another look. 'The Madonna was unframed [sic], the gallery was closed to the public, and I could dedicate a whole day to the examination of the painting from top to bottom,' he later remembered.[21] He had been invited to Dresden by Dr Hans Posse, the director of the Dresden Gallery. Eleven years later Posse would be in charge of collecting art for Hitler's Führer Museum in Linz, and fourteen years later Grabar would be compiling a list of paintings to be removed from the Dresden Gallery and sent to Russia.

Almost all the classic masterpieces were on the list, including the Sistine Madonna. But the choice of nineteenth- and twentieth-century pictures reflected Russian taste. French paintings were numerous: Courbet's *Stonecutters* and Puvis de Chavannes' *The Fisherman's Family* were named as equivalents. But Caspar David Friedrich, so well represented in the Dresden collection, did not appeal to the experts.

Berlin had many tempting collections, but the experts singled out the Kaiser Friedrich Museum (now Berlin-Dahlem). Van Eyck's celebrated *The Virgin in a Church*, Petrus Christus's *Portrait of a Young Girl*, Bosch's *St John at Patmos*, Giotto's *Entombment of Mary*, Raphael's *Colonna Madonna*, Luca Signorelli's *Pan*, Rembrandt's *Hendrickje at an Open Door* and *Man with the Golden Helmet*, along with canvases by Rubens, van Dyck, and Titian, were among the 179 paintings named as equivalents.

It was not only paintings that interested the experts. They did not forget the rich collection of drawings in the Kupferstichkabinett, choosing eighty-eight illustrations by Botticelli for the *Divine Comedy*, among other works. From Leipzig the experts chose only twenty-five paintings and three sculptures, including Rembrandt's great *Self Portrait* and Frans Hals's *The Mulatto*. When they discussed the problem of compensation for architectural losses, such as the ruined frescos in the Novgorod churches, Grabar remembered the fresco of the archangel Michael by Pintoricchio in Leipzig, and it too went on the list.[22]

During his trip to Germany in 1929, Grabar had visited Hamburg. Later he remembered the Kunsthalle with fondness, particularly Renoir's *Portrait of Mme Lerioux*, but he was disappointed with Manet's *Nana*, which he considered 'not up to the level of this painter's genius'.[23] Despite his disappointment, the Manet was included in the list of French paintings chalked up for removal to the USSR. Collections in Augsburg, Brunswick, Darmstadt, Frankfurt, Karlsruhe, Kassel, Oldenburg, Potsdam and Würzburg were also on the list.

The decorative arts were not ignored. Furniture, arms and armour, porcelain, and jewellery were all included on the list. The tenth-century Gold Comb of Henry I, from the Church of St Servace in Quedlinburg, was nominated for export.[24]

On 26 February 1945, at the moment when the first trophy brigades of the Arts Committee were receiving their new military uniforms in anticipation of entering Germany, Grabar sent the final list of equivalents to Andrei Konstantinov, deputy head of the Arts Committee of the Central Committee. The list of paintings, sculptures, and Byzantine art had been compiled by Lazarev, Vladimir Levinson-Lessing, Nikolai Vlasov, and himself. Both Levinson–Lessing and Vlasov had taken an active part in the secret sale of treasures from Soviet museums organized by the Stalin government during the late 1920s and early 1930s. Vlasov was an expert with Antiquariat, the state company created to run the operation. Their participation in the nomination of equivalents was crucial since they knew what prices the Soviet government had received for the masterpieces, many of which had been purchased by the American Treasury secretary, Andrew Mellon.

Other respectable art historians compiled the lists of ancient Egyptian objects, antiquities and drawings to be removed from the museums of Germany, Austria, Italy and Romania. The final list named 1,745 masterpieces and valued all of them in American dollars.[25] Grabar and Vlasov explained why in a letter to Konstantinov:

> In 1935 Andrew Mellon, the well-known American collector, had to publish the prices he had paid for the masterpieces of Raphael, Titian, van Eyck, Rembrandt, Rubens, van Dyck, and other great masters. Mellon donated his famous collection to the state and the National Gallery in Washington was created on the basis of it.[26]

They did not mention that it was unnecessary for them to get the prices from Mellon's list, since the pictures had been purchased from the Hermitage, and both Levinson-Lessing and Vlasov knew perfectly well what he had paid for them. Mellon published the information

Despite Goering's promise that no bombs would fall on the cities of the Reich, Berlin museum officials began in 1939 to pack up their collections and move them to vaults and cellars. Heinrich Hoffmann, Hitler's personal photographer, recorded workmen stacking sandbags against the frieze of the great Pergamum Altar (top). Later it was dismantled and stored in the Zoo tower. Sent by train to Leningrad in 1945, it was returned to East Germany thirteen years later and reinstalled in its own museum (above).

The fortress–like anti-aircraft tower at the Berlin Zoo (opposite) was supposed to be impregnable. During the war, valuable objects from the city's museums were stored there, including the 'Trojan gold' (below), so named because its discoverer, Heinrich Schliemann, believed that it had belonged to King Priam of the *Iliad*. Most spectacular among the vessels, weapons, and ornaments was a delicate diadem, modelled (right) by Sophia Schliemann.

Large-scale architectural assemblages in the Pergamum Museum were too big to be moved. In 1945, after the bombardment of Berlin, an American observer described Museum Island as a 'shambles of crumbling rubble, with the great monuments from Mschatta and Miletus peering like ghosts over ruins more sudden than those they had seen before in their two or three thousand year history'.

The battle for Berlin was fierce. Nikolai Berzarin, chief of the Soviets' Fifth Shock Army, ordered his commanders to smash everything in their way with artillery fire rather than risk the lives of the troops.

Once the battle was over, the Red Army turned to looting. While soldiers were satisfied with bicycles, wristwatches, and other humble luxuries, their officers were sending home planes and boxcars full of artworks, furniture, porcelains, silver, jewellery and furs.

Architects of the plan to recompense Soviet museums for their losses with artworks taken from Germany included Igor Grabar (top left), Vladimir Blavatsky (top right), and Viktor Lazarev (bottom left). Andrei Belokopitov (bottom right, in 1968), in civilian life the manager of the Moscow Art Theatre, became head of the Arts Committee trophy brigade in Berlin and sent the Trojan gold and the Pergamum Altar to Moscow.

The Dresden trophy brigade taking a break. Standing, from left to right, Nikolai Ponomarev, Mikhail Volodin, Stepan Churakov and Sergei Grigorov. Ivan Petrov is on the ground, with two German women. The brigade established a collecting point in Pillnitz castle, outside the city, where Raphael's Sistine Madonna and other masterpieces of the Dresden Picture Gallery were stored.

A shabby three-storey building at Drachenfelsstrasse 4 in Berlin's Karlshorst suburb, the only district in the city that had electricity, was headquarters for the Arts Committee trophy brigade.

The greatest mystery involving the looted artworks of Berlin was the fire in the Friedrichshain control tower in May 1945. Over 400 large canvases from the Paintings Gallery, including Signorelli's *Pan* (above) and Ruben's *Bacchanalia* (below), were destroyed, along with the most important objects from the antiquities collection and 400 sculptures. The cause of the fire was never determined.

because of accusations in the American press that the low prices asked by the Soviets were a sort of bribe to him for arranging a trade agreement with the USSR. Mellon wanted to prove that he had never dealt directly with the Soviets and purchased all works of art with the help of an intermediary, the dealer M. Knoedler and Co., owned by Armand Hammer.[27]

The secret sale of the masterpieces of the Hermitage and other Soviet museums had damaged the collections of the country more seriously than the activities of the Nazis. The quantity of works of art sold were small compared to the quantity of looted objects, but their quality was much higher. The dealer Joseph Duveen wrote sadly: 'The Hermitage is no more the greatest collection in the world, it has gone to pieces. I do not see how a nation could sell their great pictures of that kind.'[28]

On the basis of those prices, the Soviet art historians appraised the art works belonging to the museums of half of Europe. The total value of the desired 'equivalents' was $70,587,200. The Sistine Madonna was valued at $2,000,000. The most expensive object was the Pergamum Altar, which was valued at $7,500,000, and the cheapest was a knife in the Egyptian collection in Berlin, appraised at only $200.[29] Both the altar and the knife were removed to the USSR at the end of the war.

Soviet officials never had a chance to claim paintings from Italian museums. When they made up the list, in 1943, the pictures they wanted were already in the hands of the Nazis. The famous *Blind Leading the Blind* and other paintings from Naples, evacuated by the Italians to the Monte Cassino Monastery, were looted by the Germans. Two of them, canvases by Titian and Claude Lorrain, were presented to Goering. Seventeen, including *The Blind Leading the Blind*, were sent to Berlin and chosen by Hitler for the Führer Museum in Linz. They were hidden in the salt mine at Alt Aussee in Austria and found by the Americans in May 1945. The art treasures from the Uffizi Gallery were removed by the Nazis too and hidden in the South Tyrol and in Salzburg, where they were discovered by the Allies.[30]

The treasures from Germany started arriving at Vnukovo airport in Moscow on 30 June 1945. The first plane from Berlin had the three crates containing the Trojan gold on board. Ten days later the treasure was taken to the Pushkin Museum.[31] On 10 August cargo came from Dresden. Among the boxes filled with paintings, graphics, and decorative arts was a huge crate containing the Sistine Madonna.[32] The Pergamum Altar reached Leningrad on 29 October.[33]

Two paintings named on the list never reached Moscow: Signorelli's *Pan* was burned in the Friedrichshain anti-aircraft tower in Berlin. Courbet's *Stonecutters* was destroyed during the Anglo–American bombardment of Dresden in February 1945. The museums of Munich, Cologne, Frankfurt and Stuttgart were in the British and American occupation zones. The Soviets never had the chance to collect the equivalents they had chosen from these collections. The Comb of Henry I from Quedlinburg disappeared in the spring of 1945 and was discovered forty-seven years later in Whitewright, Texas. It had been stolen by an American soldier, Lieutenant Joe Tom Meador, from its hiding place in a mine shaft.[34]

THE TROPHY BRIGADES

On 10 March 1945, Fyodor Khotinsky, an officer in the Ninth Army who in civilian life was a restorer at the Museum of Oriental Cultures in Moscow, sent his colleagues an account of his first days on German soil:

> When our truck stopped in Germany to refill water containers, and our people jumped out to stretch their legs, they paid a visit to the houses abandoned by the inhabitants and presented me with 2–3 porcelain knick-knacks. These were the first things I held in my hands on Aryan soil. A prophetic sign! Our truck continued en route. Finally we reached our destination – a hunting castle of Count Portales, one of his 90 estates. Porcelain, paintings, tapestries, antique arms, a library, crystal, old furniture. Many of the objects would be of interest to the Kuskovo Museum.

Knowing that his letter would be scrutinized by military censors, Khotinsky wrote guardedly – it would have been dangerous to state openly that Soviet troops were destroying property – but he managed to convey to his superiors in Moscow that within a few days the soldiers had broken most of the porcelains, defaced the statues, and poked out the eyes of the portraits 'in the style of Rembrandt and Greuze'. He mentioned that 'canvases by Velazquez, Antonello da Messina, Leonardo da Vinci, Bartolommeo, Lorrain, Le Nain, Murillo, and others' (his attributions were undoubtedly optimistic) were covered with darkened varnish and were 'burning very well'. At the end of the letter he apologized for using 'Aesopian language', a traditional Soviet way to veil one's meaning. But he made it perfectly clear that action had to be taken to protect valuable property.

Khotinsky asked for a government order making him responsible for the care of such property. 'The commander of Military Unit N 66569 must be informed by General Gulayev about the need to make real efforts to preserve objects and about my right to send (at least by post) at least the light things.' There would be many interesting objects for the Moscow museums and the Lenin Library. But, he warned, if the correspondence dragged on, nothing would be left of the works of art. He wanted to organize the work on a large scale and was confident that he could find the right people for the job, but the Arts Committee in Moscow had to reach an agreement with the commanders-in-chief. In the envelope Khotinsky slipped an old watercolour found in the castle as evidence of the sad tale he told. His plea was successful. Mikhail Khrapchenko, head of the Arts Committee, gave the order to take measures to prevent damage to works of art in the area occupied by the Ninth Army.[1]

What Khotinsky did not know when he wrote his letter was that dozens of art historians and specialists in theatre, music, and printing had already been sent to the front line. He may even have met them without knowing it, for they were identifiable only by their brand-new uniforms.

The decision to divide Germany into occupation zones had been taken during the Yalta Conference, which ended on 12 February 1945. The Allies discussed the reparations question, with the USSR asking for $10 billion dollars in compensation for the damage the country had suffered under Nazi occupation. The Western Allies were doubtful about the amount but finally agreed. A more detailed discussion of the problem was made the responsibility of the Allied Commission for Reparations.

Stalin, inspired by the agreement of the Western Allies, acted immediately. On 25 February the State Committee of Defence adopted a decree establishing the Special Committee on Germany, which would be responsible for confiscation of valuables in the occupied territories. Stalin appointed Georgy Malenkov, a rising star in the Party bureaucracy, to head the new body. Its members included General Nikolai Bulganin, deputy head of the Commissariat of Defence; Nikolai Voznesensky, head of Gosplan, the planning agency for the entire Soviet economy; General Andrei Khrulev, head of the Home Front of the Red Army; and Lieutenant General Vakhitov, head of the Main Trophy Department. The most influential figure was undoubtedly Voznesensky, creator of the Russian wartime economic miracle. Later, in 1950, Stalin decided Voznesensky was a potential rival and had him executed.

The Special Committee had enormous power. Under its supervision, commissions were created on every front to organize the collection of trophies. All decisions about the removal of material to the USSR were signed personally by Stalin. Moscow was in a state of fervour. Preparations for robbing Europe were in progress, and thousands of officials from state agencies and organizations were receiving orders to report for duty in the trophy brigades.[2]

Action began even before the Special Committee was organized. On 15 February, Andrei Konstantinov, deputy head of the Arts Committee, asked the deputy commander of the Red Army Home Front, Major General Baukov, to supply documents to the members of the brigade sent by the committee to the First Ukrainian Front for the 'accomplishment of a special government mission'. The next day the Arts Committee asked the staff of the Home Front to provide sixteen military uniforms for experts leaving for the front line to participate in the commission 'on the registration of trophy property'. In a letter sent on the 19th, Konstantinov asked Baukov to provide the head of the brigade sent to the First Belorussian Front, Andrei Belokopitov, with 'military rank corresponding to his position' and informed the major general that 'in a short time, the brigades of the committee will be sent to all fronts of the Red Army reaching the borders of Germany'. The brigades' mission was defined in this letter more completely: 'participation in selection and transportation to Moscow of trophy property for cultural organizations'.

Cultural bureaucrats and stage directors, art historians and musicians selected by the committee prepared for the dangerous journey. Andrei Belokopitov, manager of the prestigious Moscow Art Theatre (MKhAT); Sergei Sidorov, chief inspector of the Arts Committee's Department of Visual Arts, and deputy head Leonty Denisov; Andrei Chegodayev and Lev Kharko, curators of the Pushkin Museum of Fine Arts; Boris Filippov, director of the Moscow Drama Theatre; Yevgeny Sushchenko, a musician with the State Symphony Orchestra of the USSR; and many others received travel documents and military uniforms.[3]

The first groups set out in late February. The civilians wore uniforms because the mission was secret and they were supposed to be inconspicuous. Natalia Sokolova, an expert who was sent to the front in April, remembered in her memoirs that in Kiev, en route to Germany, she was stopped by a patrol when she was walking down ruined Kreshchatik, the main street:

'Your documents, Comrade Major!' I handed over my identity card with a casual gesture. 'You can pick it up in two hours in the commandant's office, Comrade Major.' 'Excuse me, but I need my documents, I'm leaving the city. What's going on?'

I was indignant and nervous; as a novice major I tried to follow all regulations with the meticulousness of the convert. My overseas cap was worn two fingers above my eyebrows ... My military overcoat fitted perfectly and was completely buttoned...

'Because of your shoes, Comrade Major,' the second lieutenant repeated with a smile. He saluted and disappeared around a corner. And, in fact, after walking once in Moscow in soldier's boots two sizes too large, I had thrown them away and left for Germany in simple, unattractive low-heeled shoes. And they caught the attention of the patrol![4]

Boris Filippov, head of the trophy brigade of the First Ukrainian Front, described the trip to the German border. On 15 February, Filippov was in the auditorium of the Moscow Drama Theatre, where a new play was being performed for cultural officials, when he received a message from Konstantinov to visit the Arts Committee at five o'clock. He was late because the performance overran. Konstantinov told him that 'the next day at two o'clock I would be sent to the First Ukrainian Front in Germany for confiscation of museum valuables and theatre equipment. I had to lead a brigade that included four people – experts in different fields.'

The next day Filippov was told that he would receive the rank of lieutenant colonel for the duration of his trip and that the whole brigade would receive military uniforms. 'By evening I was already dressed in the uniform of a lieutenant colonel. Our departure was delayed to 17 February.' On the 17th it was delayed again because of a shortage of railway carriages and chaos in the Department of the Home Front.

The Department of the Home Front informed us that departure earlier than 19 February was impossible. Imagine my astonishment when, in answer to my telephone call on the 19th, the same Department of the Home Front informed me that the special train had left on the 18th ... I decided to act on my own. My brigade included three majors, all of us novices: Sushchenko from the Philharmonic Music Society; Grigorov, secretary of the Committee on the Preservation of Monuments; and Chegodayev, an art historian and museum official.

Finally, two days later, after an appeal by Filippov, the brigade was ordered to be at the railway station at nine o'clock at night. A special train to transport them had been found. They shared it with only three others, experts from the Committee on the Paper Industry, sent to Germany to remove industrial equipment.

> The train departed with only seven passengers on board, because this time the Department of the Home Front had forgotten to inform all the others about the departure. The train had bed linen for 48 passengers. On the way my art historians fished out of their cases Baedekers published in 1884 and 1910, which gave detailed information about landmarks of southern and southeastern Germany. The Germans, who published their guidebooks with their traditional pedantry, could not have imagined that such unexpected tourists would use them.

Filippov could not resist making a political point. 'The Baedekers of both editions turned out to be accusatory documents against German Fascist aggression. They called Breslau, where we were going, an OLD SLAVIC CITY. The Fascist historians from Goebbels' chancellery tried to change its history.' Breslau, an old Slavic city, had been annexed by the Germans in the Middle Ages.

The brigade reached Kiev, passed through Lvov, and soon crossed the border. This was the first time most of them had been abroad. Their first impressions were mixed. In Rzeszow they came across a group of Czechs and Hungarians liberated by the Red Army from Auschwitz. Among them were doctors, artisans and young girls, many still dressed in their striped prison rags. They showed the Russians the tattoos on their arms.

But if the survivors of the camps aroused the Russians' sympathy, the Poles provoked very different feelings: 'We seemed to be in another world, strange and unknown,' Filippov remembered of the brigade's short stay in Krakow. The military commandant and his staff were housed in the palace of Count Potocki, which impressed them with its grandeur. In the Soviet Union, Filippov commented, it would have been turned into a palace of culture. Everything looked strange: the churches, the priests and nuns in the streets, the little stores selling icons and statues of the saints. 'In the centre was a crowd of frivolous young men and women promenading with dogs. I remembered that in Leningrad in 1942 most of the dogs were eaten.' Finally the brigade reached Katowice. The German border was nearby. 'A tram crossed the city and stopped at the German border. We left it and took places in the German tram, which was going to the German city B ... We entered German territory by TRAM. Who could imagine that?' The brigade was in Germany, or actually in territory that would remain German for a few weeks longer and then be annexed to Poland. The mission had begun.[5]

During their first months in Germany the trophy brigades were in a difficult situation. The Red Army was advancing. In front of them the Allies were bombing German cities. Artillery duels were in progress. For works of art, however, the greatest danger was not bombs or shells but pillaging soldiers. Belokopitov reported that in every city and every district the commandants were busy

> collecting watches, typewriters, bicycles, carpets, pianos, which of course is a necessary undertaking, but being so occupied, they leave without control or security the museums, the big country estates, and theatres, where important museum valuables are destroyed or stolen, and most of the buildings as a result of this neglect are burned out. I think it is necessary for the military commanders to give a special order to the front units that in case of occupation by the army of the big country estates and palaces, they must be taken under protection ... Otherwise, important museum valuables will be left for destruction and pillage.[6]

In the second part of March, Belokopitov's brigade, which was working in the area of Meseritz, discovered an underground shelter not far from the village of Hohenwalde. In the shelter they found the works of art belonging to the Kaiser Friedrich Museum in Posen. It was the first large depository on German territory to be removed by the experts of the Arts Committee.

The fate of this collection was dictated by the dramatic events of the twentieth century. Posen belonged to Germany from the end of the eighteenth century until the signing of the Versailles Treaty, when it reverted to Poland and became Poznan. The Kaiser Friedrich Museum became the Museum Velikopolskei v Poznani. In 1939, when Poland was partitioned according to the Molotov–Ribbentrop pact, the city was returned to Germany. All the museum objects purchased before 1939 had both German and Polish seals and labels. When the bombardments began, the collection was evacuated from Posen and sheltered in the underground halls of the Focke-Wulf factory, which produced military aircraft in the caves near Hohenwalde.

Along with paintings and sculpture, there were graphics, furniture and tapestries, porcelains and glassware, coins, arms and armour, Greek vases, and the museum library. The collections of the museums of Tallinn and Riga, which had been removed by the Nazis, were also stored there. This huge underground storeroom of works of art and military aeroplane engines was put under the control of the Sixty-Ninth Army. The head of the Trophy Department of the Front, Major General Nikolai Zhilin, informed the staff of the Special Committee on Germany about the find, and a member of Belokopitov's brigade, Major Sergei Sidorov, was sent to Hohenwalde. While other experts examined aeroplane production lines (later removed to the Soviet Union and used to manufacture planes for the Red Army), Sidorov explored two tunnels forty-nine metres underground.

Despite the guards sent to protect the art treasures, the Hohenwalde shelter was in a state of chaos. Crates that had contained paintings and porcelain were smashed open, and stretchers from which canvases had been roughly cut were strewn around. Coins and jewels had been dropped everywhere. Large carved pieces − armoires, chests, and tables − stood along the walls, all the locks broken. Painted wooden sculptures were jumbled together on the right side of the tunnel with an ancient marble well enclosure. Greek vases, some damaged, were lined up under the tables along the walls, and Oriental vases stood on the floor. Porcelain and glassware were shattered. Church chalices, tabernacles, and goblets were standing on crates or jumbled up among them. The guards stationed near the entrance had a fire going all day long, and they fed it with boxes and wooden objects from the tunnel. They were cooking and storing water in fine porcelain vessels and using embroidered Oriental textiles and rare hangings as bedclothes.

When Sidorov returned to Hohenwalde a week later with an order from the Special Committee to prepare the works of art for transportation, he found about forty soldiers working hard in the tunnel. 'The aim and character of this work were unclear to me,' he wrote in his report. He soon discovered that the soldiers had been sent by the army commanders to collect 'trophies' for them. The chaos was worse than it had been the week before. Objects had been moved and damaged, crates had been opened, and more porcelain was broken.

With the help of the commander of a platoon of the Twentieth Trophy Battalion, Sidorov expelled the uninvited guests and began to prepare the works of art for transportation. In the light of one carbide lamp and three candles, he opened crates to check their contents and then nailed them shut again. The soldiers of the trophy platoon tried to mend the broken crates. It was almost impossible to move in the dim, crowded tunnel, and the group worked slowly. One of the soldiers accidentally discovered a third tunnel, also filled with works of art, located 200 metres away from the others.

At the end of March, the Soviet Sixty-Ninth Army was preparing to cross the Oder river. The patrols left Hohenwalde. Soon the district would be handed over to the Polish military administration, and there was no time for Sidorov to be selective. He was ordered not to pick out the most valuable objects in the depository but to send everything to Moscow. The Department of Special Transportation of the Front gave him twenty-two railway carriages, and the Twentieth Trophy Battalion sent 120 soldiers and trucks. For six kilometres from the shelter the railway was camouflaged against possible air strikes. Crates filled with works of art were lifted by winches from the tunnel. German bombers were swooping overhead as the trucks were being loaded. Another train nearby was being filled with equipment from the Focke-Wulf plant.

An unexpected convoy of trucks arrived at the last moment. To his surprise, Sidorov recognized its commander, Alexei Belousov, the former chief political editor of the Department of Music Halls and Circuses of the Arts Committee, who had been sent to the front with the rank of major in Belokopitov's brigade. Belousov was transporting works of art he had collected in Panzin Castle in the district of Stargard. Sidorov had not been informed that the castle treasures had to go to Moscow by the same train, but after a short argument the soldiers were ordered to load the crates into the already overloaded carriages. There was no inventory for them, so by the time the train reached Moscow it was impossible to tell which crates had come from Hohenwalde and which from Pansin.

Belokopitov arrived a few hours before the departure. Feverishly supervising the loading, the exhausted Sidorov learned that he would travel with the 'art train' to Moscow as the convoy officer. He was told that there had been no time to prepare transportation documents and that he would receive them at a station en route. As the trains departed Belokopitov and Belusov stood together in a forest clearing under pine trees draped in camouflage netting, watching the first major transportation of works of art wend its way towards Moscow.[7]

BERLIN

The Destruction of the Museums

Despite Goering's promises that no bombs would fall on the cities of
the Reich, Berlin museum officials began as early as 1939 to hide
their most valuable possessions in the cellars of museum buildings. In
1940 important objects were sent to the Reichsbank, the Prussian
State Bank, and the Imperial Mint, where they were locked in safes.
The newly built anti-aircraft towers, or Flakturms, at the Zoo and in
the Friedrichshain district, each connected to a smaller Leitturm, or
air defence command tower, became the main shelters for the treasures
of the Berlin museums in 1941, and it was not until the end of 1942
that curators began to prepare smaller shelters outside the city, despite
accusations of defeatism from Reich Minister Goebbels.[1]

The evacuation from Berlin began after the night bombardment of
1 March 1943, when hundreds of British bombers rained explosives
and incendiaries on the capital. More than 700 people were killed
and 35,000 were left homeless. It was the first sign of the armageddon
that was waiting for the Third Reich. 'Hitler's doctors and staff
reported that far into the nights that followed, he was troubled by
anguished images of humble Berlin families who had lost not only
their homes but two or three children before their eyes as well.'[2]

From Pomerania to Württemberg, from Silesia to Hesse, more than
twenty warehouses were feverishly refitted as depositories for works
of art. Museum staff members rushed to microfilm inventory books,
catalogues and files. The most important museum buildings were
measured and photo-documented. In the Old Museum (Altes
Museum), the New Museum (Neues Museum), and the Palace of
the Crown Prince (Kronprinzenpalais), frescos were copied. But
the major museum collections remained in the city. Widespread
evacuation came only in the middle of 1944, when the bombardments
were especially devastating and the front line was inching closer and
closer to the German border. Then treasures from the Berlin museums
were sent to the salt mine of Grasleben near Helmstedt (situated on
the future border of the Soviet and British occupation zones). Other

objects were sent to the Schönebeck mine near Magdeburg and to Ransbach. Museum valuables and the gold stock of the Reichsbank were sent to mines in the area of Merkers.[3]

'Night after night,' the American Monuments, Fine Arts, and Archives (MFAA) officer Richard Howard wrote in an unpublished memoir,

> under cover of darkness, but interrupted by air raids, the museum people labored to pack and load the material. They were hampered by shortage of transport – trucks and gasoline were desperately needed by the army, and parts were almost non-existent to repair break-downs ... Few of the laborers were really able-bodied. Old men, women, and wounded soldiers packed the cases, manhandled the heavy loads through the buildings and onto the trucks in the court-yards, crunching the broken glass under their feet, stumbling over piles of brick and stone and plaster fallen from the walls and ceilings, always in the gloom of a blacked-out city. The convoys had to be under way by midnight or soon after, so that they wouldn't be caught in the open road in daylight. (Allied planes could not tell what a truck convoy carried, and dove on such columns with glee, machine gunning their entire length and dropping small bombs whenever they could catch them.)
>
> At the mines, the full cases had to be unloaded again, carried to the elevators, and lowered painfully into the bowels of the earth. Long corridors (usually abandoned by miners long since) had to be traversed, balancing the loads precariously on narrow tracks. Most of the mines had electric light, fortunately; at least in the large chambers. They were awesome sights, great caverns hollowed out of the salt, with vaulted roofs high overhead, and sometimes as big as a football field. Boxes and uncrated pictures and statues were stowed as neatly as possible, and the workers breathed freely for the time they were there, for no bombs could reach two thousand feet underground.
>
> Yet the pressure of time was always on them. Tremendous quantities had to be moved by these few workmen. At least twenty-five hundred packing cases, for instance, were stored in Grasleben. And that was not all. Storage space was carefully allotted, with priorities, so that not only the museums, but the State Archives, the Libraries, the University often struggled to fill the same space ... The banks, too, were hiding away their gold and their records. Private collectors with influence brought their things to the museums or direct to the repositories, and begged for

places of safe-keeping. (Military Government later estimated that far more than fifteen million works of art shared in this exodus, in the United States Zone of Germany alone.)

So it went, right up to the time the Soviet armies surrounded Berlin. With typical German attention to detail, attempts were made to complete records, and tons of paper were filled with lists and catalogues. It was a hopeless task, however, since no sooner were lists made than fires would destroy parts of them, or water would seep into the basements where they were kept, washing away the ersatz ink and reducing the paper to pulp. Slowly the old men watched their life's work sink into chaos, chaos of fire, rubble, dirt, water and the unutterable messiness of destruction. They grew accustomed to it, and puttered and muttered in their ruined offices, wrapped in all the clothing they owned, striving, by burying themselves in scholarly problems of complete ineffectuality, to forget the fantastic reality about them.[4]

The Berlin museums suffered the most serious damage since the beginning of the war on the night of 10 March 1945. A single British bomb aimed at the State Mint, where art treasures were stored, destroyed a large part of the Ornamental engravings collection of the Art Library, most of the porcelains of the Museum of Decorative Arts and the finest exhibition porcelains of the Berlin Porcelain Factory, twelve superb Islamic carpets, musical instruments, and a large part of the East Asian collection of the Ethnographic Museum, among many other treasures.

At the beginning of 1945 the Schlossmuseum had been seriously damaged by bombardment. Sixty of the best faience vessels, furniture, and about 500 Byzantine and Coptic textiles from the collection of the Museum of Decorative Arts were destroyed. Part of the Ethnographic Museum collection was lost on 3 February, when two bombs exploded in the museum building on Prinz Albrecht Strasse.[5]

The British bombardment of 22 November 1943 had taken 2,000 lives. It also destroyed the Monbijou Palace, opposite the Kaiser Friedrich Museum, and blew away the museum's roof. Three of the buildings on Museum Island were lost within a few months. In January 1945 a bomb exploded in the Pergamum Museum and destroyed the left tower of the most important exhibit of the Islamic Collection, the façade of the Ummayad Mschatta Castle.

On 25 February 1945, as Richard Howard described it,

in broad daylight, American bombers, trying to hit Gestapo headquarters and saturating the governmental section of the city, scored more than twenty five direct hits on the buildings of the 'Museum Island', leaving the entire area a shambles of crumbling rubble, with the great monuments from Mschatta and Miletus peering like ghosts over ruins more sudden than those they had seen before in their two or three thousand year history.[6]

The effect of all this on the old men whose life's work was sinking into chaos was terrible. 'Death released some from their nightmare,' Howard wrote.

Thirteen department heads or assistants died 'natural' deaths in two or three years. Five were killed in action. Three are missing, and several more committed suicide. This doesn't count the little fellows, the guards, workmen, and general help who didn't hold resounding titles. All the rest sat in terror, waiting without hope for the end. To the last possible minute they packed and shipped nightly loads out to the repositories, but as the Soviet troops surrounded the city, terror mounted higher and higher, fear became hysteria and then a numbing, senseless resignation. They lost power to plan, to think, or even to move, for a time. Finally, the ring of the savage enemy was complete, the siege of Berlin began, and at least the bombings stopped.[7]

The popular Soviet writer Vsevolod Vishnevsky, who had been in Leningrad during the blockade and was sent in 1945 to the front line to describe the victory of the Red Army, had a different perspective: 'We burst through the borders of Great Berlin at daybreak', he wrote.

It was a delightful dawn. The city, fourth largest in the world, lay before us ... The ill-omened, resentful city, where there were about three million Germans ... And the first discharges of the guns rumbled in the direction of Berlin ... For you, our Russian land, for all our trampled fields, for peasants' huts, for all our orphans, for all widows, for the pain that burdened us all during four years of war! Oh, how furiously we shot and how constantly! Berlin, we will spare no one ... And the battle began inside the city ... The roar in the city was incessant. Glass splinters and dust flew in all directions, an awful dust clouded this huge battle.[8]

The first Soviets to burst into the city were the troops of the Fifth

Shock Army attacking from the east under the command of Colonel General Nikolai Berzarin. They crossed Berlin from the Marzahn district on the outskirts to the Brandenburg Gate and occupied the largest part of the city. Berzarin's troops took almost all of the depositories and hidden stores of works of art in Berlin.[9]

On the morning of 25 April, when the city was surrounded and the Soviet forces met the Americans on the River Elbe, tanks began the bombardment of the Flakturm and the command tower, where the art objects were hidden, in Friedrichshain. The infantry was ready to storm the tower, but Berzarin, who the night before had been appointed the first Soviet military commandant of Berlin, gave the order to surround it and then move in the direction of Alexander Platz. Berzarin did not want to risk the lives of his soldiers and ordered the commanders to destroy every force in their way with artillery fire and to protect their troops.

The command tower became a target of Soviet artillery. One of the shells, aimed at a window, crashed through the steel shutters and exploded in the corner where the glass collection from the Museum of Decorative Arts (located before the war in the Schlossmuseum) was sheltered. One of the world's greatest collections was destroyed; only eleven objects survived the explosion.[10]

Big guns were moved to the Berlin–Lichtenberg railway station, and the bombardment of the centre of the city began. The same day, 1,500 Russian bombers took part in the air strike on the Citadel, the centre of the Reich capital. There was another strike that night. Fifty blocks were taken by Berzarin's forces.[11]

After fierce hand-to-hand fighting, the First Battalion of the 1042nd Rifle Regiment, commanded by Major Alikhan Makoyev, captured the New Mint. A German soldier who was taken prisoner during the battle told the attackers that the garrison of the building was holed up in the cellar. Shouting 'Death for death', the Soviet soldiers threw hand grenades into their midst. When it was over, they swarmed over the badly damaged building. Some rooms had huge iron doors. These were promptly blown up, and behind them the Soviets discovered vaults filled with German banknotes.[12] In the cellar, where the hand grenades had exploded, there were hundreds of works of art: Egyptian, Greek and Roman sculptures, dozens of crates containing antique vases, terracottas, and glass vessels. The famous Roman copy of the Wounded Amazon by Polyclitus, the architectural parts of the

Pergamum Altar, the granite sculpture of the New Kingdom architect Senemut holding Princess Nefrua on his lap, an antique mosaic depicting a battle of centaurs and tigers – all these were witnesses to the last battle of the staff of the Nazi garrison.[13]

The palace and park of Monbijou, in front of the Kaiser Friedrich Museum, was also taken on 25 April. From 29 April to 2 May two Soviet divisions, the 266th and the 416th, attacked Museum Island from opposite directions. Lieutenant General Fyodor Bokov recalled the fighting: 'In the area of the old political centre of Berlin on an island surrounded by two arms of the River Spree, the battles were extremely fierce. This was the site of the palace of Kaiser Wilhelm [the Schlossmuseum, the Museum of Decorative Arts], the cathedral, and the museums that had been transformed by the Nazis into powerful defensive positions.'[14]

On 1 May the 416th Rifle Division, which consisted mainly of Azerbaijanis, began the assault on the palace of Kaiser Wilhelm.

> The day before the attack the storm units ... reached the Schlossplatz – the square in front of the palace. The Palace of Wilhelm! The word spread down the line. The artillery began the bombardment ... Our heavy tanks and assault guns, manoeuvring with difficulty on the narrow streets blocked by heaps of broken bricks, arrived at the Schlossplatz. A continuous shower of fire was launched on the Nazis defending the palace and other buildings. A hurricane of fire howled around the palace. Then the storm began. From different sides the reinforced battalions under cover of our fire rushed the palace ... They cleared the way with the help of hand grenades and machine-gun fire, and in some places broke gaps in the old walls with the help of sappers.

Bloody clashes took place everywhere around the palace: on the main stairway, in the Renaissance Erasmus Chapel, in the study of Frederick the Great, in the ornate Wilhelmine halls. Many objects that had survived the Anglo–American air strike in February were destroyed. The soldiers acted according to the instructions on street fighting in their soldiers' booklet: 'How to enter buildings: First throw a hand grenade into it, then enter it.' After such fighting, little remained of the furniture designed by Schinkel, the music books and notes of Frederick the Great, and the other exhibits.

The palace was soon occupied, but German soldiers in the cellar continued to resist. The division commander considered withdrawing his troops and calling in bombers to destroy the building from the air, but at the last moment he agreed to send negotiators into the cellar, and the surviving Germans surrendered. The palace, which housed two museums, was saved, only to be destroyed by the Communist government of Otto Grotewohl in 1950 as a symbol of Prussian militarism.[15]

On 1 May, the 266th Division took the northern part of the island and occupied three museum buildings. During the night they took the Armoury and the Prussian State Library. The same night a regiment commanded by Colonel Ivan Kozlov occupied the Reichsbank, where collections of drawings and prints and other objects remained. The gold stock of the Reich had been evacuated to the salt mines in Thuringia together with 150 paintings, but in the big safes the Soviet soldiers found canvas sacks secured with black wax seals. Inside were gold crowns of teeth collected from the mouths of victims in concentration camps. The shocked and furious soldiers kicked the only cashier who remained in the bank out of the building and began to question him about their find. They intended to shoot him, but he was rescued by counterintelligence officers who wanted to interrogate him more thoroughly.[16]

The Nazi garrison that defended the Modern Art Department building of the National Gallery in the Kronprinzenpalais resisted longer than other German troops. It was not until the morning of 2 May that the 295th Division cleaned out the building.[17]

Thousands of masterpieces of world art were stored in the cellars of the great museums around which the battles raged. In the Kaiser Friedrich Museum there was a collection of mosaics. Egyptian sculptures were stored in the Neues Museum. A collection of furniture was in the Schlossmuseum, and in the Pergamum Museum were canvases of French Impressionists from the private Siemens Collection, paintings by Ghirlandaio and Goya, sculptures by Luca della Robbia and Rossellino from the Berlin museums, and other valuables. The Ishtar Gates, the Babylon reliefs, the figure of Athena Parthenos from Pergamum, and other large monuments that were impossible to hide or evacuate, remained in their half-ruined halls during the bombardments and hand-to-hand fighting. In the yard of the Armoury, among the shell craters, was a collection of souvenirs of former wars: the famous sixteenth-century cannon called Schöne Taube, or Beautiful Dove, the cannon of Charles the Bold, and

another sixteenth-century cannon from Nuremberg. All these masterpieces remained in the part of the city occupied by the troops of
the Fifth Shock Army.[18]

BERLIN

Gold in the Tower

The first Soviet tanks of the Eighth Guard Army reached the Zoological Garden on the evening of 27 April. They took up positions outside the hippopotamus house and the planetarium and opened fire at the huge Flakturm nearby, aiming at the steel shutters over the windows. The Flakturm was overcrowded with terrified civilians who had sought shelter inside – about 30,000 men, women and children crammed into every available corner. The strain had become intolerable for most of them. Some had quietly committed suicide. Two old women sitting side by side had taken poison but remained propped up by the press of bodies. It was days before anyone realized they were dead. A military hospital located in the tower kept operating for all five days of the siege, and the doctors did what they could. When the number of wounded reached 1,500, the hospital overflowed, and people were put wherever there was space. Corpses remained in the tower because the intensive bombardment made it too dangerous to take them out.[1]

Dr Unverzagt, the director of the Museum for Pre- and Early History, was on the first level, on the more secure north side, in room No. 11, worrying about the boxes of antiquities that were still there, including the three crates containing most of the Trojan gold from the Schliemann Collection. The hospital commander, Dr Walter Hagedorn, had told orderlies to place the overflow of wounded on stretchers on top of the museum crates. Their moans could be heard above the constant boom of explosions and gunfire.

Unverzagt's collection was not the only one still sheltered in the tower.[2] From the Armoury, there were the elaborate arms and armour of the kings of Brandenburg and Silesia, a unique collection of helmets, and Napoleon's hat and military decorations. From the Ethnographic Museum were carved totem poles and boats from British Columbia; and from the Egyptian Museum, the famous head of Queen Nefertiti and a collection of gold jewellery and scarabs. There were hundreds of portfolios and rolled-up drawings, including

Botticelli's illustrations to the *Divine Comedy* and Grünewald's studies for the Isenheim Altar. Large paintings and the best portraits of the National Gallery were stored here. But most of the depository was occupied by antiquities and Far Eastern objects: Japanese sculpture and temple paintings, Chinese porcelain and lacquer work, seventy bronze mirrors of the Chou dynasty, and hundreds of other exhibits. There were terracotta figurines and painted vases, cupboards full of gemstones and cameos, and the gigantic reliefs of the Pergamum Altar.[3]

When all these things had been moved to the Flakturm late in 1941, everybody thought it would be for a short time only. Now, three and a half years later, Russian tanks were only a few metres away from the treasures to which Unverzagt had dedicated his life.

The Zoo tower that became his shelter was one of three built during the summer of 1941. The designers in Albert Speer's workshop had made them look like medieval fortresses. Hitler had intended them to be the first buildings of the future capital of the Reich, to be called Germania, that would rise on the site of Berlin after the war. These Nazi castles were bombproof, with walls made of reinforced concrete two metres thick. The window slits were protected by steel shutters, and before the assault on the city many of the windows were bricked up. The towers had electricity, water, and enough stored food and ammunition for a twelve-month siege.

The Zoo Flakturm, forty metres high, was the largest of the three. On the roof were platforms for the anti-aircraft guns. The gunners' barracks were immediately below, on the fifth level. The hospital was on the fourth level, and museum treasures were stored on the third and first levels. On the two lower levels were air-raid shelters, kitchens, and emergency quarters for the staff of the national broadcasting station. There were six levels below ground, for service and communications equipment and ammunition stores. Near each Flakturm was a Leitturm, a smaller tower with a radar dish on the roof that functioned as a communications and radar control centre. From the smaller Zoo tower, separated from the main Flakturm by the Landwehr canal, Luftwaffe officers directed the air defence of the capital.[4]

In his memoirs, Albert Speer wrote a vivid description of watching a British raid from the top of the Zoo communications tower:

I was having a conference in my private office on 22 November 1943, when the air-raid alarm sounded. It was about 7.30 p.m. A large fleet of bombers was reported heading toward Berlin. When the bombers reached Potsdam, I called off the meeting to drive to a nearby flak tower, intending to watch the attack from its platform, as was my wont. But I scarcely reached the top of the tower when I had to take shelter inside it; in spite of the tower's stout concrete walls, heavy hits nearby were shaking it. Injured anti-aircraft gunners crowded down the stairs behind me; the air pressure from the exploding bombs had hurled them into the walls. For twenty minutes explosion followed explosion. From above I looked down into the well of the tower, where a closely packed crowd stood in the thickening haze formed by cement dust falling from the walls. When the rain of bombs ceased, I ventured out on the platform again . . .

From the flak tower the air raids on Berlin were an unforgettable sight, and I had constantly to remind myself of the cruel reality in order not to be completely entranced by the scene: the illumination of the parachute flares, which the Berliners called 'Christmas trees', followed by flashes of explosions which were caught by the clouds of smoke, the innumerable probing searchlights, the excitement when a plane was caught and tried to escape the cone of light, the brief flaming torch when it was hit. No doubt about it, this apocalypse provided a magnificent spectacle.[5]

Friedrich Tamms, the architect who designed the Zoo Flakturm, warned the museum curators in 1945 that it was bombproof but could be damaged or even destroyed by heavy artillery fire. Fortunately for the Germans, General Vasily Chuikov's army, which was advancing toward the Reich Chancellery from the west, had no heavy artillery. The tower survived the tank bombardment. On 1 May the commanders of the Eighteenth Panzergrenadier Division, under pressure from Dr Hagedorn, decided to send negotiators to discuss the conditions of surrender. Everyone had already heard about Hitler's suicide the day before. When the negotiators left the tower to meet a Russian captain, a fanatic Nazi began to shoot at them, but the surrender took place anyway. By evening the civilians and the soldiers had left the tower; only hospital personnel and the museum guards, led by Unverzagt, remained.

A few hours later the Flakturm was overrun by Russian soldiers. Three of them burst into room No. 11 and aimed their machine guns at Unverzagt. 'Wo ist Gold?' they shouted. Fantastic rumours were circulating among the Russian troops about the tower and its treasures, but Unverzagt was lucky. The soldiers who burst in on him were called away by their fellows, who had discovered the stores of food and ammunition. Unverzagt realized that the only way to save the treasures was to ask for the protection of the military administration of the victorious army. He had made this decision some time before, when he concluded that defeat was unavoidable. After the end of the First World War, Unverzagt, then a twenty-six-year-old art historian, had taken part in the work of the restitution commission that had spent six years trying to resolve questions concerning museum exhibits according to the Versailles Treaty. He knew that it was better to give the art treasures to the enemy, who would probably return them eventually, than to let thieves and pillagers take them.

But Unverzagt could not contact military authorities because it was impossible to leave the gold in the tower, which was in the hands of unruly soldiers. He decided to wait, hoping that responsible officers would arrive. Two hours later, when someone appeared on the threshold of room No. 11, Unverzagt saw with relief that he was wearing gilded shoulder boards. The young officer was polite and listened attentively. He immediately ordered the soldiers who had followed him to guard all museum valuables in the tower. Two machine gunners were stationed at the doors of Unverzagt's depository, and the officer ordered them to allow entry only to the medical personnel who were tending the wounded in the room. And so Unverzagt spent the first night of the occupation sitting on the crates containing the gold treasure of Troy, surrounded by wounded and dying people, with two Soviet guards at the doors.[6] He did not know that the well-mannered officer and the guards securing the depository belonged not to an ordinary military unit but to the sinister special service, SMERSH.

SMERSH – the name was an abbreviation of the Russian words 'death to spies' – was the military counterintelligence service established by the NKVD. The brainchild of Stalin, it was as dangerous to Soviets as to Germans.[7] There were rumours that high-ranking Nazis were sheltered in the Zoo tower, and the SMERSH men were looking for them.

The next day, 2 May, Andrei Belokopitov, head of the Arts Committee trophy brigade, arrived in Berlin from Potsdam, where he had left Lieutenant Yevgeny Ludshuveit, who was in charge of military administration in the Trophy Department of the Forty-Seventh Army. An expert in Oriental history, Ludshuveit had been a lecturer at Moscow State University before the war. Together he and Belokopitov had examined Sans Souci and the other palaces in Potsdam. They had questioned the German museum officials who remained in the city, including the former director of the Berlin Picture Gallery, Dr Carl Justi, who gave them invaluable information about where objects were hidden in the capital.

Belokopitov hurried to Berlin, confident that Ludshuveit, who spoke excellent German and got along well with the military administration, could handle things in Potsdam. In Moscow he had been told what to hunt for, and now, thanks to Justi, he knew where to look. The Zoo tower was closer to Potsdam than the other main depositories of works of art. It was impossible to reach Museum Island from the southwest outskirts of the city because a battle was still raging in the area of the Reich Chancellery and the Brandenburg Gate, but the road to the Zoo, controlled by the Eighth Army, was free. Belokopitov's jeep passed the smoking ruins of the Kaiser Wilhelm Memorial Church and turned in the direction of Tiergarten. The streets were blocked by heaps of broken bricks and burned-out tanks and trucks. Corpses lay among the ruins. During the three months of his life on the front line, Belokopitov had become accustomed to landscapes of death and destruction, but he was shocked by the scale of the devastation in Berlin.

The jeep stopped. The road was blocked by piles of rubble. Belokopitov jumped out, ordered his driver to wait, and entered the Zoological Garden through a gap in the wall. Almost all the animal houses and administrative buildings had been destroyed by the Allied bombardment and four days of Soviet shelling. Everywhere the bodies of dead animals lay together with the corpses of the defenders of the capital. The ruins of the exotic elephant house, built in the style of an Indian temple, suggested an episode from Rudyard Kipling. All but one of the elephants were dead. Clambering over shattered trees and making his way among shell and bomb craters, Belokopitov passed the pool where dead hippopotami drifted, killed by shell fragments. One huge beast had survived, and swam in slow circles through water that was bright red with blood. The largest gorilla in Europe, the famous Pongo, lay dead on the concrete floor of his cage. Unearthly noises sounded over this bizarre kingdom of death: the last elephant, Siam, had been driven mad by the bombardment and continually trumpeted his terror. Frightened monkeys flitted about the ruins and a few exotic birds darted from tree to tree, trying to escape the clouds of acrid black smoke.

The massive tower stood at the corner of the garden, between the Landwehr canal and the foundations of the S-Bahn. The steel shutters over the windows, crumpled by shells, were closed. On the wall, pitted by bullets and shrapnel, two slogans were written in white paint: 'Better dead than slaves' and 'Our honour is our fidelity.' The entrance was a dark hole between two massive buttresses. Over it was a balcony, accessible by an iron staircase. Belokopitov read the warning over the entrance, 'Halt-verboten' – Stop, forbidden – and to his immense surprise at that moment heard the same words in Russian. He had not seen the patrol, armed with machine guns, hidden in the trees.

'Why forbidden?' Belokopitov asked, surprised that his colonel's shoulder boards did not impress the lieutenant commanding the patrol.

'The Gestapo hospital is situated here,' the lieutenant answered, checking Belokopitov's papers. Only then did he understand that he had been stopped by SMERSH.[8] The last thing Belokopitov wanted was any involvement with this organization, whose first priority was to spy on Soviet troops through a huge network of informers, and to pounce on signs of disaffection or 'cowardice'. Belokopitov did not know that Stalin, when he was told that Hitler had committed suicide, had ordered a special group of SMERSH officers to find the body. They had scoured the city for eyewitnesses of Hitler's last hours and minutes, locating the man in charge of the Führer's personal security, SS Brigadier Johann Rattenhuber. They had arrested Hitler's body-guard, SS Brigade Leader Wilhelm Mohnke, and his naval adjutant, Admiral Hans-Erich Voss.[9] They held Hitler's personal pilot, Hans Bauer, who had tried unsuccessfully to carry out the Führer's order to rescue from Berlin his favourite portrait of Frederick the Great.[10]

A group of people who would be able to identify Hitler's body wandered among the corpses, shepherded by SMERSH officers. The Führer's remains were not found until 4 May and were identified a week later. SMERSH found a man who had seen Hitler's burial, a guard named Harry Mengershausen, but the final identification was based on dental evidence.[11]

On 2 May, when Belokopitov wanted to examine the Zoo tower, SMERSH personnel were still questioning the staff of the hospital based there and looking for high-ranking Nazis among the wounded. They suspected that the Führer, or his body, might be hidden in the tower. Nobody was paying any attention to the art treasures. Belokopitov pleaded with the patrol for permission to enter. He told them that it was his responsibility to look for the valuable works of art he had been informed were inside, but neither his documents nor his agitation had any effect.

'All right. If you do not want to let me in, call someone who can describe what he saw inside the tower,' Belokopitov begged. The guard agreed and disappeared inside. Half an hour later a military investigator with the rank of colonel came out. They sat down on a blasted tree trunk.

'I can say,' the investigator offered, 'that there are some sculptures. They are very big.'

'What kind of sculptures?' Belokopitov asked. 'Statues?'

'No, not statues, but some huge pieces of stone about three or four square metres each with some images.'

'What kind of images?'

'Some muscular backs, they are almost three-dimensional, but not separated from the stone. They depict some kind of action – something mythological.'

Belokopitov did not recognize the Pergamum Altar frieze from this description, but he understood that the tower was full of valuable old reliefs. The SMERSH colonel advised him to come back a few days later and promised him that the works of art would be protected. He pointed to the armed patrol. 'You see,' he said, 'everything here is guarded and your stones will be completely safe.' And he returned to the search for Hitler.

Belokopitov was still not able to reach either Museum Island or the Flakturm at Friedrichshain. He returned to Potsdam. The streets were filled with rubble and barricades made of burned-out tramcars filled with broken bricks and stones. In the yawning windows of the surviving houses white banners fluttered as signs of surrender. On the top of every tall building the Soviets had affixed a red flag. Big guns still boomed in the centre of the city, but in the Tiergarten the victory celebration had begun. Soviet infantrymen were dancing to the wild music of accordions, either brought from native villages on the Volga

or looted in Germany. The cheerful Russian tank drivers gave cigarettes to the shocked prisoners and let the boys of the Hitler Youth,
whose Panzerfaust rockets had caused them such grief, run away.
Night came to the burning city. It was the first night of peace – a
night of robbery, rape, and suicide.[12]

BERLIN

Ali Baba's Cave

Professor Otto Kümmel, the seventy-year-old director of the Berlin museums, was an expert on Far Eastern art. He was also a Nazi. He did not think that his museums would survive the fall of the Third Reich, but his curator's instinct goaded him to fight to save the collections that remained in the ruined city. At the end of April, before the street fighting ended, he had tried to explain to the Russian officers in charge that the buildings they were shelling contained valuable works of art. They paid no attention to the excited old man who sputtered and waved his hands incomprehensibly.

Kümmel was not frightened during the street fighting, but he was afraid to go outside after the battle ended. The foreign workers had been freed, and 800,000 of these slaves of the Reich became for a time the masters of the city.[1] Organized groups of Poles, Ukrainians, Russians, Dutch, and French labourers, united by the common struggle for survival during the long years under Nazi rule, now hunted their former despots. Kümmel stayed indoors until 5 May, when he made his way to the Zoo tower. To his surprise, the Russian guard commander, Major Lipskerov, not only listened to him but even let him in. He spent a short time in the tower and then was escorted by Lipskerov to Museum Island.[2]

Andrei Belokopitov's goading had convinced SMERSH to pay some attention to the art treasures of Berlin, but the main impulse was given by Colonel General Nikolai Berzarin, the military commandant of the city, who paid a visit to the Zoo tower the day before Professor Kümmel arrived. On 3 May, Berzarin, together with Marshal Zhukov and Lieutenant General Bokov, looked out over defeated Berlin from the Victory Column in the Tiergarten, where Hitler had usually greeted military parades. Arthur Pieck, son of the German Communist leader Wilhelm Pieck, pointed out the sights of interest to the Soviet commanders. He had fought in the Red Army and wore the uniform of a Soviet officer. Berzarin's attention was arrested by the Flakturm that loomed above the Zoological Garden.

The next morning the commandant took part in a military parade of the Thirty-Second Army Corps on Museum Island. The troops were drawn up in parade formation on the Lustgarten square, between the Schlossmuseum and the cathedral. Traditional Russian dances were performed and a military orchestra played. After the parade Berzarin ordered his driver to go to the Zoo. They drove down Unter den Linden. Passing the university, Berzarin noticed that a commissar with the rank of major was standing on a truck and with the help of soldiers was attaching to the entrance arch of the building a banner printed in both German and Russian: 'Karl Marx, the founder of scientific communism, was a student at this university 1836–1841.' On the neighbouring building, the state library, another banner was already fluttering, and a group of soldiers, led by another commissar, was observing with enjoyment the result of their efforts. The banner said 'Vladimir Lenin, the founder of the All-Union Communist Party (Bolshevik) worked here in 1895.' Satisfied with the work of the political department, Berzarin continued on his way.

His desire to pay a visit to the Flakturm was the result of his meeting that morning with Walter Ulbricht, one of the leaders of the German Communist Party. Ulbricht insisted that it was crucially important to prevent conflicts between the Russian forces and the German population. Berzarin agreed and ordered him to visit various army units to explain the policy.[3] He decided to visit the Flakturm himself, where one of the largest military hospitals in Berlin was located. In the tower he met Unverzagt, who told him at length what kind of valuables were stored there. Berzarin calmed him down by promising that 'very soon the Special Committee will remove everything to storage'.

Major Lipskerov, the SMERSH commandant of the tower, treated Unverzagt with sympathy. On 3 May he had accompanied him to Museum Island, where there was complete chaos. The directors and curators of the museums had escaped, but in the cellars they found some guards and their families who had taken shelter from the bombardments. Unverzagt found the keys to the vaults and opened them. The counterintelligence officers checked the contents, found nothing of interest, and left in disappointment. The coin collection of the Münzkabinett and the paintings did not interest them. SMERSH was still hunting for Hitler and for documents containing the secrets of the Reich. As Unverzagt locked up, he noticed that the

Russians had begun to secure Museum Island, and their patrols were in control of its territory. After Berzarin's visit to the Zoo the next day, the Arts Committee brigade was finally given permission to organize normal work in the Berlin depositories.[4]

The Arts Committee sent more experts to Berlin from Moscow. Two of them were art historians in major's uniforms: Serafim Druzhinin and Alexei Mikhailov. The third was Lieutenant Colonel Alexander Voloshin, in civilian life the stage director of a circus. He became Belokopitov's deputy and the main organizer of the brigade's daily life. They lived and worked in a shabby three-storey building at Drachenfelsstrasse 4 in the suburb of Karlshorst, the only district in Berlin that had electricity. The building housed up to eight art experts, four engineers, and seven specialists in printing. Their mission was not only to collect works of art but to prepare for shipment to the USSR theatre costumes and equipment, machinery for making prints, strings for musical instruments, sheet music printing presses – all kinds of equipment that had some connection with culture. Two German translators and two typists assisted them. Six local carpenters were hired to make crates and pack works of art. Two attendants cleaned the apartments and offices every day.[5] A driver kept the brigade's cherished car, a new Opel Admiral, meticulously polished.

The little kingdom of the Arts Committee in defeated Berlin was always crowded with visitors from Moscow. Some came for brief periods to select art treasures from the city's museums for shipment to Russia. Others visited Drachenfelsstrasse to spend time in congenial company. In late spring and early summer a group of prominent artists came to record the victory of the Red Army. Alexander Deineka and Dmitry Mochalsky, Konstantin Finogenov and Pyotr Sokolov-Skalya, who were sketching the ruins of the Reichstag and other government buildings for their future pictures commemorating the victory, enjoyed the parties in Karlshorst, where they could drink a glass of vodka and listen to the stories about mines and shelters packed like Ali Baba's cave with art treasures.[6]

In August the operations of the Arts Committee were expanded. The Soviet military administration decided that German workers, who had been conscripted during the first months of the occupation, must be paid, and Voloshin included in his new budget the price of vacuum cleaners and equipment for measuring humidity, needed for the storerooms. One depository was situated in a huge abbatoir.

Another was in the Treskov Palace in Friedrichsfelde. Neither building was ideal for storing the thousands of works of art collected for transportation to the Soviet Union, but at least they were undamaged by bombardment or artillery shells.

Voloshin's estimate for salaries and wages, special packing materials, vacuum cleaners and office renovation came to 597,400 rubles. It was a lot of money, but he was sure his superiors would agree that the return would be worth the expenditure.[7]

On 7 May Belokopitov returned to Berlin. He met his new colleagues and ordered them to go to Potsdam the next morning to begin preparing the collections of the palaces for transpo. .tion to the USSR.[8] After their departure, Belokopitov composed his report to Major General Pyotr Zernov, the representative of the Special Committee on Germany in Berlin, and Lieutenant General Konstantin Telegin, a member of the Military Council of the Soviet Occupation Forces in Germany. He wrote that he had examined the palace museums of Potsdam with the help of Ludshuveit. 'Summarizing the results of the inspection,' he said,

> we can say that we have several thousand original pictures . . . of German, French, and Italian masters and a large quantity of valuable copies of the works of world-famous artists, several hundred marble statues . . . a very large quantity of old palace furniture and *objets d'art*. There are several thousand miniatures. There are about fifty thousand rare (some antique) editions of books . . . The value of all counted objects, which could be deconstructed and removed to the Soviet Union . . . is about 150,000,000 golden rubles.[9]

Not until Belokopitov had completed his report did he decide to inspect the depository in the Leitturm at Friedrichshain. His delay had tragic consequences. While he was counting the Potsdam valuables, the real treasures were lost for ever. Their fate would disturb the imagination of historians and journalists for the next half-century.

BERLIN

Fire in Friedrichshain

The greatest mystery involving the looted works of art of Berlin was the fire in the Friedrichshain Leitturm, or control tower. It began on 2 May 1945, when the last defenders of the tower escaped. Soviet military officials and SMERSH were more interested in the Zoo tower. Friedrichshain had been cut off from the centre of the city on 27 April, and it was clear that neither Hitler nor other high-ranking Nazis could have hidden there. The Soviets shelled the tower but did not storm it. In any case, they had no information about the works of art stored there.

What happened in the tower after it was deserted by its defenders is not known. The museum curators responsible for the collections sheltered there slipped away. Museum guards visited the tower from time to time, on 3, 4, and even 5 May. They saw that the tower had no security and was being robbed by foreign workers and by Germans, whose main target was the food supply on the first level. On the same level were stored the most important objects from the Berlin museums antiquities collection and from the Art Gallery: 8,500 antiquities packed in boxes and 2,800 glass objects of exceptional value. The 411 large canvases from the Art Gallery – pictures that were too big for the mines – included the highlights of the collection. The 160 Italian paintings – a quarter of the Italian collection – included works by Fra Angelico and the famous *Pan* by Luca Signorelli. Flemish art was represented by the huge canvases of Peter Paul Rubens. There were seventy paintings of the German school and works by Chardin, Zurbarán, Murillo, and Sir Joshua Reynolds. There were also 400 sculptures and reliefs from the Sculpture Collection, from a *Lamentation* by an anonymous German master of the early fifteenth century to the *Madonna with Christ and Cherubs* by Donatello. Pre-Columbian figurines shared the space with Egyptian statues and oversized, rolled-up prints from the Kupferstichkabinett.[1]

Otto Kümmel was finding it impossible to deal with the Russians. They assured him that they wanted to take care of things but did nothing. 'One never gets anywhere with them in attempting to go through their channels of command,' he later told the Americans. 'The lowest echelon says it will refer a matter to the proper higher echelon, but one never hears anything further and action is never taken.' It was difficult to learn the name of any Russian who was responsible for anything.[2]

On the night of 5 May, a few hours after Kümmel had visited the Zoo tower, a fire began in the tower at Friedrichshain. The first level, including the food stocks and most of the works of art, burned. Kümmel got there two days later and learned that the fire had not damaged the second or third levels. He tried unsuccessfully to convince the Soviet military administration to secure the building, but once again the Russians said they would take care of things and did nothing.

Belokopitov also failed to convince them. He came to the tower a short time after Kümmel, between 7 and 14 May, and walked up the only surviving staircase to the first floor. The lift and the second staircase had been ruined by fire. The remains of paintings, tapestries and prints were still smoking, but the foreign workers were digging in the debris, looking for something to loot. Shards of antique glass and pottery crackled under Belokopitov's boots. All the doors were open. In every room he saw the same picture of destruction: fragments of terracotta mixed with shards of antique vases, wooden sculptures transformed into charcoal, and stone reliefs broken in pieces. Only ashes remained of the Mexican feather mosaics and the Peruvian textiles.

Among the ruins Belokopitov saw that a few things had survived. The Roman Caffarelli Sarcophagus stood near a collapsed stairway. Its marble walls were crumbling and black with soot, but it was still possible to recognize the skull of an ox, symbol of death and sacrifice. One of the heavy iron doors was closed and barricaded by debris, which Belokopitov pushed aside. As he opened the door, the marble statues standing in the small windowless space began to fall apart before his astonished eyes. A marble hand fell to the floor and dissolved to dust. It was like entering a bewitched castle in a fairytale. Hands and heads and then torsos disappeared. Belokopitov stooped and picked up a handful of dust that a few seconds before had been the face of a serene Italian Madonna. It took him a few minutes to understand what had happened. As a result of extreme heat, marble is transformed into lime in the absence of oxygen. When Belokopitov opened the door, oxygen entered and the chemical reaction ruined the statues. The head of the brigade was the last human being to see these masterpieces intact. Sergei Sidorov, the chief inspector of the Arts Committee's Department of Visual Arts, did not receive a list of the objects stored in the Friedrichshain tower until the end of June.[3]

On 9 May Belokopitov and his brigade temporarily forgot their problems. Not far from brigade headquarters in Karlshorst, in the building that housed the staff of the Fifth Shock Army, the Act of Unconditional Surrender was signed. The hall in the former military engineers' school was specially decorated for the occasion.

A few minutes before his death, Hitler had given an order to his adjutant Otto Gunsche that his bunker was to remain untouched. 'I want the Russians to realize that I stayed here to the very last moment,' he said. The adjutant executed the order. The Russians, who had surrounded Hitler during his last hours, took the bunker intact.[4]

When the surrender ceremony was being planned, General Berzarin and Lieutenant General Bokov had an idea that pleased them immensely. They remembered that when France surrendered in 1940, Hitler had insisted that the ceremony take place in the railway carriage of Marshal Foch, in which the German generals had signed the surrender of 1918. Berzarin ordered his staff to take some furniture from the Reich Chancellery and the huge carpet that had decorated Hitler's office. 'Let Hitler's intermediaries sign the surrender on the same carpet on which they used to report to their Führer,' Bokov later wrote. 'The commandant of the Reich Chancellery selected the necessary quantity of furniture, and it was transported to staff headquarters with a 120-metre-long dark brown carpet from Hitler's study, which was carried with effort by fifteen of our soldiers.'

The Soviet generals observed with interest the reaction of the Germans during the ceremony.

We noticed that Keitel looked briefly at the carpet, became lugubrious, and whispered something to Friedeburg. He looked down attentively and shuddered . . . The face of the adjutant who stood behind Keitel was transformed, and he began to cry soundlessly. They recognized it – how could they not recognize it? The furniture was familiar. Not so long ago it was an honour for them to sit on it, but now they feel as if they are sitting on pins.[5]

Hitler's personal belongings were sent to a special storage facility, where they were shown from time to time to high-ranking visitors from Moscow. Hitler's remains were sent to Moscow by special plane. Stalin wanted the identification completed by highly qualified doctors. The Führer's skull was kept in a paper bag in the so-called State Archive of the Russian Federation in Moscow in complete secrecy until 1992. The paintings from his private collection were turned over to Belokopitov and transported by him to the brigade's collecting point in the abbatoir.[6]

Serafim Druzhinin, whose unit was billeted in Potsdam, heard about the surrender the same day. An employee of the propaganda department of the Tretyakov Gallery, Druzhinin had been sent to Germany in 1945 as an expert with the trophy brigade. On this warm sunny day in May, he wrote in his memoirs, he was awakened by the sound of gunfire. His first thought was that Nazi holdouts had made their way through the forest, but when he ran outside everything became clear.

' "It's the end!" someone shouted. "It isn't an alarm. This is it, the long-awaited victory!" Kisses, embraces . . . An old German walking down the street doffed his cap and bowed to everyone, saying "Hitler kaput!" ' Dinner was a boisterous banquet, with wine, speeches, and cheering. But in the afternoon came more news. 'We received information that in the "am Zoo" bunker some ancient stones, apparently valuable, had been found. We packed and set off quickly for Berlin.' Belokopitov had summoned them.

As they approached Berlin they passed streams of liberated Poles heading east, in overflowing cars and trucks or on foot pushing handcarts. Many of the vehicles had homemade Polish flags attached. People jumped out to embrace the Russians and cried tears of joy. Finally the brigade neared the desolate, empty city. It was a shocking sight. The black skeletons of bombed-out houses stood stark against the red twilight sky. Fires were still burning here and there. They heard explosions, then saw a pillar of fire, and another ill-fated building collapsed.

They crossed Berlin from east to west: the Frankfurter Allee, the Alexander Platz, the Schloss Platz, Unter den Linden. The Brandenburg Gate was still bricked up, but the central span was open. Druzhinin noted that the damaged Reichstag was covered with graffiti written in chalk and charcoal. Finally they reached the Zoo Flakturm and ran up the stairs, through double doors, and into a huge windowless hall. 'The hand lamp was switched on,' Druzhinin wrote. What he saw astonished him.

'A giant, crying, screaming in torture, and the proud victorious Athena above him are in front of me, on the left side of the entrance. Zeus, stormy and triumphant, is on the right. And so "the ancient stones" meant the frieze of the Pergamum Altar!'

Druzhinin was overwhelmed.

The battle of the gods and the giants! The eternal subject – the fight of life and death, of light and darkness. I was frightened – the artist spoke two thousand years ago about the events of yesterday, the memories of which were alive for us that day ... Victory and catastrophe, destruction and the passionate ecstatic success of life ...[7]

BERLIN

The Gold Disappears

Wilhelm Unverzagt had been told that he would be responsible for the treasures in the Zoo tower until the arrival of a competent Soviet commission. Unverzagt had replied that he could not take the responsibility as long as the hospital remained in the depository and medical staff moved freely about. General Berzarin promised to move the hospital elsewhere, and Unverzagt was appointed director of a new institution, the Flakturm Museum. He received identification papers from the Soviet military administration along with other documents declaring that all art objects stored in the tower were under the protection of the military commandant's office and any attempt to loot them would be punished by a military tribunal.

The wounded were moved from the art storage areas to other rooms in the tower, but the Flakturm Museum did not exist for long. Unverzagt was soon told to prepare his treasures for transportation. Together with the chief museum guard, Dietrich, and one of his staff members, Frau Rove, Unverzagt opened crates, checked the objects against inventories, and then packed them again. Later he wrote that the occasional theft of a few objects was possible only during the preparation of the works of art for transport.

In the other storage areas, objects belonging to the Kupferstichkabinett were packed by Dr Arnolds. Professors Carl Weickert and Carl Blumel had the job of sorting out immense numbers of objects from the antiquities collection, which included 6,000 Greek vases alone. Museum guards helped their supervisors. On 13 May the first convoy of treasures left the Zoological Garden. During the next week Unverzagt wrote in his diary only one word each day: 'Abtransporte' – Transportation. By 19 May the depositories on the first level of the Zoo tower were almost empty. The German museum officials did not know where the works of art, whose preservation had been their occupation for so many years, had gone.

On 21 May the collection of the Ethnographic Museum was removed, and Unverzagt finally discovered that the trucks were going in the direction of Karlshorst. Very soon eight cupboards full of Egyptian papyri, armour belonging to the French kings Francis I and Henry II, from the Armoury, and many other valuable objects were taken there. Although most of the collections of the Museum of Pre- and Early History had already been removed, Unverzagt refused to part with the three crates containing the Trojan gold. He was waiting for competent Soviet authorities. Finally, on 26 May, a group of people in military uniforms arrived at the tower. Unverzagt heard Serafim Druzhinin, who had already been there, explaining some- thing to his comrades and concluded from the major's confident tone that he was the leader of the group. He did not know that it included Andrei Konstantinov, the deputy head of the Arts Committee, who was personally responsible for the removal of art trophies from Germany. Another important person present that day was the art historian Viktor Lazarev.

Konstantinov and Lazarev were in civilian clothes. Unverzagt, accustomed to military uniform as a symbol of high position, did not pay much attention to these two inconspicuous figures. But the Soviet officers and soldiers treated them with respect and caution. In those days only very high-ranking Soviet citizens could appear in Berlin in civilian dress, so Lazarev, a former lieutenant in the czarist army, seemed to the waiting drivers a more powerful person than Lieutenant General Nikolai Antipenko, the head of the Home Front of the First Belorussian Front, to whom Lazarev was talking, behaving in a professorial manner. Finally the crates containing the Diadem of Helen of Troy and the treasures of Eberswalde and Cottbus were loaded into the Studebaker truck. Unverzagt watched it move off among the trees.[1]

Andrei Belokopitov's battle with SMERSH dragged on. Despite General Berzarin's support, SMERSH refused Belokopitov per- mission to organize large-scale work in the Zoo tower. He removed small objects to the collecting points, but the sculptures on the third level remained untouched. The SMERSH officers allowed the brigade to use German museum personnel in the tower but would not let in other people, limiting access even to members of the trophy brigade.

It soon became known that at the beginning of June the Western Allies would take control of their zones of the city. The Zoo tower would be in the Western sector, and Belokopitov knew that he had a very large problem. On one hand, he was getting nowhere with SMERSH, which had no intention of leaving the tower. On the other hand, SMERSH would surely arrest him if he left a rich collection of antique sculpture in the Western zone. Belokopitov visited the Zoological Garden again, but the visit gave him no relief. The scene there was chaotic. 'The Zoo was overcrowded with people of all possible nations,' he later remembered.

> All the liberated displaced persons organized a camp there. Their tents were everywhere – ecstasy, drinking, sex. Some soldiers, probably Americans, organized trade there. God knows what was going on. You could count the days that remained until the Americans would take over the territory. American journalists were running around the tower. They, and of course American intelligence, knew that the Pergamum Altar was inside. They probably believed that all these treasures would be left for them. What to do?[2]

Belokopitov's belief that the Pergamum Altar would be removed by the Americans (in fact, the area of the Zoo tower was in the British zone) reflected a new state of affairs. The Western Allies were already regarded as enemies – but not yet openly. The cold war had started even before the real war was over. Vladimir Yurasov, an officer of the Soviet military administration who defected to the West in 1946, later described a meeting of high-ranking officers of the First Belorussian Front on the eve of the storming of Berlin:

> General Nikolai Bulganin [later Premier] was the first to speak: 'The war is not over. We have defeated Hitler but not Fascism. Fascism exists all over the world, especially in America. We needed a second front and the Capitalists refused to give it to us! And it cost us millions of our brothers!' As Zhukov sat silent, general after general got up to exhort the listeners. 'America is now the primary enemy,' one of them said. 'We have destroyed the base of Fascism. Now we must destroy the base of Capitalism – America.'[3]

Later Yurasov, who was a *demontagenik* – a dismantler of factories and industrial installations to be shipped back to the USSR – was supervised by the deputy for economic problems of the Soviet commander in Berlin. His orders were clear: 'Take everything from the Western sector of Berlin. Do you understand? Everything! If you can't take it, destroy it. But don't leave anything to the Allies. No machinery, not a bed to sleep on, not even a pot to pee in!'[4]

Belokopitov had one advantage over the representatives of the various state agencies and commissariats who swarmed over Berlin at the end of May, annoying the military administration with demands for help in removing everything from large industrial installations to small pencil factories. He had known many of the high-ranking commanders before the war. In those days they had had to curry favour with him in order to get tickets to new performances at the Moscow Art Theatre, where he was the manager. It was Stalin's favourite theatre and one of the very few he attended regularly. He had a special armoured box there for his use only. To be present at a first night was an honour for high-ranking apparatchiks and a necessity for the political and cultural elites of Moscow. Belokopitov, who was even known to Stalin, could always provide a ticket for a friend. Now, in a difficult situation in Berlin, he decided to call in some favours. Lieutenant General Nikolai Antipenko, head of the Home Front of the First Belorussian Front, was an old acquaintance. Belokopitov explained his problem to Antipenko, and then warned him that if the sculpture collection remained in the tower, there would be a major scandal. 'I will be accused, and everybody will have problems.'

'I can do nothing,' Antipenko answered. 'You know what kind of organization it is. The business is not my responsibility. This is the first problem. And the second problem is that I simply have no transport or equipment. All the transport and the labour force have been sent to remove factory equipment.'

They agreed that Marshal Zhukov was the only person who could intervene, but Antipenko did not want to bother him with Belokopitov's problem, especially since SMERSH was involved.

'In that case, please arrange a meeting for me with Zhukov,' Belokopitov said. This was risky, but Belokopitov had decided that a collision with SMERSH was unavoidable. Antipenko was also frightened because SMERSH was controlled personally by Stalin and led by General Viktor Abakumov, a man who had become famous for his ruthlessness during the purge years. He was a crude, corrupt man who liked spending his time in the circle of his harem and boon companions. But he was undeniably efficient, jesuitical, sharp, and of course devoted to Stalin. During the May days of 1945 his star was rising. Less than a year later Stalin would appoint him the head of the Ministry of State Security (MGB).

Both Belokopitov and Antipenko knew that Abakumov bitterly resented any interference in counterintelligence activities, especially if it came from representatives of the army.[5] Plus, they could not be certain that the conduct of SMERSH was not simply camouflage for the removal of Abakumov's own private loot. He was a well-known lover of art, and there were many rumours about his private collection. In 1951, when he was arrested by his arch competitor Lavrenty Beria, he was accused of 'moral decadence and the use of his position for personal purposes', among other sins. The main evidence for this charge was his collection.

Belokopitov decided that appealing to Zhukov was less dangerous than giving in to SMERSH. He knew Zhukov personally because the marshal too was a theatregoer, and he was aware that Zhukov, who had survived the purge of 1937 only by luck, hated the secret police. (After Stalin's death he helped Khrushchev arrest Beria and, according to popular legend, he and members of his staff personally shot Beria and Abakumov.) In May and June of 1945 he had reached the culmination of his career and the height of his power.

The next day Belokopitov met Antipenko, who was pessimistic. 'The only thing I can promise is to take you into the Central Staff building in Karlshorst, and escort you to Zhukov's door. But I'm sure that it will end with scandal and you'll be sent from there directly to military prison.'

'For this business I'm willing to take the risk. And the military prison is not Lubyanka anyway,' Belokopitov answered.

Nearly fifty years later, Belokopitov described what happened next.

I returned to our office on the Drachenfelsstrasse and told our people, you must find me a civilian suit. Where they found it I don't know; perhaps they undressed some German. But it fitted well. The next day I met Antipenko. He was surprised: 'What happened? Why aren't you in uniform?' 'It's better to be dressed like a civilian for this business.' 'My God, then do what you want. The only thing I'm afraid of is that you will create trouble for me too. I'll never let you in if you don't promise me now that in no circumstances will you mention my name in your conversation with Zhukov.' 'I give you my honest word,' I answered.

He came with me to Zhukov's door; the guards saluted us and let us in – everybody knew Antipenko. When we reached the door of the marshal's office Antipenko disappeared. I went in. Some generals were sitting in the waiting room. It seemed that they had just arrived from Moscow. They didn't look like battle generals. Judging by their faces, I understood that they were important. I bravely walked up to the adjutant and showed him my MKhAT [the theatre] ID; by lucky chance I had taken it with me to Germany, and it really was useful on this occasion. He read my ID and immediately went to Zhukov's office. In a few seconds he was back: 'The marshal is waiting for you.' The waiting room reminded me of the silent scene from Gogol's comedy *The Inspector General*. All the generals who had been waiting there for a long time stared at me with surprise . . .

Zhukov stood up and walked over to me with the words: 'Finally MKhAT has come to Berlin.' I stood to attention and answered: 'No, MKhAT didn't come to Berlin, and I'm not the theatre manager now . . .' And I explained to him why I had been sent to Berlin. The friendly expression on Zhukov's face changed. 'Is this a masquerade?' he asked. 'I've organized this masquerade because it was the only chance to see you, comrade marshal,' I answered and then explained to him the problem of the Zoo tower. Finally I lost patience and said, 'If the Americans get this collection, you'll regret this mistake.'

Zhukov became grim and ordered his adjutant to call General Antipenko. When Antipenko came in, he pretended not to know me and I pretended, too, that I didn't know him. Zhukov briefly explained the problem, which was actually well known to him, and then asked in a stern voice: 'Why aren't you helping to evacuate these valuables?' Antipenko looked blank but answered: 'The tower is under SMERSH control. They wouldn't let us in.'

'Call the head of SMERSH,' Zhukov shouted to his adjutant. A general came in. 'You have twenty-four hours to evacuate everything from the Zoo Flakturm,' the marshal said to him. The general was stunned. I lost control and interrupted their conversation. 'Twenty-four hours is not enough. The objects are very big.' Zhukov looked at me disapprovingly and then again addressed the SMERSH general: 'If not in twenty-four hours, in forty-eight hours everything must be removed. In two days the tower must be empty.' After this we all left the office. The SMERSH general looked at me with antipathy but remained silent. Antipenko whispered, 'You gave me a hard time.'

That same evening the sappers unit was moved to the Zoo. It was led by Major Kulakovsky, from the Trophy Department of the Fifth Shock Army. We looked at the friezes and sculptures that were stored on the third level. Our sappers were not very young: these were old men who had constructed the pontoon bridges on the Vistula and the Oder. Kulakovsky asked them: 'How can we get all this stuff out?' 'Very simple,' they answered. 'Let's smash one wall and put a crane there and we can fish them out.' They immediately began to cut down old trees in the park and made wooden frames 3 by 2 metres each. The hospital was quickly evacuated by SMERSH. We took mattresses and luxurious plush blankets from the hospital rooms. We put the mattresses on the frames; we put the reliefs packed in blankets on the mattresses and then let them down carefully through the hole in the wall our sappers had blown out. In a day and a half everything was removed to the abbatoir. We controlled the work. I begged the drivers: 'Comrades, please try not to break them!' The displaced people surrounded us, talking loudly all the time. And the Americans were jumping around. They were furious when they noticed that we were moving the Pergamum Altar . . .[6]

Walter Andrae, a professor and the curator of the Far Eastern collection, wrote in his diary: 'The Russians said that they would remove the Pergamum Altar in two days with the help of 300 soldiers. It is impossible. Forty German masons needed four weeks to dismantle it.'[7] But the professor did not know the Russians. The American MFAA officer Richard Howard recalled:

Their most spectacular job in Berlin was the Pergamum Altar . . . Major Druzhinin nodded taciturnly and forty soldier workmen joyfully attacked the sculptures with pickaxe and crowbar. The friezes were ripped anew from their walls, loaded upon flat cars, and were never seen again. About a hundred other first class Greek sculptures and architectural pieces, from Olympia, from Samos, from Priene and Miletos, from Didyma and Baalbek, brought by the devoted labor of archaeologists to Berlin, went with them. In guttural accented German, Lazareff directed that more be taken. Seven thousand Greek vases, eighteen hundred statues, nine thousand antique gems, sixty five hundred terracottas and Tanagra figurines, and thousands of lesser objects were removed from the Department of Greek Antiquities alone.[8]

Most of the objects were removed in two days. At the beginning of June the 'remains' were collected. Only bare walls remained in the

Zoo tower. But Belokopitov's fears were ungrounded. The Allies did not take control of their zones for another month.

On 28 July an American officer (probably Lieutenant Kenneth Lippman from Supreme Headquarters, Allied Expeditionary Forces) reported to his MFAA colleagues about a meeting with the Russians. The Americans visited the Flakturm a few days later and were shown a big room from which, they were told, the Soviets had removed works of art. On the door was a sign reading 'Staatliche Museen'. It was Otto Kümmel who told them what had happened to the collections. The Pergamum Altar reliefs had been removed without harm, he said, but the paintings and other things had been thrown into trucks without packing materials, so that friable limestone Egyptian reliefs and Romanesque sculptures had come apart in the Russians' hands. A Chinese bronze drum had been rolled down a flight of stone steps, 'and so on and so on until one became rather sick at the recitation'.[9]

While the Zoo tower collections were being taken away, removals from the other storehouses in the future Western zones were in progress. Objects belonging to the collections of the Ethnographic Museum, the Art Library, and the Museum for Pre- and Early History were removed from the depositories on Prinz Albrecht Strasse and Arnimallee in Dahlem.[10] When the transportation of works of art from the Western part of the city was completed, the most trying period for the trophy brigades was over. The objects from the Berlin museums that had not been removed to Soviet collecting points were secured in the cellars of the well-guarded Museum Island and the New Mint. It was time to decide what to do with these treasures too.

On 16 May Professor Ivan Galkin, the rector of Moscow State University, received an unusual telegram, signed by Andrei Konstantinov: 'Because of a special assignment from the state boards, corresponding member of the Academy of Sciences of the USSR Comrade Lazarev V.N. must immediately leave for 10–15 days. I am informing you that Comrade Lazarev V.N. is on a confidential mission.'[11] When Galkin received the telegram, Viktor Lazarev had already been in Germany for two days, having flown to Berlin with Konstantinov on 14 May. Andrei Belokopitov met them at Tempelhof airport. His two reports about the art treasures of Potsdam and the situation in the museums of Berlin had made the famous art historian drop everything to come to Germany.

Konstantinov and Lazarev immediately began to work. Officially, Konstantinov was the head of the Commission of the All-Union Art Committee, as their mission was called, but Lazarev, who had an excellent knowledge of the Berlin collections, played the main role. He wrote all the commission documents. Efficient and inspired by his task, he travelled around Brandenburg, inspecting shelters. He personally selected paintings in the monastery church in Lehnin, removed works of art from Reinsberg Castle, and examined the ruins of the burned-out depository of the Palaces Department in Barkow.

Lazarev was pessimistic about the future of the Berlin museums:

> All museum buildings are in half-ruined condition. Most of them were so seriously destroyed as the result of air strikes that their reconstruction seems impossible. This group included the National Gallery, New Museum, Old Museum, Schlossmuseum, Museum of Pre- and Early History, Ethnographic Museum, and the Museum of Far Eastern Art.[12]

Lazarev was the most prominent art historian in the Soviet Union. During the 1930s he had protested against the secret sale of masterpieces from Soviet museums organized by Stalin's government. He would suffer during the campaign against cosmopolitans of 1948, losing his position and being prevented from publishing. He had taken an active part in drawing up the lists of equivalents, and now he drew up a plan for the removal of cultural trophies from Germany. He believed that selecting the works of art was a job for experts, and he personally agreed to select the Western European paintings and sculpture. Lazarev paid serious attention to the preservation of the objects and their safe transport. He recommended better security for the museums and protested sharply against the removal of museum records. He even insisted that the records of the Sculpture Collection, which had already been confiscated, be returned. He also protested against private looting by high-ranking military commanders, making no exception for Antipenko or Bokov. As an art historian, Lazarev understood the importance of the German school of art history and tried to save it. But he had no sympathy for Nazis. He asked Berzarin to fire Otto Kümmel, who had been an active member of the National Socialist Party.

Lazarev proposed a logical plan for the removal of works of art. He recommended that important pieces in limited quantities be taken from the state museums, leaving representative collections behind. 'I would select 50–100 of the best pieces in the cellar of the New Mint,' he wrote, 'and from the territory of the museums I would take only the statues of Meleager, Demeter, and Aesculepius.'[13]

In his report addressed to Georgy Malenkov, the secretary of the Central Committee, Lazarev expressed his opinion even more clearly:

> Because the best and the most valuable museum exhibits were removed by the Germans to the Western occupation zone, it makes sense to limit the selection from the half-ruined museums and cellars only to the most interesting objects (not more than 300–400). The works of the German masters, as a rule, shouldn't be removed.[14]

In his report about the palaces of Potsdam, Lazarev recommended that these historic buildings should not be ruined.

> It is impossible to separate the monumental sculpture, tapestries, chandeliers which are connected to the architecture. It is reasonable to limit the removal to the most valuable ... statues and paintings (not more than 250–300 exhibits) created by foreign masters ... It makes sense to remove 20–30 objects of furniture of the eighteenth century, which could be used to enrich our palaces on the outskirts of Leningrad, which were ruined by the Nazis.

In all the documents composed during trophy operations, this was the only reference to compensating Soviet museums for their losses with works of art confiscated from German collections.[15]

But in the same letter we find Lazarev giving stern orders:

> To work all the time to find private collections belonging to the Nazis, representatives of the bourgeoisie, and art dealers. All things must be transported to Moscow immediately ... To remove to Moscow everything that can be found in the Friedrichshain flak tower ... Immediately send to Moscow everything that was removed from the Zoo flak tower and the museum objects situated in our depositories.[16]

Lazarev tried to help the museum officials of Berlin:

> We must give the officials of the central museums food coupons and salaries. More than 90 per cent of these officials are not party members.

They work honestly and help us in our job. Many of them are inter-
nationally known art historians.

But in the same letter he insisted on the establishment of an additional
checkpoint for searching museum staff to prevent theft.[17]

Without hesitation Lazarev confiscated works of art belonging to
private owners and even the property of other countries that had
been allies of the USSR during the war. He ordered two paintings
sent to Moscow that had been looted by the Nazis from Poland: a
Lamentation by an anonymous fifteenth-century German master and
a portrait of a woman by Largillière, found by the Russian experts on
Museum Island. The same fate was waiting for 'the paintings from the
Siemens Collection and the paintings of the French Impressionists'.[18]

But at the same time Lazarev took an unexpected step, which was
extremely risky. He demonstrated great bravery in the case of the
Koenigs Collection, which had been purchased, in a more or less
forced sale, during the Nazi occupation of Holland. In a secret report
addressed to the American occupation authorities in 1947, Hans
Röthel, the curator of the Bavarian State Picture Collection, who
worked at the Allied Collecting Point in Munich, wrote: 'Prof.
Lazareff, at one time Russian Representative at the Collecting Point
Munich, admitted to Colonel Vorenkamp of the Dutch Mission that
the Russians had the Koenigs Collection in their possession.' If the
Ministry for State Security had learned about this conversation,
Lazarev would have paid a very high price.[19]

During a short trip to Munich, Lazarev impressed the young
American art historians of the MFAA by his hunger for information
about developments in art history in their country. He asked them
about new publications; since the end of the 1930s Soviet scholars
had had no access to Western publications. He was ready to talk for
hours about new ideas and discoveries.[20]

The art historian, with his sharp eyes, grey hair combed back, and
guttural voice, always made an impression. He was not a traditional
academic type. Later, talking to his students, Lazarev gave them an
ironical self-characterization: 'I would kill a man for an old master
drawing, but I would exchange the drawing for a ticket to a soccer
match.' As with every joke, this one had a grain of truth.

Lazarev's visit to Germany coincided with the reorganization of
the administration of the Soviet occupation zone. On 6 June 1945

the Council of People's Commissars of the USSR created a system of various authorities for the Soviet military administration in Germany. The heads of military administration in the regions of East Germany were formally the commanders of the army units based there, but the real rulers were the political commissars, not the battle generals. They were under orders from Lieutenant General Bokov, who was based in Berlin. He had been actively involved in the removal of German art treasures. He had helped Belokopitov's brigade equip their depositories and transfer to them the objects from the Berlin museums found in the Zoo tower. After June 1945 all decisions about the fate of the art treasures of the defeated country were made by Bokov.

The Special Committee on Germany was not disbanded. It continued to strip German industrial installations and remove everything from agricultural products to freshly produced German goods. Hundreds of representatives of Soviet ministries, commissariats, and organizations were sent to Germany with only one task: to remove, remove, remove. Special military units as well as 60,000 German POWs were engaged in the work, and 90,000 railway carriages were used to transport the loot. Stalin was most interested in heavy industry. Entire factories were dismantled and transported from Thuringia, Saxony and Brandenburg to the Urals and Siberia. Millions of dresses, coats, men's suits, and even hats were sent to Moscow, Leningrad and Kiev. By the end of July, trains overloaded with loot were leaving for the east day and night.[21] It was not until this flood of 'material valuables' ebbed that the stream of cultural valuables picked up speed. Works of art took time to collect, and there was always a struggle for space in the overloaded railway carriages.

BERLIN

The Friedrichshain Disaster

On the recommendation of Viktor Lazarev another important Russian art historian and archaeologist, Vladimir Blavatsky, was sent to Berlin. Richard Howard, the American eyewitness to events in Berlin, remembered Blavatsky more kindly than the authoritarian Lazarev: 'Professor Blavatskii ... greeted his old colleagues with warmth. He had once studied art history in Berlin. Of Polish extraction, he had become a thoroughgoing Communist, and was the "expert" of the Soviet forces.'[1] Howard did not know that Blavatsky felt guilty for the rest of his life about his activity in the occupied capital in 1945. He confessed later to one of his students that fate had forced him to take part in the 'raid' on German museums.

Blavatsky's major assignment was the excavation of the burned-out Friedrichshain Leitturm. At the beginning of July he visited the tower with the restorer Mikhail Ivanov-Churonov. The soldiers would not let them into the top floors because it was widely believed they were mined, but they described to them the immense eight-level cellar, connected by tunnels with other bunkers. 'The heaps of plaster fallen from the ceiling and the walls created a layer 50–80 cm thick, lying on the floor,' Ivanov-Churonov wrote later.

In some places the floor was covered with a layer of flaky white ash, 90 cm thick. In various places on top of these heaps lay porcelain statuettes. With the soldiers we gathered them together in one place but did not pack them because we had no crates. Then the archaeologist and I began to scrape the plaster dust to a depth of 20–30 cm. We found some statuettes made of clay. The archaeologist called them terracottas. Becoming more and more interested in this job, we began to penetrate into the depth of the layer of plaster, gathering little shards with interesting decorations painted in black and brown ... Blavatsky, with the skill typical of an archaeologist, poked his hands into a crack in the heaps of plaster and fished out a clay vessel with a long spout. He held it in both hands and asked me: 'Do you know how old this pot is?' 'No,' I answered. 'This pot was made 2,000 years before our millennium.' Our work was finished that day with the discovery of the pot. Two days later I and the archaeologist took crates and workers with us and came there to organize real excavations.

The experts filled fifteen crates with objects found in the heaps of ash and plaster. On the second level they discovered damaged and dusty statues. In a heap of ashes Blavatsky found a strange object that looked like a vase of unusual shape. When the ash and dirt were cleaned off, the archaeologist discovered to his surprise that the exotic 'vase' was an anti-tank rocket, a Panzerfaust, which had not exploded during the fire.[2]

Blavatsky's reports create a very gloomy picture. He concluded that the fire had started with the help of flammable liquid. 'The crates were concentrated mainly on the first level, most of which was occupied by them. A smaller number of crates were stored on the second and the third levels ... It seems that the crates were burned from the bottom and burned out completely. During the fire the majority of the works of art burned up, and the rest were damaged by the fire.' Objects made of iron were partly melted, thin-walled objects were burned through (like pots after very long use), some ceramic objects were deformed, plaster was transformed into dust. Roman glass vessels were melted and misshapen. Vessels made of clay, terracotta and porcelain were fractured and broken. Objects made of limestone and marble were transformed into lime. The bronzes were melted down. Things that had fallen, especially large pieces of plaster and parts of the building, ruined the fragile objects.

Later, Blavatsky wrote, crowds of people visited the burned-out storage, walked around it, and dug through the debris, with the result that many of the objects were completely crushed and lost all artistic value. Blavatsky found many objects of antique art, mainly from Cyprus, in the rubbish: terracottas, protomes, masks, little altars and architectural details, vases, glass vessels, bronze statuettes. He found a total of 1,500 objects (forty crates). 'Among them are such first-rate pieces as bronze statuettes from the island of Paros, dated to the 4th century BC, "Spinners" dated to the 5th century BC, and the "Satyr" from Pergamum.'[3]

Blavatsky thought he would need at least two archaeologists and ten labourers to complete the work. However, the final excavations did not take place until six months later, because Blavatsky was 'urgently' sent to Dresden and then returned to Moscow.[4]

At the end of September, Colonel General Alexander Gorbatov, the military commandant of Berlin, sent a report to Marshal Zhukov: 'The season of autumn rains is coming. Many of the things that remained [in the Leitturm] are being ruined as a result of dampness. It is necessary to begin ... excavations immediately ...'[5] But the Arts Committee officials could not understand what was clear to the generals. The excavation was delayed, and they would not agree to use German archaeologists for the work. Only after Georgy Malenkov personally intervened was Blavatsky sent back to Berlin on 28 December 1945. He brought with him an archaeologist, P. Sokolsky, and finally professional excavations began in the ruined depository.

On 16 March 1946 he summarized the results of his work: about 10,000 objects of ancient and Western European art and applied art had been found.[6] Some were sent back to the Pushkin Museum, where they were described on the list compiled when they were received as 'partly burned', 'seriously damaged', and 'broken'.[7]

In July Zhanetta Matsulevich, head of the department of modern sculpture at the Hermitage, opened a crate that contained:

> 1. A relief of rectangular shape, made of marble. Half-figure of the Virgin and Child by Rossellino. Broken. Many of the parts are missing. 2. Bas-relief of rectangular shape made of marble. Half-figure of the Virgin and Child by Donatello. Broken in many pieces. The marble is burned on the surface. The right elbow of the Virgin is covered with soot. 3. Statuette of the Virgin and Child made of marble by Giovanni Pisano. The heads of both figures are broken off, all projecting parts are seriously damaged, sides are crumbling.

The curators noted similar damage when they opened dozens of other crates that arrived in July from Berlin.[8]

Who was responsible for the fire in the Friedrichshain Leitturm? It seems clear that the tragedy was a result of the sluggishness of the Soviet trophy brigade and the irresponsibility of the German museum curators who were supposed to be responsible for the works of art stored there. The experts of the Arts Committee were so engrossed in their fight with SMERSH over control of the Zoo tower and so occupied by their work in Potsdam that they did not find the time to put the Friedrichshain tower under control. The German curators, unlike their colleague Unverzagt, abandoned their treasures to fate.

The Americans were also very keen to know what had happened in Friedrichshain, which was in the Soviet zone, and they too were investigating the matter. Their most important informant was Professor Kümmel, who told them that there had been heavy fighting in the area on 5 May. This was probably a mistake – it is unlikely that there was fighting in the area after 2 May. The tower was guarded by elderly museum employees who had gone without food or water all day, and in the evening they slipped away, leaving the building unguarded. 'On 6 May,' Kümmel told the MFAA officers, 'a German or Germans' – Kümmel is firm on this point, and sadder on this account – 'set fire to the contents of the Flakturm. He does not know who did it and supposes that it was a manifestation of the last ditch fanaticism of the Schutz-Staffel, or that it was a Werewolf job.'[9]

Kümmel described to the Americans the state of the tower when he saw it the day after the fire. 'It was still quite warm,' they related, and through some good fortune only half of its contents had been cremated. Ashes and debris to the depth of one metre covered the floors of the rooms that had been burned, and perhaps a few objects may have resisted the heat and may be buried under the ashes.' Kümmel urged the Russians to remove the remainder of the objects, which they said they would do but did not. They declined to have a German guard posted, and during most of the following days posted none of their own.' Kümmel managed to send an employee of the museum, named Fuchs, to the Leitturm on 15 May, and Fuchs found that everything in the Leitturm that had not burned on the 6th had been burned in a second fire sometime between the 7th and the 15th.

Professor Kümmel had an illustrated catalogue of the Berlin collection and he ticked off the paintings that had been destroyed. It was 'sickening', an American officer wrote, to think about the lost masterpieces: 'the vanished Rubenses and the glorious things of the Cinquecento; but to be told that Donatellos have also been lost, and about fifty other absolutely first rate sculptures of the Italian Renaissance . . .'

But was Kümmel's suspicion right? Had the arsonist been German? The American officer was unsure. 'A mystery second to that surrounding Hitler's finis will remain to haunt the art historians of the future,' he wrote, 'and I don't think that they are temperamentally able to surmount such anguished uncertainty.'

Kümmel knew that the Russians, who had no torches, lit twisted pieces of paper and then dropped them when they burned down. They had already accidentally started a fire in a warehouse. So why was he so sure it had not been Russians who started the Leitturm fire? 'I couldn't tell you,' the American wrote. 'I could guess about something that he thought strange: the Russians removed catalogue cards from the museums on the Museuminsel, and from the Museum für Völkerkunde, for many objects that weren't in Berlin but had been evacuated to Merkers. I think that the answer to this is perhaps easy.'[10]

Richard Howard, who was well informed about rumours making the rounds in museum circles, believed that thieves had probably started the fire in the tower and that the stored ammunition had turned it into a conflagration. He provided this version of events:

> The Flakturm was the magnet for robbers. The people, curious and rapacious, wandered through its dark waste halls, stumbling over Greek vases, Rubens paintings too large to have been evacuated, Roman sculpture and uncounted treasures. With no light, it was impossible to penetrate far into its artificial caverns. Torches took the place of bulbs. Torches twisted off old newspapers, fired from cigarette lighters, and held overhead until they burned out, when new ones were lit. Thus raging fires were started, holocausts within walls. Demolition charges, probably set by German soldiers before the capitulation, eventually exploded, blasting all that remained to bits. The Soviets accused the museum officials of setting the charges, much to their hurt bewilderment, and in turn they hinted the Russians themselves had done it. There was much confusion as to the actual happenings.[11]

The MFAA officers wanted to see the burned tower with their own eyes – a risky venture, since it was in the Soviet sector. They left their jeep at a distance and strolled leisurely through the grounds, as if they had no particular aim. But they had no problem getting into the tower. 'A Polish DP (Russian slave-labour specimen) with a rifle and one eye received us with genuine Slavic hospitality, offered us to come right in and showed us around with a grand gesture. Everything in here is yours (his actual words, in Polish naturally).'

Inside they found 'the most pitiful scene' they had ever seen. Scattered around in the rubble of fallen plaster, bricks, and concrete illuminated by their torch, they could recognize the remnants of the porcelain and ceramics collections, both European and Oriental, of the Berlin museums, marbles, bronzes, and terracottas. Almost everything they saw was in very bad condition.

In one room they found pottery, sculpture, and various small objects along with wrapping paper and other materials that suggested a packing operation was in progress. The Pole assured the Americans that nobody had been inside the tower since he had been living there, but they did not believe him. 'As this was Sunday afternoon, we were inclined to think . . . that the Polish gentleman was not quite true to facts, and that weekdays may well reveal a feverish activity in the Flakturm.'

The Pole had a generous nature and an appetite for cigarettes. The Americans left with a number of 'souvenirs' of the visit: a large early Italian marble relief in perfect condition; an Italian Renaissance bronze horse minus one leg; several Greek terracotta heads; a few Meissen fragments and other objects.

The next morning the Americans returned to retrieve the torch they had left behind. They found the Pole and his female companion still asleep at eleven in the morning. Nobody else was there, and they got the impression that nobody cared about the things remaining in the tower. They did not find the torch, but neither did they leave empty-handed. They took 'a bronze Aphrodite (not too good), a personal gift from Polish one-eyed host which I could not refuse and several potteries, bronze figures etc.' Later they checked their finds against the catalogue of the Kaiser Friedrich Museum.[12]

The Americans made a third trip to the tower, this time coming away with Italian sculptures: two polychromed terracotta heads by Michelozzi Michelozzo, bronzes by Riccio, and 'a delightful' St John by Francesco di Giorgio, unfortunately in two pieces. All of these objects were turned over to the German curators.

But there was nothing the Americans could do to prevent looting in the tower. They could not decide whether to 'inform the Polish DP of the importance of his job, or whether this would give him ideas of a "souvenir"-peddling kind. Actually our position is rather powerless as we cannot get the Russians to take serious interest in something they do not seem to care much about as they leave it to a DP controlled fate. One should allow the Germans to get their stuff into their own responsibility . . .' But this the Russians never did.[13]

BERLIN

Cleaning Out the City

Another scene of devastation was the New Mint, which had been badly damaged by grenade explosions. The summer was rainy, and conditions in the basement, where antiquities were stored, were very bad. Blavatsky was shocked when he went there. Sculptures and crates standing on the floor and on low shelves had been underwater for a while and were covered with dirt and mould. Egyptian reliefs, stacked like firewood, were flaking. Statues that had been restored had lost their modern repairs when the glue dissolved: noses, ears, and fingers fell off. There were treasures of Egyptian and classical art: the famous figure of Aphrodite with a tortoise and the only Roman copy of Polyclitus's Amazon, parts of the columns and entablature of the Pergamum Altar. Blavatsky used his battered copy of Gisela Richter's *Sculpture and Sculptors of the Greeks* as a guide. He also found the filing cabinets containing the catalogue of the sculpture collection in the Berlin museums. In all, Blavatsky selected for removal 219 objects stored in the cellar of the New Mint. In his report, composed later, he mentioned that some crates containing 'vases, terracottas, glass, and small statuettes ... were opened before my arrival, and their contents were turned upside-down. Some vases were broken a short time ago, many of the shards are gone.'[1]

Blavatsky's concern about conditions in the cellar was well founded. On 25 September Alexander Voloshin and Sergei Sidorov completed the transfer of the exhibits selected by Blavatsky from the New Mint to the abbatoir depository. They discovered that the works of art were in very poor condition, and not only because of the dampness. Thieves had broken into the cellar again. Most of the crates were smashed and the objects in them had been thrown around. Many of the vases were broken, and statues and reliefs were damaged. The floor was covered with shards of antique pottery. The German curators told the Russians that the Architectural Committee had been there and removed crates. Indeed, on 3 August, Stalin had ordered the Architectural Committee to remove from Berlin 220 crates of archaeological and museum valuables, including porcelain and Majolica collections. But it was never clear who had created this mess: the representatives of the rival committee, thieves, or the soldiers who guarded the cellar. The 'Germans', as the curators of the Berlin museums were called in the Soviet documents, were not allowed to enter it.[2]

The Americans were also very interested in what was going on in the New Mint. Their German museum friends told them that the Russians had returned it to German jurisdiction and left it in the care of a German guardian, who

> let seventy cases of stuff out a few weeks ago on the request of a Russian WAC officer. The stuff was not important but, nevertheless, it was released without demanding any official or unofficial 'dokument', and moreover without taking down the license plate number of the Russian truck. The Russian authorities deny all knowledge of this removal as well as of the WAC officer involved.[3]

The MFAA people applied for more information to Dr Settegast, the newly appointed director of the Berlin museums. Although he introduced himself as a 'socialist', Settegast was a communist, which was widely known in museum circles, and he was in direct contact with Soviet military officials. He invited the Americans to his office in the Magistratur and told them seriously that there were no art objects deposited in the New Mint. He was asked to repeat this statement three times 'in a similar form (pour marquer le coup)', but he stuck to his story.[4]

After six months in Germany, Colonel Andrei Belokopitov was home-sick for his family and his theatre in Moscow, but the representatives of the military administration liked him too much to let him go. The story of his visit to Marshal Zhukov in civilian dress had become a legend among the troops. When Belokopitov realized that he would be unable to refuse an offered promotion, he decided once again on a risky step. He asked the theatre administration in Moscow to send him a letter ordering him to return immediately, waited for a time when all the responsible military administration chiefs were absent, and then presented the letter to an officer who did not know about his pending promotion and gave him permission to make a short visit to Moscow. There was a scandal, but the influence of Stalin's favourite theatre was strong enough to suppress it.

Belokopitov's replacement was Lieutenant Colonel Alexander Voloshin, who was appointed acting head of the trophy brigade but worked in the position longer than any of the 'permanent' heads. It was not until November 1945 that Alexander Zamoshkin, an art critic and the director of the Tretyakov Gallery, was sent to Berlin to head the brigade. He remained until March 1946 and then returned to Moscow. After his departure and until the end of operations in August 1946, Voloshin was again appointed acting head. During its last two months Fyodor Petrov held the position.

Zamoshkin did not like the job and did not get on with the military administration. His cool, correct manner repelled the generals, who had become accustomed to the hearty, gregarious Belokopitov. The brigade's experts did not like him either. But in reality Voloshin continued to run the organization. Zamoshkin's only improvement was the more readable and professional reports sent to Moscow during his tenure.[5]

There was one major change after Belokopitov's departure. In general, Belokopitov had tried to act according to Viktor Lazarev's guidelines for making selections, but Voloshin's idea was to remove everything possible, ignoring the advice of the professors and art historians from Moscow. Later he explained his policy as follows:

> We were guided by one feeling – not to leave the valuables to the Germans but as fast as we could and by every possible way to export them to the USSR and save them from theft. The decision was dictated by a difficult situation that required from us not panic and delay but reasonable risk, operational bravery, quick decisions, and initiative.[6]

And initiative was demonstrated. Zamoshkin sent the military administration a letter that apparently was dictated by Voloshin:

> In Berlin, on Museum Island, in the cellars of the big museums (Pergamum, Kaiser Friedrich Museum) and in the New Mint, masterpieces of Antique, Egyptian art, art of the Renaissance and Byzantine epochs are stored ... It is very necessary to remove to the USSR the paintings, the sculptures, and the collection of coins stored there among some thousands of other works of art. Such an enrichment will make it possible for our museums to be on the same level as the best museums of

the World. It is essential to remove all remaining parts of the Pergamum Altar, which was transported to the USSR according to the decision of the government. It is impossible to reconstruct the whole complex of the Pergamum, a famous monument of World art, without the details mentioned. I ask you to give an order to the Soviet military administration to confiscate the works of art from the depositories on Museum Island and from the New Mint according to the recommendations of the Representative of the Arts Committee of the Council of People's Commissars of the USSR and to give help in their removal to Moscow.[7]

Marshal Zhukov scrawled 'I agree' on the letter and signed it. The second attack on the New Mint and Museum Island began. Some days later, at the end of November, a special plan of operations was drawn up. It covered everything, from the quantity of nails that would be required to the number of guards. The Berlin commandant's office drafted German workers and supplied the brigade with military guards and trucks. Packing and control of the operation were the responsibility of the trophy brigade.

The logistics of the confiscation and removal were precisely described in the plan:

1) A representative of the commandant's office gives the order to the director of the Pergamum Museum and to the cashier of the New Mint to give up the works of art mentioned in the lists composed by the representative of the Arts Committee. 2) They must collect the works of art mentioned in the list . . . in one room. After inspection and comparison of the works of art with the list, all selected works of art must be packed in the same room according to the order of the commandant's office. The director of the Pergamum Museum must give up all crates which he has at his disposal. 3) Dismantling, packing, and loading on trucks of large sculptures and architectural elements must be organized with the help of officials of the Pergamum Museum who . . . took part in constructing them.[8]

On 7 January 1946 the packers went through the cellars of the New Mint. From the Egyptian collection 200 objects were confiscated (instead of the seventeen Blavatsky had specified). Tomb reliefs, the mastaba of Manofer and the ship from Deir el Bahri, painted pottery and many other objects were removed to the abbatoir along with the remains of the antiquities collection.[9]

On 17 December operations began on Museum Island. Special passes to the museum for the selection of objects were given to Zamoshkin and a group of Arts Committee officials and representatives of major Soviet museums. They were joined by Blavatsky, who had just returned from Moscow. The most interesting person in the group was the experienced Lieutenant Colonel Sergei Sidorov, who had taken part in the frontline operations of the brigade and earned military medals along with high military rank. Richard Howard recalled that during those days in Berlin:

> In civilian clothes he would look no different to anybody else, but in the mud-colored uniform, clanking with medals, the inevitable pistol, sagging from his belt, and with the professional sullen dead-pan affected by Soviet officers, he must have been rather terrifying to old Justi, who now headed the former Prussian Museums since Kümmel was dismissed as a Nazi. Justi himself was tired. He longed for the good old days, and talked interminably of the times of the Kaiser, long before the First War. Sidoroff ... didn't give him much chance to reminisce. Quietly, but sternly [he and his colleagues] began their work.[10]

At the end of May 1945 Viktor Lazarev selected for removal from the cellars and halls of the museums situated on Museum Island only 146 works of art, including paintings, three antique statues, and Renaissance sculptures. In July Blavatsky proposed for export not three but nine statues and the remains of the Pergamum Altar. By the end of June all paintings belonging to private collections and all paintings looted by the Nazis from Poland, which were stored on Museum Island, were removed, at Lazarev's order, to the brigade's depository. On 30 June the first painting from a private collection – El Greco's *John the Baptist* from the Koehler Collection, was on its way to Moscow. At the end of October the curators of the Hermitage were unpacking yet another batch of crates filled with the riches of private German collections that had just arrived by cargo train.

The fifty-four canvases selected by Lazarev from Museum Island did not satisfy Zamoshkin and Voloshin. They removed more than 200 paintings from the cellars there, including works by Mantegna, Lorenzo di Credi, and Ercole de' Roberti. The *Maypole* by Goya and a Crucifixion by Ghirlandaio were sent to the USSR, followed by Madonnas by Rossellino and Benedetto da Maiano and works by Luca, Andrea, and Giovanni della Robbia. Byzantine and Early Christian objects, Coptic textiles and icons, Italian furniture, and hundreds of other art objects were transported to the abbatoir.[11] In light of the 'new policy', Blavatsky drastically enlarged his list of antique sculptures to 100 and added eighteen large vases from the cellar of the New Museum. He prepared 122 crates of works of art, three strongboxes of coins, and sixty-nine boxes of books for transportation. The library of the German Archaeological Institute was taken too. The last trucks did not leave the Museum Island until May 1946.[12]

The American MFAA officers began to gather information about Soviet activities after 5 July 1945, when the Western Allies took control of their occupation zones. Their initial contacts with the Russians made it clear that there would be no cooperation. Although German museum people had told the Americans about the removal of works of art, the Russians insisted that they had found nothing of importance. On 28 July an American officer (probably Lieutenant Kenneth Lippman from SHAEF) reported to MFAA that a meeting with the Russians had been

> discouraging in that we were given such a different, and unlikely, story about German works of art not evacuated from Berlin. As you will know from German museum-staff reports already sent to you, considerable material is claimed to have stayed in Berlin. But our USSR people told us that they have found nothing of any importance in Berlin.

It was Otto Kümmel who finally told them exactly what had happened to the art treasures stored in Berlin. They found him in the Magazinebau, a depository building. Thirty GIs had commandeered the building and were playing darts with South Seas arrows until their officers ordered them to leave. 'How this miracle of good sense happened I don't know,' wrote an MFAA observer.[13]

There was something else that surprised the Americans. From their first days in the city, they had noticed antique shops selling old paintings and other valuable objects that operated with the blessing of the Soviet military administration. One shop, at No. 3 Teltower Damm, offered to buy or sell pictures, furniture, jewellery, and gold and silver objects. There were two notices on the door, one saying that it was a Russian firm and the other that it was off limits to US Army personnel. The Americans did not know that these shops were run by the Soviet Ministry of Foreign Trade.[14]

The Teltower Damm shop was involved in a major scandal a year later. In February 1946 an American officer confiscated an important painting from Dr Winkler, an art historian who had received it for evaluation from the 'Russian art shop'. The painting – *The Donor with Saint Augustine and Saint John the Baptist* by Dieric Bouts – came from the Kaiser Friedrich Museum and had been stored in the Friedrichshain tower. The Americans were alarmed because everyone knew that the paintings stored in the Friedrichshain tower had been burned in the fire of May 1945. So how had this masterpiece appeared on the black market?

The owner of the Teltower Damm shop was a mysterious Graf Kamensky, who claimed to be a stateless person born in Russia. He told the Americans that he had bought the painting from a Soviet officer, Captain Evdokimov, in November 1945 for 25,000 Deutschmarks. Kamensky was arrested, having violated a number of regulations prohibiting the movement of works of art from one sector to another, but he was soon released on bail.

To Dr Winkler's surprise, he was summoned to the Soviet commandant's office at Luisenstrasse 56 and questioned by an unknown Soviet major, who had a photograph of the painting and a letter written in Russian. Winkler thought the letter had probably been written by Kamensky. The major told him that he should have served 'German interests' by informing Soviet authorities about the painting and ordered him to return it within three days, although it had been confiscated by the Americans.

When Winkler told them what had happened, the Americans counterattacked. They arrested Kamensky again, and he admitted that he had informed the Soviets about the confiscated painting. But he did not stay in American custody long this time either. The chief of staff of the Soviet military command in Berlin sent an official request that he be turned over to them because he was a Soviet citizen, although he claimed to be a stateless person. That same day Kamensky disappeared into the Soviet zone.[15] The Americans sent an angry letter to the Soviet military authorities demanding to know how Captain Evdokimov had acquired the painting and how he had brought it into the American sector and sold it, but no satisfactory answer was received.

The Americans believed that the Soviets would eventually return the German art treasures. This optimism is expressed in a special report on restitution prepared in 1949 in which the Soviet government is compared to its czarist predecessor. The writer recalled that the czarist government had proposed the original and basic article contained in the Declaration of Brussels of 1874 and the Hague Conventions of 1899 and 1907 for the respect and protection of cultural property under international law, and that after the First World War the Soviet government had drafted admirable treaty articles for the return of cultural property to their rightful owners. The writer pointed out that the USSR recognized the czarist signature to the Hague Convention of 1907. Furthermore, 'the USSR shows great pride in the cultural heritage of its own people and has scholars of high attainments in art and archaeology'.[16]

In the course of the next two years the Americans realized the difference between Soviet foreign policy and the policy of the czarist government. In August 1951 a secret report, called 'The Fate of Art Treasures in the Soviet Zone of Occupation and in the Soviet Sector of Berlin', was delivered to the responsible American authorities. It summarized what the Americans knew about events in the Soviet zone:

> In the East ... many items of museum property were destroyed during military operations. Others were destroyed after the war, and still others were finally taken to the Soviet Union as so-called 'trophies' by special Trophies Commissions. Where and how they were housed there and what fate awaits them there is, with few exceptions, unknown.

The report noted 'a very great lack of clarity' regarding the numerous privately owned works of art and private collections that had disappeared. Many had been taken from the vaults of private banks. 'This booty must have been of very considerable value,' the report stated.

There had also been cases of vandalism, such as the fire in the castle of Sophienhof, near Berlin, caused by Soviet soldiers, which destroyed the entire archive of Wilhelm Humboldt as well as many valuable museum objects. The medieval arms and cannons in the yard of the Berlin Arsenal had been cut up with oxyacetylene torches by order of the Soviet military authorities. In the park at Karinhall, Goering's country estate near Berlin, statues by Pigalle, Houdon and Boizot were broken or used as targets. The kitchen staff in Teupitz hospital was ordered to burn a cache of paintings by Emil Nolde, which represented years of work. This was probably an aesthetic decision on the part of the Soviet commander.

The behaviour of the new German political elite in the Soviet zone was not much better. The report noted that government officials had commandeered thirty-three paintings and three sculptures from the National Gallery and twelve paintings from the Kaiser Friedrich Museum to decorate their offices and apartments. It seemed that the czarist ideals of 1874 and 1907 had been forgotten.[17]

SILESIA

Radios and Violins

On 2 March 1945 the trophy brigade of the Arts Committee of the First Ukrainian Front, led by Boris Filippov, crossed the border of the Third Reich by tram. Silesia had been annexed by Germany in 1939 according to a secret protocol signed by Molotov and Ribbentrop. Now it was occupied by the Red Army, and it would soon be handed over to the Poles. But before the transfer, a brigade was sent from Moscow to remove cultural property that would be of value to the victorious Soviet Union.

Unlike other occupied areas, Silesia was no longer rich in art treasures. But the trophy brigades were not looking only for masterpieces. Theatre equipment, musical instruments, art books – anything of cultural importance was packed up and sent to the USSR. It was congenial work and not very dangerous. Filippov and his experts enjoyed the comfortable hotels and good food.

The brigade arrived in Gleiwitz a few weeks after it was taken by Soviet troops. The battle for the city had its humorous aspects, as Marshal Konev recalled in his memoirs. He and General Ribalko watched from an observation point on the top of a hill.

In front of us was the battlefield, and both of us could see it as clearly as if it were on the palm of our hands. We could see the manoeuvres of the tank units of Ribalko ... The actions of large military masses are impossible to comprehend with the field of vision of the human being, even if he is at an observation point. Usually it is possible to see them only on the map. Because of this my pleasure was so great when I could observe the rapid advance of the battle units of the tank brigades, brave and strong, despite the fire and resistance of the enemy. Special shock troops and infantrymen were sitting on the attacking tanks, some of them playing Russian accordions. It is interesting to mention that the tanks during this operation were camouflaged by lace curtains. The tanks and the lace curtains were at first sight a strange union, but it had its logic. It was wintertime and the fields were covered with snow, and the tank crews had occupied a textile factory on the eve of the battle. They found a lot of lace curtains and decided they could be used as decent camouflage. I can see this picture with all its contrasts even now: the smoking chimneys of Silesia, the artillery shots, the sound of the tank caterpillars, with the accordions of the paratroopers playing but unheard.[1]

Filippov was astonished by the hotel in Gleiwitz – the servility of the lift operator, the 'orderliness, so different from the chaos of the destroyed city . . . Complete cleanliness, order, an excellent restaurant and a wonderful dinner with vodka and beer. By the way, everything is served perfectly,' he wrote in his diary.[2]

Comfortable accommodation was not the only pleasure. Hundreds of radios had been stored in the cellar and abandoned. Everybody grabbed them. 'We listen to the whole world,' Filippov wrote, 'and of course we don't lose contact with our native Moscow.' To Soviets in those days, a radio was a symbol of almost inconceivable Western luxury. Later, when the trophy brigades returned home, many of the men were accused of smuggling these 'abandoned' radios.

The brigade inspected libraries, theatres and castles, looking for objects worthy of removal. Andrei Chegodayev, an expert in Filippov's brigade, later remembered that he did not bother looking for works of art because he knew this area had no masterpieces. Instead he concentrated on art books, with great success. In the deserted villas and castles he found everything upside-down. 'First the Germans retreated and then the Russians advanced, but the books were thrown around on the floor; nobody needed them. I exported to the [Pushkin] museum 40,000 art books, and after 45 years these books still make up a third of the museum's library.'[3]

The city library of Gleiwitz was very good, according to Filippov, and the brigade selected 10,000 rare art books. A collecting point was set up in the library. It was run by SMERSH, which 'dealt with the detention of Soviet and European POWs and Ostarbeiters in the occupied territories and organized the transportation of both real and false "collaborators" to the GULAG. We organized the packing and loading of the books using people who had been arrested.' The head of the collecting-evacuation point, a dynamic and lively captain from Odessa, told funny stories about people he had arrested for identification checks. 'Some time ago a beautiful, overdressed lady from France tried to convince him that she and her father had

Marshal Georgy Zhukov, chief commander of the Soviet Occupation forces in Germany, in a portrait by Pavel Korin. Zhukov's dacha outside Moscow was furnished entirely with trophy artworks, including a shocking picture of two nude women over his bed. It was all confiscated when Stalin, jealous of his popularity, turned against him.

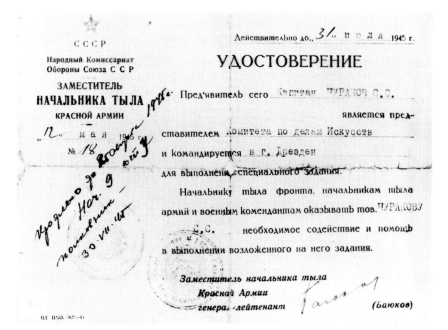

Stepan Churakov's identification document is signed by Lieutenant General Baukov, deputy head of the Home Front of the Red Army. A restorer, Churakov was a member of the Dresden trophy brigade.

Thousands of artworks from Dresden collections were brought together in Pillnitz castle. Undamaged and isolated in an English-style park, it became the main Soviet collecting point in the area.

Lieutenant Leonid Rabinovich in the ruins of the Zwinger palace in Dresden in May 1945. He claimed to have been the first to discover that the Dresden Gallery had survived. Later he created the myth of its 'rescue' by the Red Army.

Natalia Sokolova on a visit to Dresden a year before her death in 1975. As a major in the trophy brigade sent to Silesia, she decided to look for the Dresden Gallery collection and became the first Arts Committee expert to see the Sistine Madonna after its discovery.

In the summer of 1945, Viktor Baldin took these drawings, Albrecht Dürer's *Christ Child Enthroned* (left) and Luca Cambiaso's *Woman with Three Children* (below), from the cellar of Karnzow castle, north of Berlin, where they had been stored for safekeeping by officials of the Bremen Kunstalle. He tried unsuccessfully for years to persuade the Soviet government to help him give them back.

The young Captain Baldin (left) in the park of Karnzow castle in May 1945. He traded a pair of 'really good boots' for a painting by Dürer. Baldin (at work in his studio, below) still hopes that the drawings will be returned to 'the real owner – the museum in the city of Bremen' before he dies.

Dozens of trucks bearing artworks from Germany arrived in the yard of the Pushkin Museum in the summer of 1945 (above). A young staff member, Irina Antonova (below, lower left) helped unload the treasures and was one of the first people to see the Trojan gold after its arrival in Moscow. As the director of the Pushkin today, she bitterly opposes the restitution of artworks to Germany.

Millions of books, along with artworks and archival collections, were hidden in mines all over Germany for protection against Allied air raids during the war. They went from German hiding places, like the Ransbach mine near Merkers (above), to Soviet ones, like the secret depository in the Uzkoe church in Moscow (below, in the early 1990s), where they remain to this day.

All Soviet museums have trophy artworks in their collections. *Susanna and the Elders* by the Master of the Prodigal Son, from a Berlin private collection, decorated the office of the director of the Museum of Western and Oriental Art in Kiev when Konstantin Akinsha worked there in the 1980s.

accidentally stumbled onto German territory,' Filippov wrote, but investigation proved that the French lady was really a Russian from Kharkov who had a perfect command of French and that her fake "father" was in reality a former inspector of Laval's police.' Filippov did not bother to mention the fate of the woman and her 'father' because it was perfectly clear.

In Gleiwitz the brigade visited the depository belonging to the military commandant's office. Among the upright pianos and concert grands, radios, sewing machines and bicycles, Filippov noticed four violins. Two of them were in shabby cases and looked old but not damaged by time. Inspecting them closely, he noticed a label inside one of the cases that said 'Stradivari 1757' and in the other 'Amati' with a partially illegible seventeenth-century date. The 'Stradivarius' was immediately removed to a more secure location, but a few days later the experts found more 'Stradivarius' and 'Amati' violins and realized that they were all fakes.

The brigade inspected the local villas and castles that had belonged to aristocrats and industrialists. For many of the Moscow experts, it was a trip to another world. On 17 March Filippov wrote in his diary that he had inspected the mansion of an important industrialist named Berve.

> A Frau Kemler was housed there temporarily because her villa was occupied by the commandant's office. This Frau, together with her husband, an important manager of a local corporation, a well-groomed and phlegmatically polite German, made a very strange impression on us. What happened? Why and for what reason did they stay here when almost all of their acquaintances fled? They behaved as if nothing impressed them after our arrival. When the works of art were confiscated from the Berves' mansion, the Frau acted as if we were in a shop, buying all these things. She showed us with courteous politeness the porcelains, carpets, valuable books, and silver, and provided explanations about every object. I could find only one reason for this behaviour. Apparently the most important, the most valuable things were already hidden somewhere else ... The Frau escorted me around other villas. Thanks to this, I had a chance to see how the German bourgeoisie lived. I saw excellent two-storey villas with large rooms, winter gardens, rich furniture, and great comfort.

But Filippov was disappointed by the works of art; he thought they reflected bourgeois tastelessness. He was most impressed by the convenient modern furniture and commented on bookcases with lights inside that switched on when the door was opened and desks equipped with bookshelves. 'Oh, yes!' he concluded. 'They lived for their own pleasure and lacked for nothing. If I could have imagined a month ago that I would take part in this excursion to capitalism!'

Occasionally, important works of art were found during such excursions. In one villa Chegodayev found a bronze mermaid by Georg Kolbe, which went to the Pushkin Museum.

In Gleiwitz the trophy brigade came across a group of Ostarbeiters. They were Russian and Ukrainian girls who had been conscripted for hard labour in Germany. One of the girls, called Zina, sang them a song that was popular among the Russian prisoners and labourers. Filippov wrote down the words of this plaintive slice of camp folklore:

> I send you greetings my dear
> From Kolyma far away.
> How are you my dear?
> Please send me a letter soon.
> I lived near the Sea of Okhotsk,
> On the edge of the Far East,
> I lived there without want or grief,
> Building bunkers, digging sand.
> We didn't have time to finish the bunkers,
> We didn't have time to mix concrete,
> Because the Germans declared war on us,
> And my song sounds different now.
> I will sing in this song, my dear,
> How we lived as prisoners in the camps,
> How the soldiers hit us with sticks,
> How the policemen smashed in the doors.
> We learned the rules of the day
> From dawn to dusk.
> Standing in line for prison soup,
> We could hardly move our feet.

Neither the girls nor Filippov knew that soon most of the Ostarbeiters would indeed be on their way to the terrible camps of Kolyma and the Far East, branded as potential collaborators and traitors to the motherland simply because they had involuntarily spent so much time in Germany. The song's sad message was true. The fate of these people was to travel from one camp to another camp.

Filippov and his men witnessed many strange events during the first days of the occupation. 'On the road to Gleiwitz we had an interesting encounter,' he wrote in his diary on 17 March.

> A truck driver had in his cabin an unusual companion – a chimpanzee of medium size, with lively eyes and a slightly injured nose, dressed in warm clothes. The history of this exotic passenger was incredible ... Arriving at some country estate left by the Germans, the driver found a company of our drunken soldiers who had caught a monkey left by its owner and decided to hang it because of its Nazi past. It happened that one of the soldiers shouted, jokingly, to the monkey, 'Heil Hitler'. The monkey immediately stood erect and raised an arm in the Nazi salute. The soldiers didn't like this – they didn't understand the ironic side of this odd event. The driver had been a dog trainer and had a good sense of humour. He saved the monkey and it became his devoted companion. He explained the situation very simply. 'I can survive without the monkey, but when it's with me everybody is ready to help me, give us accommodation, warm us, and help with the truck in case of emergency.'

In Silesia Filippov met the all-powerful Maxim Saburov, who was one of the real rulers of the occupied country. During the early years of the war Saburov had been head of Gosplan, the national planning board that ran the economy of the USSR. Later he was appointed to the top-secret Special Committee on Germany. His responsibility was very simply to loot the occupied country. After the war he was again appointed head of Gosplan, then became deputy head of the Council of People's Commissars and a member of the country's ruling body, the Presidium of the Communist Party Central Committee.

This meeting had important consequences for the art collectors. Filippov tried to explain to Saburov that the removal of cultural property was just as important as the removal of industrial equipment. 'When I introduced myself,' he wrote,

> his reaction was not very traditional. But first a few words about Saburov. He is a short blond middle-aged man. Among the numerous representatives of the People's Commissariats, only he was in civilian dress. But it didn't stop him from commanding military men, including generals and colonels. In Saburov's group you could find a reflection of the interests of the whole of our country. All the main sectors of industry are

represented there. Only culture is represented in a very limited way. And it's a very big mistake. Representatives of the Academy of Sciences, librarians, cinema engineers should be there. Their absence has bad consequences. Some fields are not covered at all.

Saburov was not immediately convinced. 'The meeting with Saburov was equal to a cold shower for me,' Filippov wrote.

'I have no intention,' Saburov told me, 'of dealing with your questions. I am responsible for industry. Act autonomously and as you want! I can't give you a car.' Saburov was in a hurry. His speech was taciturn and I realized that it was impossible to 'cook kasha' with him.

But Saburov announced his intention of visiting the trophy brigade, and Filippov decided to try to use the occasion. He could not resist noting in passing that the hotel in Beuthen where Saburov's staff was staying 'has the proud name Kaiserhof – Imperial court. It means that I have become a part of the court and that I am a "courtesan".' At Saburov's request, he gave a speech to an assembled group of representatives of various state organizations about the brigade's work. It was apparently successful, because afterwards Saburov changed his mind and promised his help. To impress the gathering, Filippov had used a bit of theatrical business: he had taken along as an exhibit a huge, heavy book, called *History of the German Wars*, that was lavishly illustrated and impressive looking although not very valuable. The meeting was suspended while everyone, including Saburov, examined the book, dazzled not by its contents but by its weight. The battle was won.

Thanks to his persuasiveness, Filippov and his group finally received a lend-lease American jeep and other manifestations of official support. But the political situation was changing rapidly. Silesia was reverting to Poland.

On 19 March the cities of Gleiwitz, Hindenburg and Beuthen were handed over to the rule of the Polish administration. The houses were decorated with white and red Polish banners. Everywhere popular demonstrations were organized. It would make our work more difficult because the Poles would certainly 'veto' the removal of all valuables. And we didn't want to create any conflict on this ground.

The Russians quickly transported all the property they had confiscated to the commandant's depository. Unwilling to leave anything useful behind, they found three trucks and with great difficulty removed the box with the control board from the Konzerthaus, lifting the three-ton box out of the building with cranes through a hole in the wall made for the purpose.

Operations in Silesia were completed. Three cargo trains were on their way to Moscow bearing furniture, paintings, sculptures, prints and reproductions, stained-glass panels, porcelain, concert pianos, old arms, carpets and, of course, books. But things did not go entirely smoothly. On 1 May an unfortunate signalman named Vopasenko made a mistake and a railway carriage full of porcelain overturned. It is not difficult to imagine what happened to the cargo.[4]

Natalia Sokolova, an expert on the Arts Committee who took an active part in Dresden operations, spent her first days in Germany with Filippov's group.

> In Gleiwitz, in the officers' hotel, I met my brigade. It included Lieutenant Colonel Filippov, Majors Grigorov and Chegodayev – the art historians and one representative of the Philharmonic Society – Sushchenko. Every day we visited the depository to which they had already transported objects selected for export to Moscow, addressed to the Arts Committee. With the help of German women and boys, who were escorted to the depository for work, they packed carpets, chandeliers, filling crates with all kinds of things removed from nearby castles. Among all these things were some bad paintings. Soon the whole brigade returned to Moscow, believing that their mission was completed.[5]

Sokolova stayed ... and found a far bigger prize.

DRESDEN

Masterpieces in a Mine

The discovery of the masterpieces of the Dresden Gallery in a mine in Gross Cotta, near Pirna, was the greatest achievement of the Soviet trophy brigades. This was one of the world's most glorious collections, containing one of the world's most famous pictures, Raphael's Sistine Madonna. The discovery was reported directly to Stalin, who responded that the collection had 'state importance' for the Soviet Union and personally ordered it to be sent with all possible care to Moscow.

In later years the discovery became the subject of numerous myths about the 'rescue' of the Dresden Gallery, with many of the participants claiming leading roles for themselves and disputing the claims of others. People were so anxious to share in the glory that they sometimes crossed the boundaries of exaggeration into outright falsehood.

The gallery's prize possession, and the focus of so much Russian attention, was a picture whose fame had endured for centuries. Raphael painted the Sistine Madonna in about 1513, to be placed over the bier of Pope Julius II. He wanted the figure of the Virgin holding the Christ Child to seem like a vision, revealed behind parted curtains. Serene and majestic, she seems to be wafted forward on billowing clouds, as St Sixtus bows before her on one side and St Barbara kneels on the other. Two cherubs (reproduced on thousands of Christmas cards) rest their elbows against the bottom of the frame. Raphael painted many beautiful and beloved Madonnas, but no others had the universal appeal of this one.

In the eighteenth and nineteenth centuries the Sistine Madonna was regarded as the highest manifestation of heavenly beauty. Hundreds of copies and uncounted engravings, etchings and lithographs of the picture circulated around Europe. Tolstoy had one hanging over his desk in his country estate at Yasnaya Polyana. At the end of the nineteenth century rebellious art students began to scorn the ubiquitous image as a symbol of academic stagnation. The Russian

Futurists made her a representative of the old, corrupt culture that had to be destroyed. But after the victory of Socialist Realism as the only approved art style in the Soviet Union, the Sistine Madonna once again became the standard of beauty for Russians. Dmitry Nalbandyan, court painter to Soviet officialdom from Stalin to Brezhnev, even produced a large picture of Lenin admiring the Madonna, a picture he had never seen.

When Marshal Ivan Konev described his descent into the Gross Cotta mine, he naturally made his encounter with the Sistine Madonna the climax of his account. 'I remember as if it were happening right now the sight that appeared in front of us,' he wrote in his memoirs.

> The railway that was used to carry out the stone led into the depths of the mine. It survived but looked like a place that had been abandoned a long time ago. Near the entrance to the mine two broken cars were placed to hide it . . . Nobody imagined that anything valuable was hidden here, especially not famous canvases. I can say as a military man that the camouflage was perfect. Nothing that might arouse suspicion was there. But inside the mine, after all this camouflage, after all this visible desolation, a door was found, then another one, then the electricity and even special equipment to control the temperature inside the mine was discovered.
>
> The mine was like a big cave. Probably those who hid the paintings here believed that this kind of stone gallery would be dry. But unfortunately underground water was seeping into the cracks in the stone; it seemed that the temperature changed very rapidly and the equipment to control it no longer worked when the paintings were found. The paintings (about 700 of them were there) were in disorder. Some of them were packed in parchment paper, some were in crates, some simply stood against the walls. I inspected the whole cave and saw for the first time many of the masterpieces that are exhibited now in the halls of the reconstructed Dresden Gallery. The Sistine Madonna was there. I spent a few minutes in front of her, still not believing my own eyes that we had finally found her.[1]

But this dramatic event Konev described so feelingly never took place. By the time he entered the mine, the Sistine Madonna had already been removed and taken to the depository of the trophy battalion in Dresden. The marshal saw the picture for the first time in the castle of Pillnitz, the collecting point of the Arts Committee trophy brigades.

Konev's 'mistake' created a serious problem for the editors of the book *Saved Masterpieces*, published in Moscow in 1977 and dedicated to the 'rescue' of the Dresden Gallery. Finally the editors simply left out the Sistine Madonna from the famous commander's recollections of his visit to Gross Cotta.

Marshal Konev's armies took Dresden on 8 May. The next day Natalia Sokolova left for the city, escorted by Colonel Sergei Piankov, who was on the staff of Maxim Saburov, the powerful representative of the Special Committee on Germany. Dresden had been largely destroyed by the Anglo–American bombardment of 13 February, which had taken 300,000 lives. Most of the palaces, museums and churches of the old town were gone. The city that had once been called the Florence of the Elbe was a wasteland, with the ruined Frauenkirche looming over the desolation.

The Soviet administration set up headquarters in Neustadt, and experts began to strip the city of any surviving industrial installations. Sokolova, who spent her first days with the *demontageniks* – the dismantlers – recalled that:

> The German engineers showed their factories to our 'demontageniks' with pleasure. Piankov 'bought' them for a mess of pottage. They gave our [experts] their inventions, sometimes showed the secret projects they had hidden from Hitler. Almost all of them kept exclaiming 'Hitler kaput!' whether it was appropriate or not. And only one chief engineer of some big factory said, 'You have your ideology, we have ours,' and asked the sarcastic question, 'Frau Major, can you explain why none of the Russian experts have watches?'

'Translate for this bastard,' Piankov answered, 'that we have no watches but we have a free motherland.'

Sokolova walked around the old town centre, inspecting the ruins of museums and palaces. Only the walls remained of the so-called Japanese palace, with its famous graphics collection; everything inside had been burned. Walking around it, she stepped on earth shattered by shell craters and trenches and had to manoeuvre among tangled cables and rolls of barbed wire. The nauseating smell of corpses was everywhere. Not far from the ruins of the Japanese palace were the remains of the little museum of folk art.

The Japanese palace was situated on the bank of the Elbe. There was a garden here too, a blossoming, luxuriant garden full of magnolias and lilacs situated on the embankment. Near the entrance an iron plaque was erected with the words: 'Entrance prohibited to Jews'. 'The German who was escorting me,' Sokolova wrote, 'immediately threw himself forward to remove it when he noticed that I was drawing it in my notebook. "Too late," I told him. "Leave it for the Dresden museum." He pretended that he was very confused and raising his hands exclaimed: "Oh, how we blame ourselves!"'

Thanks to her good relations with Saburov's people, Sokolova was given a car and an escort to go to Meissen. There she inspected the famous porcelain factory, met the director, and gave the order to resume production. She visited the town's military commandant and persuaded him to send patrols to secure the factory.

> The acting director, called Neigaus ... told me that he had visited Moscow and that he was a supporter of Communism, and then complained that the factory was not guarded and that they [Russian soldiers] had broken in, looking for valuables. With his help we learned that the Meissen museum (which included all the most valuable examples produced since the first years of the factory's existence ...) was packed and stored in the cellars of Meissen Castle. The castle was used by the Germans as an evacuation point. Later some of the Dresden Gallery paintings were found there.

Porcelain production did not resume for a very long time, because the *demontageniks* stripped the factory's equipment and sent it to the Soviet Union. The same fate awaited most of the objects in the Meissen museum.

Sokolova's major success was the discovery of Pillnitz Castle, which later became the main collecting point of the Soviet trophy brigade in the area. The castle, fifteen kilometres from the centre of the city, was undamaged. Surrounded by an English-style park, it was an ideal depository. 'Pillnitz was not secured,' Sokolova remembered.

> Germans whom we found in the garden told us the name of the manager and we sent for him. Very soon he came – little, sweet Herr Schobel. He informed us that the director of Pillnitz Castle had fled, but the keys were in the possession of Schobel. We gave the order to open the museum and for a long time wandered around the galleries and halls, both empty and filled with various things. Paintings were in the palace – bad portraits of

various electors, copies of Italian masters, two works of Jacopo Bassano. In one room were collected harmoniums, grand pianos, and other musical instruments. As Schobel explained to us, all these instruments, including a cupboard full of violins, belonged to the Royal Opera. One room was completely filled with boxes of books. I was extremely happy with the building's many empty halls, with the loneliness of the palace, situated on the outskirts of Dresden in a big, shady park. I already knew that the collection of the Dresden Gallery had survived, and my task was to remove it to a secure place.

Sokolova learned that the gallery had survived from Second Lieutenant Leonid Rabinovich, of the 164th Battalion of the Fifth Army. The young man, who had been an artist in Kiev before the war, told her an exciting story. As a member of the trophy battalion, he had visited the Zwinger Palace on 9 May. There he met a German artist who was sketching the ruined building. The artist told him that the collection of the Albertinum had been hidden in the museum's cellar and had survived the bombardment. The next day Rabinovich found the curator of the Albertinum collection, who showed him documents. Among them was a coded map of secret shelters situated in Saxony. The curator told Rabinovich that officials in the castle of Weesenstein could help him to decipher the map. At Weesenstein Rabinovich found a Dr Hammler, who indeed helped him decode the mysterious map. It led him to the village of Gross Cotta. There in a tunnel he discovered a railway carriage with a large crate inside. A thermometer was attached to the crate. Rabinovich realized immediately that he had found the treasure of the Dresden Gallery – Raphael's Sistine Madonna. The same day he transported the box to the Dresden abattoir, where his battalion was based.[2]

Later, in a book he published under the pseudonym Volinsky, Rabinovich described the removal of the crate from the quarry near the village of Gross Cotta, which took place on 14 May:

It was standing near the wall of the carriage, flat, not painted, carefully covered with plywood 10 millimetres thick. The padlocks on the clamps securing the lid were unusual.

The padlocks are combination locks. Zakharov is waving his head, raising the lantern.

What is in this crate? We tried to move it from the wall, it was pretty light.

I measured the long side by the steps – it was about three metres . . . And suddenly, the flash of a guess: Is it possible?

'Hey,' I said, trying to be calm, afraid to believe it myself. 'It seems that we must take this crate to our battalion. We can't manage to open these locks here . . .'

We jump out of the car and together push it to the entrance of the gallery. The rusty wheels screech. [Rabinovich 'forgot' that it was impossible to move the car to the entrance of the gallery because the railway was obstructed by a wooden construction housing paintings.] 'Careful' sounds constantly, but it is not necessary: if there were glass as thin as the wall of a soap bubble in the crate, it wouldn't be cracked.[3]

Rabinovich's story impressed Sokolova. She immediately paid a visit to the Trophy Department and asked its chief, Colonel Kurganov, to put Rabinovich under her command and to permit her to use Pillnitz Castle as a depository of art objects. The colonel agreed to everything. Then Sokolova and Rabinovich went to the abattoir. She wanted to see the crate he had rescued from the mine.

'Imagine the old black–red block of buildings,' Sokolova remembered.

In the centre of the yard was a black statue of a bull – the symbol of this mighty institution. In the left wing, in the block of flats, there was something like a hotel. We ran up a few steps and were met by the shout of a guard: 'Back!' It was the patrol put here by Rabinovich the day before. We greeted the patrol commander and showed our documents. The guard lowered his rifle, and I approached the mysterious crate with two padlocks. The room in which it was standing was a grim, dimly lit anteroom. Cigarette butts and empty champagne bottles wrapped in straw were strewn on the floor. Now I understood why the commander of the patrol was blinking with inflamed eyelids and walking gingerly. An examination of the place horrified me. A garage and a wine cellar were situated nearby; it was pretty late and it was impossible to remove the crate immediately. We called the guards and the patrol commander and ordered them to throw away the bottles, clean the room, and regard the crate as the apple of their eye. For half the night I couldn't fall asleep, and then I had nightmares because on this night in the frontline city we were responsible for the priceless treasure packed in the stout wooden crate. The next day Rabinovich, with a group of the soldiers, took the crate to Pillnitz . . .

The activity of the collecting point had began. The first painting delivered there was the Sistine Madonna.[4]

Like many of the stories later told about the Dresden rescue, Rabinovich's was not entirely truthful. It *was* true that the crate had been found in the mine near Gross Cotta. Rabinovich really had visited the Albertinum and talked to its curator and then gone to Weesenstein Castle, but he was not the person who discovered that the collection had not been destroyed during the bombardment. The exciting story about the secret map exaggerated the exploits of the young painter from Kiev.

The true story of the discovery was somewhat less dramatic. It was told by a Professor Wachs from Rostok, who came to Weesenstein Castle on the eve of the Soviet occupation. The Soviet armies advancing toward Dresden passed the castle, unaware that it was one of the most important art depositories in the area. Part of the collection of the Dresden Gallery, the collection of prints and drawings of the Kupferstichkabinett, and part of the graphics collection purchased for the Führer Museum in Linz, including the Koenigs Collection of drawings, were stored there.

Wachs was not a professional art historian, but he was interested in art and often visited the castle to talk to Hermann Voss, the director of the Dresden Gallery and the last head of the Führer Museum. On 11 June 1945 Wachs described the events that had taken place on 8 May:

Until Monday, 7 May 1945, the castle and the town of Weesenstein happily escaped military danger. On Tuesday, 8 May, at three o'clock in the afternoon, the ceasefire had to begin. After this any resistance was no more than crime and banditry. The castle and the town of Weesenstein received an order not to resist during the Russian offensive. Despite this order, on Tuesday, 8 May 1945, about twenty SS men from Werewolf [which operated behind the lines] armed with guns and anti-tank grenades hid in the grove behind the castle, waiting for the Russians ... I took my bicycle and went towards the Russians, who were expected from the direction of Heidenau. Before the town of Dohna, where the road turns to Pirna, I met the first Russian patrol – three officers on horseback and about fifteen people on bicycles. One of the officers jumped down from his horse, and with the help of his and my maps and a Russian woman I explained the situation to him. The officer immediately understood what I was talking about and rode with two of his comrades in the direction of Gross Sedlitz (Meizegast). I followed them, escorted by eight soldiers on bicycles. When we reached the top of the hill, I met the Russian officers again . . .[5]

Wachs apparently told the Russian officers not only about the Werewolf trap but about the masterpieces that were stored in the castle. When Mikhail Volodin, a member of a special brigade sent from Moscow to Dresden by the Arts Committee, was questioned in 1955, after the 'rescuers' of the Dresden Gallery had started arguing about who had played the major role in the event, this is the account he gave to the Ministry of Culture officials. Volodin arrived in Dresden in late May. He said that the brigade members believed Rabinovich's version of the discovery story until one day a group of officers headed by General Shtikov arrived in Pillnitz and asked the art experts to show them the paintings. 'We are free now and we want to see what we saved,' the officers said. The art experts related Rabinovich's story of the secret map, but General Shtikov told them that it was untrue and offered a completely different version of events.

Before Dresden was taken, Shtikov said, Weesenstein Castle was occupied and Voss was detained. Terrified, and hoping to save his life, he told the Russians about the mine where the Sistine Madonna was hidden. According to Shtikov, the SS tried to resist his troops but were defeated. Shtikov ordered the trophy battalion to secure the castle and check the information about the Sistine Madonna.[6]

Arthur Graefe, head of the Department of State Collections of Art, Science, Castles, Gardens, and Libraries of Saxony, who was in the castle at this time, recalled that:

On 10 May a major general escorted by two Russian officers and an interpreter arrived at the castle of Weesenstein. They wanted to see the depository of the castle and requested information about the places where the art treasures of the State Dresden Collections were hidden. The general and his escort examined the museum treasures belonging to the province of Saxony, stored in the castle . . .[7]

The general issued an order that nothing be taken from the castle without the permission of the trophy battalion and that entrance to the castle be forbidden to everyone else. He made Voss responsible for saving the collection. It seems that SMERSH was involved in this operation. The head of the trophy brigade operating in Dresden, Alexander Rototayev, later wrote to Khrushchev: 'When we arrived in Dresden we met Marshal Konev and General Petrov ... General Petrov told us that the first depository containing paintings had been discovered, according to the special order of the commanders of the Front, by Soviet intelligence – the officers of SMERSH.'[8]

Mikhail Volodin was not fond of Voss: 'We did not trust Voss, but intelligence ordered us to use him in our work because he gave them information.' Voss told them that there was nothing left in the castle of Weesenstein, but later the Russians found three rooms filled with paintings and the collection of the Kupferstichkabinett.[9]

Another version of events was based on the report of the restorer Heese, who said that on 8 May, when the first Soviet tanks appeared in the area of Gross Cotta, he had informed the Red Army officers that the masterpieces of the gallery were hidden in the mine.[10]

When SMERSH learned that the Dresden Gallery collection had not been destroyed, they ordered the trophy battalion to secure the paintings and informed the staff of Marshal Konev. On 10 May the commander of the First Ukrainian Front sent a telegram to the Arts Committee in Moscow informing them that the treasures of the gallery had been found.

The committee immediately decided to send a special brigade to Dresden, a group that included Mikhail Volodin, Stepan Churakov, a restorer, Alexander Rototayev, at that time the assistant to the head of the Arts Committee of the CPC of the USSR, and the art historian Sergei Grigorov.[11] They paid a visit to the quarry tunnel in Gross Cotta. 'A German who was a restorer in the Dresden Gallery, Alfred Unger, came up to us from a little house,' Sokolova recalled.

We went to the inconspicuous wooden gates that led to the tunnel. A German came with keys and opened one door and then another. We were immersed in darkness and dampness. A simple freight wagon was in the tunnel. The German gave me a candle. Rabinovich switched on an electric lantern. In this dim light we saw gilded frames standing very close together. We directed the light onto them and I felt myself becoming deathly pale: in front of me were the outstretched wings of the eagle and Rembrandt's *Ganymede* lit by the golden ray. Rabinovich carefully moved the painting to the right and another canvas appeared.

'Do you see?' he whispered. 'Wunderbar,' the German said. And, really, in front of me was *The Sleeping Venus* by Giorgione ... Then the *Self Portrait with Saskia* by Rembrandt followed, then a little silvery landscape by Watteau, a Dresden landscape by Canaletto, Titian's *Young Woman in White*. My teeth were chattering because of the cold, because of emotion, and because of this awful spectacle ... It seemed that the Germans believed that the paintings would remain here for a long time, because the tunnel had electricity, heating, and ventilation. The day we visited it, neither heating, ventilation, nor electricity worked. The temperature in the tunnel was about 8 degrees [Celsius], it was dark and damp, and in this place were stored masterpieces that had been preserved in museum conditions through the ages, in constant temperatures, in the stately silence of cathedrals and museum halls. The Germans lost any moral right to own them. Now they belonged to the Red Army.[12]

The same quarry was visited some days earlier, on 12 May, by Arthur Graefe, escorting two Soviet officers. His impression was not so dramatic. 'The restorers Unger and Heese, responsible for the security of the tunnel, were there. The valuables in all senses are in normal condition. Only the heating equipment didn't work because of the lack of electricity, which is completely inadmissible for an extended period of time.'[13]

On 26 May the Arts Committee brigade finally began its operations. According to Sokolova, there was a reason for the urgent removal of the paintings from the shelter in Gross Cotta:

A rumour spread that some athletic American had appeared in the old quarry and that he had had some negotiations with the restorer who showed us the paintings in the tunnel. Everybody was disturbed by this rumour, and a reinforced patrol armed with a submachine gun was sent to the quarry. We came to begin the urgent evacuation of the paintings.

Who the 'athletic American' was has remained a mystery.[14]

Stepan Churakov constructed special platforms to cushion the paintings in the trucks. Plenty of transport was made available, as well as soldiers to load the paintings. To the surprise of the experts who had just arrived from Berlin, during their first day on the job they met Marshal Konev and General Petrov in the tunnel. The two high officers wanted to see the already legendary cache.

'As we were going down to the stone-pit,' Sokolova remembered,

we noticed a few cars. It appeared that Marshal Konev with his escort was observing the pictures. When we came to the tunnel at the first moment we were a little confused. I suggested that the artists wear their overcoats properly (as representatives of the fine arts, for whom no law exists, they were wearing their military overcoats thrown over their shoulders), and we moved toward the marshal. I reported in a keen voice that the commission from Moscow had arrived. He smiled and said, 'A little late. The Red Army has left you behind.' 'There's no keeping up with the Red Army, Comrade Marshal!' I answered.[15]

The work was organized very quickly. 'All the soldiers understood that they were dealing with glorious masterpieces of art,' Churakov wrote. The brigade spent the night in Unger's house and continued loading the next day. The Pirna power station was working again, and there was light in the tunnel. On 28 May the last paintings were finally removed to Pillnitz.

> We took out all the paintings there and Sergei Pavlovich Grigorov compared them with the catalogues of the gallery. Closing all the doors and windows to prevent air currents, we stood the paintings along the walls. We did this to give them a chance to acclimatize and to dry not quickly but gradually, because otherwise the paint might swell and flake off.[16]

Finally the brigade decided to open the crate containing the Sistine Madonna. Relations among the brigade members were not entirely harmonious. Since the arrival of the Moscow group, there had been a competition between Rototayev on one side and Sokolova and Rabinovich on the other. 'Perhaps there is no Madonna there,' Rototayev had said angrily to Sokolova, observing the mysterious locked crate. She told him that she did not want to take the chance of opening it without a restorer. Finally, she later wrote,

> at 12:30 on 27 May the complete brigade gathered in the main hall of Pillnitz ... The crate was standing near the wall. The soldiers and the artist members of the brigade slowly put it down according to command. We were standing around as if we were keeping a guard of honor beside the coffin of an important man ... The top of the box could be opened like the extendable top of a dinner table. Inside the box, two holes had been made in the gilded frame [of the painting]. We had to fit pegs, which were inside the crate, into the holes, and after this it was easy to take the painting out. It was done. The pegs were in place ... and in dead silence the painting, which faced the back of the crate, began to rise

slowly. We were stunned . . . Somebody whispered: 'It's her.' We were all silent, speechless.[17]

The masterpieces had been unpacked and lined up against the walls: Ribera's *St Agnes*, Rembrandt's *Rape of Ganymede* and *Self Portrait with Saskia*, Giorgione's *Sleeping Venus*, and Rubens' *Diana*. One day when Sokolova was absent, Marshal Konev paid a visit to the castle to see the Sistine Madonna. 'Returned from Albertinum,' Sokolova wrote.

> In Pillnitz I met the generals headed by Marshal Konev. The marshal was sitting in front of the Madonna, enjoying the painting and asking Rototayev and Grigorov to provide him with the necessary information. The marshal wasn't satisfied with their explanations because he was accustomed to a military directness of speech. I was impressed that such deep interest in art was demonstrated by a military man, I was touched by the attention paid to the painting by people busy with questions of war and peace.[18]

The marshal was extremely interested. On 30 May he sent a telegram to Stalin reporting that the treasures of the gallery had been found. Thinking about it, he became nervous. What if something happened to them? He paid one more visit to Pillnitz to check the Madonna again. In an unpublished diary, Mikhail Volodin wrote: 'The marshal came for the second time. He warned us that we were dealing with Germany, that the Germans might give us a copy instead of the original.' Konev was particularly nervous because the painting was unsigned, but the experts finally convinced him that the Madonna was the real one despite the lack of a signature.[19]

After the operation in Gross Cotta, the brigade began the removal of the collections stored in the castle of Weesenstein. Voss led them on a tour of the castle, where they found the specially equipped cabinet of prints and drawings and some of the paintings of the Dresden Gallery stacked on wooden shelves. Voss, wrote Sokolova, 'spoke German and French, using English words and Italian proverbs. He was calm and emphasized that he did not admire Hitler because he was a person of bad taste.'[20]

The brigade members disliked Voss and sometimes played practical jokes on him. Volodin mentioned in his diary that one day he and his colleagues decided to do some target shooting. On the way to the park they met Voss and ordered him to go with them. Voss thought they were going to kill him. Some local villagers who saw the Russians armed with rifles taking him into the forest also assumed that they were going to shoot him, and sent a boy to see what was happening. In the forest Voss understood that it was a joke and took part in the competition. 'After two of us shot five bullets each, we gave a rifle to Voss. He began to shoot, stretching his hands in a very funny way. Two of the five bullets hit the white part of the target. Compared to us it was very bad.'[21]

Volodin wrote that Voss 'had been in Leningrad in the Hermitage, but this "important specialist" in the Italian Renaissance could not name any Russian artists. A typical Aryan! He can't see beyond his nose. All right, it's his problem, not ours, but such absence of curiosity is shocking.'[22]

The brigade spent two weeks in the castle of Weesenstein. 'It was very difficult to load the Kupferstichkabinett because it included so many prints and drawings,' Sokolova recollected.

> Every portfolio looked like a big thick book ... We asked the Germans to drag out all that stuff. They worked joyfully because as payment for the job we promised them one bottle of wine for two people and one bottle for one person for the outstanding workers. The wine was found in the cellars of Weesenstein. When the work was completed the Germans stood in line. Volodin, skilfully fishing the bottles out of the boxes, gave prizes ... to the best workers. He was standing, very tall, cheerful. The German girls stared at him, laughing and flirting. At the same time our trucks were departing. I was talking to Voss observing this rejoicing. 'It's a real rural feast,' he said. 'A real rural feast.' ... A long time ago Voss visited Lipgart [a curator] in the Petersburg Hermitage. I recommended to him to visit Tsarskoe Selo and Peterhof now, after the Nazis had been there. Using this occasion I began to describe the horrors of the German blockade of Leningrad and the barbarism of Hitler's army ...
>
> Trying to change the topic, he said: 'Frau Major, we are people of art, we are higher than politics.'
>
> 'Unfortunately, Professor, I must disappoint you. We Russians suffered so severely from Hitler's barbarians that we can't be indifferent to politics. Especially since I'm a member of the Bolshevik party.' Voss was struck dumb. He became silent and open-mouthed.[23]

Sokolova, if her memoirs are to be believed, often had that effect on people.

DRESDEN

'The Cargo Is of State Importance'

The Weesenstein depository included a part of the graphics collection of the Führer Museum in Linz, including the Koenigs Collection, the unique collection of German nineteenth-century drawings bought from Prince Johann Georg of Saxony, forty etchings by Rembrandt formerly belonging to Robert Gutmann in Vienna, and the Palmier Collection. All of this was removed by the brigade. The records of the Linz museum were found in Weesenstein, including catalogues, correspondence, and photographs, and these too went to Moscow. But many of the works of art were simply looted. Numerous prints and drawings of the Kupferstichkabinett were torn out of their mounts and disappeared.[1]

The third major depository for paintings from the Dresden Gallery was discovered at a distance from the city, not far from the Czech border. Early one morning the brigade received information from the commandant's office that paintings had been found near Pockau-Lengefeld, and Sokolova, Rabinovich and Churakov set off immediately with soldiers. It was not a very secure depository, and it had been breached. The Russians found an old wooden barn standing near a ravine. An open padlock was hanging on the door. Inside the barn were paintings from the Dresden Gallery, including Rubens' *Bathsheba*, but there were also two empty frames. It was clear that someone had been there and left again with some of the property.[2]

Sokolova later remembered the empty frames. She examined the labels, which identified the missing pictures as portraits by van Dyck. She called Schmidt, the assistant manager of the mine, and asked him sternly what had happened to the pictures. 'He said that some Russians were here and took the paintings. It seemed that they had been taken by Schmidt himself.'[3]

It is not certain who stole the paintings. The museum guards who were with them during the first part of May but were absent on the day when the paintings were removed by the experts were questioned later. They stated that two portraits had been taken by Second

Lieutenant Rabinovich during his first visit to the mine.[4]

After a thorough examination of the barn, the brigade approached the ravine. 'It was very deep,' Churakov wrote.

> The lift, as it was explained to us, didn't work ... On the sides of the ravine yawned the black holes of tunnels ... Helping Major Sokolova, we went down. One of the miners showed us in which tunnel the paintings were hidden. It was damp and dark. For lighting we used carbide lamps and thick candles made of gunpowder that burned very slowly and gave a lot of light. On the bottom of the tunnel was a stream of groundwater. Walking some steps along the main tunnel we turned to the left in the corridor and immediately saw a blasted layer of rock – the place where the paintings were stored was camouflaged by it. They were in complete darkness, dampness, without any kind of ventilation.

They had been stacked upright in a makeshift room made of rough boards, and their condition horrified Churakov and Sokolova. The backs of some of the paintings were completely covered by a coating of white mould. In other cases, the mould was on the front, especially in the minute cracks in the paint surface.[5]

A simple lift had been built on one side of the ravine consisting of two parallel rails on which a board with a shelf was lifted with the help of a windlass. The brigade used it to lift the paintings from the bottom of the ravine. 'We shared the responsibility: N. I. Sokolova stood in the tunnel with the lantern and registered the masterpieces. The soldiers carried them to the lift and loaded them, L. N. Rabinovich observed the operation ... I loaded paintings on the trucks.' In this shelter the brigade found *The Tribute Money* by Titian, a Rembrandt *Self Portrait*, and a Botticelli Madonna.[6]

The brigades inspected other places where paintings were stored. In Barnitz they found a group of canvases by Gauguin, Meunier, Max Liebermann and Lovis Corinth that had survived by a freak of fortune. A shell aimed at the top floor of the house where the canvases were sheltered had not exploded in the building but flown right through it. The huge holes through which it had entered and exited gaped in the walls. The paintings were covered with a layer of shattered plaster but were otherwise not badly damaged.[7]

In the castle of Meissen twenty-three large paintings were discovered. Churakov, Grigorov and Volodin had a very difficult job getting them out. They had to take the canvases off their stretchers and carefully roll them up on special rollers. But the depository also contained treasures in the form of three oversized panels by Correggio: *The Holy Night*, *Madonna with St Sebastian*, and *Madonna with St George*.

'It was very difficult to carry out the long rollers with the paintings rolled on them, and the paintings by Correggio, down the narrow staircases of the castle,' Churakov remembered. 'But it seemed that this test was not enough.' The route of the loaded trucks lay along the embankment of the Elbe. An overpass had been damaged by an explosion, and there was not enough head room for the loaded trucks to pass underneath. The art experts and the drivers had to unload the trucks, carry the paintings under the bridge, and then load them again.[8]

The collection of paintings brought together at the collecting point in Pillnitz was becoming richer and richer. The news that Marshal Konev had personally paid a few visits to the castle spread quickly among the Soviet commanders, and others developed a desire to see what all the fuss was about. The generals and high-ranking officers of the First Ukrainian Front began to drop in frequently to the head-quarters of the Arts Committee brigade to look at the famous pictures. 'Once when I guided such an excursion,' Sokolova remembered,

> the generals asked me ... 'Comrade Major, have we such masters today in our country?' I answered pretty obscurely that we had a lot of very gifted artists. 'Who, for example?' I began to name well-known painters beginning with 'People's artists' and 'Honored artists'. The general who asked the question shook his head disapprovingly every time I named an artist ... 'Here is an example of how they should paint,' the generals said, pointing to St Agnes, the *Sleeping Venus*, and the Dutch still lifes, which were extremely popular among them.[9]

But the interest in art demonstrated by the generals was not com-pletely objective in character. 'Once the commanders asked me to help select for the generals works of art that had no museum value. I received an order to go to Lomnitz, where the Dresden commandant had been informed that a depository of paintings and porcelain had been found,' Sokolova remembered. The cave depository was situated in the grounds of a factory that produced soft drinks. It was well hidden. 'We came to a rock that had two entrances – one false and one real, well camouflaged. The doors were opened, and we appeared like Aladdin in a deep cave ... The cave was perfectly equipped. We found there some excellent carpets, crates with not bad porcelain and very nice dishes, and some dozens of paintings of German artists of the 1860s and 1870s ...' These things were selected for the generals.[10]

But it was not only works of art without museum value that were appropriated by the generals and other commanders. The defector Vladimir Yurasov later described his trip to Saxony:

> The commandant was drinking but not eating. He got drunk and again began to propose that I take something from his belongings as a present. 'If you want, take that picture. You're an educated person, you need it more than me.' The large painting depicted a nude woman with a huge peacock in the background. The skin was painted so well it looked real. 'Take it, Major! It's from the Dresden Gallery. When the Allies were bombing, the whole gallery was transported to various villages. This one turned up in Dahlen.'

Yurasov's commander was not an exception.[11]

From the moment the Dresden Gallery arrested the attention of Marshal Konev and he reported its discovery directly to Stalin, Moscow began to treat the Dresden operation as a special case. Inside the brigade, competition became very intense. Rototayev understood clearly that a career could be based on the 'rescue' of the Dresden masterpieces, and he did not need people like Rabinovich and Sokolova, who had been in Dresden before him. At the end of May he decided to liberate himself from their presence. Sokolova was sent back to Moscow. Rabinovich, who had been rather uncomfortable since General Shtikov's visit had given the lie to his Indiana Jones-style tale of discovery, was sent back to his trophy battalion. Pillnitz was guarded now not by simple soldiers but by the NKVD.

When the castle was chock full of paintings, Rototayev decided to send Ponomarev to Moscow to ask the Arts Committee for advice on how to select and transport pictures to Moscow. According to Mikhail Volodin's diary, Ponomarev returned at the beginning of July with a decree of the State Committee of Defence, dated 26 June, concerning the removal of art objects from Dresden. Works of high quality worthy of exhibition in the best Soviet museums were to be chosen. The Arts Committee specifically recommended that not many German pictures be taken.

On 12 July Marshal Konev received a telegram signed personally by Stalin: 'GIVE NECESSARY HELP IN TRANSPORTATION TO MOSCOW OF THE CARGO PREPARED BY THE BRIGADE OF COLONEL ROTOTAYEV. REMEMBER THAT THE CARGO IS OF STATE IMPORT-ANCE, PROVIDE THE NECESSARY SECURITY, REPORT THE ACCOMPLISHMENT. STALIN.'[12]

At the beginning of August three experts were sent to Dresden to help with the selection. One of them was Professor Blavatsky, who came from Berlin. Another was Professor Mikhail Dobroklonsky, the deputy director of the Hermitage, who had been in the city during the blockade and taken care of the museum while its director was evacuated with a large part of the collection. The third was Boris Alexeyev, an expert on porcelain, who had been a curator at the Kuskovo Museum before the war. Blavatsky selected statues in the cellar of the Albertinum, Dobroklonsky was responsible for choosing the paintings, and Alexeyev selected porcelain. This almost became Blavatsky's last trip. Someone tried to shoot him, but the bullet made a hole in one of his shoulder boards, leaving him unhurt.

From about 400 paintings found in Gross Cotta, about 500 canvases removed from Weesenstein, and about 350 pictures sheltered in Pockau-Lengefeld, more than 600 paintings were selected. On 30 July a train loaded with paintings, sculptures, drawings, prints, and *objets d'art* belonging to the Dresden collections left the city. The works of art remaining in Pillnitz were placed under the control of the Soviet military administration.

At the end of 1945 Sergei Merkurov, director of the Pushkin Museum, sent the Arts Committee a list of the paintings from the Dresden Gallery that had not been found by Rototayev's brigade. Among them were such major masterpieces as Vermeer's *Girl Reading a Letter by a Window*; the van Eyck Triptych; two works by Dürer: *Portrait of a Young Man* and the Dresden Triptych; *Mercury and Argus* by Rubens; the central part of the St Catherine Altarpiece and the *Portrait of Duke Heinrichs des Frommen* by Lucas Cranach; the *Portrait of Morette* and the *Double Portrait of Sir Thomas Godsalve and His Son* by Hans Holbein.[13]

Konstantinov, the deputy head of the Arts Committee, wrote on the list: 'It was reported that these valuables are hidden somewhere in the area of Leipzig or Dresden. Give order to find them.' The order was apparently given. On 18 January 1946 Vladimir Sventsitsky, the head of the publishing company of the Pushkin Museum, and

Ivan Petrov, a restorer from the same museum, left for Germany. Petrov, who had already visited Dresden during the last stage of the activity of the Rototayev brigade, was sent to help with the packing of the paintings selected for removal. But Sventsitsky's mission was unsuccessful. He sent a number of things back to Moscow from the depository in Pillnitz, but he did not find the missing masterpieces.

Most of them were discovered later not in Germany but in the centre of Moscow. In March 1946 a group of curators in the Pushkin opened six crates they had just received from Gokhran, the State Treasury. They contained twenty-two Dresden Gallery paintings, including several of the missing masterpieces, which had been found in the castle of Königstein.

Beginning in 1945 the museum received more than 500 crates containing forty-eight Western European paintings, thirty-one minia-tures, 117 sculptures, and thirty-two objects of furniture. Fifty-two crates contained 146,258 coins and medals (4,137 gold and 84,759 silver coins). The Dresden Historical Museum collection filled 104 crates: arms, costumes, paintings, and furniture. This collection was sent to the Hermitage along with 104 crates that had been received from the Commissariat of Finance and 280 crates containing additional objects from the Dresden Historical Museum. The official reason for this transaction was the absence of a department of arms and armour in the Pushkin Museum. But the real motive was that the Pushkin was so overloaded with trophy works that it looked for opportunities to share them with colleagues. The palaeontological and ornithological collections of Dresden, found in the Gokhran crates, were given to the Palaeontology Museum of the Academy of Sciences of the USSR.[14]

In May 1945, two Soviet officers, accompanied by Arthur Graefe, who was in charge of the state collections of Saxony, visited the castle of Königstein, thirty-five kilometres from Dresden. In the picturesque fortress on a hill over the Elbe the officers confiscated six crates. It was Graefe's last visit to the castle. Very soon it was occupied by the Gokhran trophy brigade. Before the war Gokhran had been under the control of the NKVD, and the Gokhran trophy brigades included NKVD officers who operated in the occupied territories, stripping banks and hunting for precious metals, gemstones and hard currency. These NKVD officers in simple military uniforms removed to Moscow jewellery, dollars, and paintings found in the safes of banks in Budapest, Vienna, and Berlin. At the same time the Commissariat of Foreign Trade created a network of special companies in the occupied territories of Germany that bought gold, jewels, crystal, carpets, paintings and other valuables, paying for them in Reichsmarks confiscated by the Gokhran brigades from German banks.

The Gokhran brigade took the castle of Königstein, expelled the Germans, and refused to admit the art experts of Rototayev's brigade. In the cellars of the castle were hidden the collection of the Dresden jewel museum, the Grünes Gewölbe, or Green Vault. More rooms were stuffed with porcelain, arms and other objects from the Historical Museum and some of the paintings and miniatures from the Art Gallery. Marshal Konev was informed about the find and visited the castle but did not mention it in his memoirs.[15]

On 13 May 1945 some old coins were discovered in the ruins of the Johanneum Palace in Dresden. In the cellar, under the museum library, the collection of the Münzkabinett was found. The coins were removed by the Gokhran brigades and sent to Moscow. Eventually, when the Pushkin Museum received a shipment of crates from Gokhran, the mystery of the lost masterpieces was partially solved. But some important paintings were not found in the crates received from the Commissariat of Finance. Among those missing were the van Eyck Triptych, Dürer's Dresden Triptych, Cranach's *Portrait of Duke Heinrichs des Frommen*, and Rubens' *Old Woman with Brazier*.

On 30 July 1946 Hermitage curators were opening crates received from the Pushkin Museum containing objects from the Dresden Historical Museum. Among the swords and sabres in one crate they found a little box. It contained the van Eyck Triptych, which Moscow museum officials had simply overlooked. The Hermitage curators decided not to make a noise about their unexpected find. The director, Orbeli, took the triptych to his office and kept it in his safe until 13 December. Then he gave it to the department of Western European art.[16]

The museums of Kiev also received gifts from Germany. At the beginning of the winter of 1945 a military cargo plane landed at the Kiev airfield. Crates were unloaded on the snow-covered field and sat there for hours until curators from the Kiev Museum of Western and Oriental Art arrived to collect them. By that time the contents were soaking wet. It was extremely difficult to arrange transport; trucks and petrol were in desperately short supply. In the boxes found in the snow was the Dresden Triptych by Albrecht Dürer, by this time seriously damaged by damp. During November and December of 1945 the Kiev Museum received 456 paintings from the Dresden Gallery, and the Historical Museum in Kiev received forty-one paintings from the same collection.

The Council of People's Commissars of Ukraine, led by the powerful Nikita Khrushchev, had sent its own trophy brigade to Germany. The brigade sent its loot by plane and train directly to the Central Committee of the Communist Party of Ukraine and the Council of People's Commissars of Ukraine. Paintings and drawings from the collections of Berlin and Dresden were removed to Kiev so quietly that the Arts Committee in Moscow had very little knowledge about the operation. In 1955 the Soviet Ministry of Culture learned that ten years before the Ukrainians had selected a quantity of objects from what remained in Pillnitz and sent them to Kiev. But this depository contained only second-rate objects by the end of 1945. Somewhere the Ukrainians had found a cache of masterpieces: Dürer's Dresden Triptych, *Christ* by Cima da Conegliano, Veronese's *Finding of Moses*, Cranach's *Nativity* and *Portrait of Duke Heinrichs des Frommen*, Rubens' *Old Woman with Brazier*, and other important paintings. Whether they had been left behind in the castle of Königstein by the NKVD or found in some shelter unknown to the Moscow brigade is still a mystery.[17]

DANZIG

Counting Coins

Early in May 1945, a Soviet trophy brigade entered the bomb shelter of the old armoury in Danzig. It was a dim cellar lit by two oil lamps, filled with hundreds of buzzing greenflies. The smell was terrible: the stench of decomposing corpses mixed with the reek of sewage. The floor was covered with pathetic objects: toys, broken dishes, clothing, all covered with a dirty white layer of feathers from torn pillows and mattresses. These things had been taken into the cellar by the people who had thought they would be safe there during the April bombardments, but a bomb ruined part of the cellar and the debris blocked the entrance. When the heap of bricks and stones was dismantled, one of the walls partially collapsed and had to be cleared away before it was possible to enter.

Major Lev Kharko, a brigade member who was a curator at the Pushkin Museum in civilian life, counted forty-eight bodies that day. Germans, mainly old people and teenagers, were carrying them out of the shelter and dumping them into a common grave, watched over by two Polish policemen who were enjoying their power over their former masters. Nobody looked for relatives or called a priest.

On 5 May, after two days of work in the cellar, the Soviets found the entrance to the hiding place they knew was there. The officers broke through a brick wall into a depository filled with crates, cupboards and old chests. It was almost impossible to carry them out of the shelter, and Leonty Denisov, head of the trophy brigade of the Second Belorussian Front, gave the order to unpack them where they were. They had no keys to the old chests, and Major Kharko tried to open them from the bottom without damaging their carved tops and sides. The work in the shelter took eight days. Art treasures from the city museum, the city hall and other collections were taken out and loaded on to trucks. Objects made of silver and ebony, miniatures, textiles from the Marienkirche embroidered with gold threads and pearls, were undamaged. But the many 15th–18th century wooden sculptures were covered with green mould. The 195 paintings had been badly damaged by a fire in the room next to the depository. The paintings that had been stored near the wall were white with decomposed varnish as a result of the heat. But there was no bomb damage. The best part of the collections was transferred safely to the office of the Soviet commandant. Some things were given to the new Polish director of the city museum, who was surprised and delighted by the unexpected gift.[1]

Kharko and Denisov had arrived at the front at the end of February. They were not welcomed by the regular army staff. 'The absence of our own transport and other equipment made us completely dependent on the military commanders, and we were forced to do only what we were ordered to do or were condescendingly permitted,' Kharko later wrote.

> Not all the commanders understood our task and gave us orders that had nothing in common with our specialization. For example, in Bromberg (Bydgoszcz), I received an order to work on the return of the archive of the Research Institute of Soil Science of the Ukrainian Academy of Sciences, which had been removed by the Germans from Kiev. In Thorn (Torun) it was proposed to us that we prepare the return of the library from Pskov and find some local 'Persian' library.[2]

The brigade in Pomerania included two more experts: Vladimir Shcherbinin, the director of the State Symphony Orchestra of the USSR, and Mikhail Petrovsky, an artist of the Bolshoi Theatre. Shcherbinin returned to Moscow in April; Petrovsky was sent on to Czechoslovakia and returned to the USSR with a rich haul of theatre equipment and costumes. Kharko and Denisov stayed in Pomerania and examined twenty-one cities and towns. They even reached the island of Rügen, in the Baltic Sea, but real luck awaited them in Danzig, where they arrived while there was still fighting on the outskirts. They immediately began searching for works of art.

They received a lot of help from SMERSH personnel, who arrested every museum official they could find in the city and interrogated them about the location of shelters. Three professors were particularly helpful, and as a result of the information they provided, Kharko and Denisov decided to organize a large-scale operation to search for the art valuables of Riga and Elbing as well as Danzig.[3]

Flemish paintings, Gothic sculpture, prints and drawings, coins and medals, tapestries and silver – thousands of valuable objects had been hidden by the Germans in Thuringia and Saxony. Lieutenant General Telegin was ordered by the Special Committee on Germany and the Arts Committee to consult with Marshal Rokossovsky about organizing a search for the hidden pieces. It was suggested that the three German professors and their families be taken to Danzig, Stettin, Berlin, and various places in Thuringia and Saxony. 'During this operation it is necessary to isolate the German experts and not let them contact the German population until the art valuables revealed by them are found (about 100 crates). A patrol, including two officers and four machine-gunners, is needed for this.'[4] But preparations for the operation dragged on. The authorities in Berlin had plenty of work already and were unimpressed by the prospect of 100 crates of valuables, which were nothing in comparison to the hundreds of factories and the entire museums that were being removed from the country.

While the state agencies were corresponding with each other, the Danzig brigade continued its work. Kharko confiscated the works of art belonging to the dealer Pachke, the valuables from Baron Arnoldi's estate at Sobbowitz, and other objects.[5] He was deeply disappointed by the loss of the famous fifteenth-century wood relief of Saint George from the Artshof in Danzig. The house had been bombed and burned, but Kharko thought that the relief might have fallen during the fire and been buried under a protective layer of tiles from the roof. They knew where in the ruins to look; the relief had been installed near a sixteenth-century majolica-decorated stove. A terrified stove setter was arrested by a military patrol and brought with his tools to the ruined house. He removed the twelve surviving majolica tiles from the old stove and then was rewarded with a good dinner and sent home. But after two days of careful digging by a work force of seven, with Kharko making sketches and marking every layer of the excavation, the expert found a layer of charcoal on the stone floor of the house and realized that nothing was left of the relief. It had been knocked down by falling debris and caught fire from the flaming beams, he wrote sadly in his report.[6]

On 27 June he had better luck in the ruins of a bank. The German museum curators had told him that the famous Marienburg coin collection had been hidden in a vault buried under the destroyed building, and Kharko was determined to find it. He was an expert in numismatics and knew the collection well. Trembling with nervousness, he watched as an old German labourer in overalls covered with brick dust attacked the rubble with his pick. Suddenly the pick struck metal with a sharp ringing sound. Everybody started. The labourer lowered the pick and looked inquiringly at the Soviet officers. Under the brick wall, a metre and a half thick, was another wall made of steel. Lieutenant Rogunkov swore and then said to Kharko, 'Damn it, the room is armoured like a tank. There's only one thing to do – an acetylene torch.'

Waiting for it to arrive, everybody sat down on the ground near the ruins of the bank. It was a hot day. Denisov was silent. He had been in hospital for a month after a serious car accident near Stettin and was still very weak.

Finally the torch was found. Fire began to eat at the steel door, making it glow bright red. The sergeant from a sapper platoon took a step back and raised his mask. A fellow soldier grasped a heavy hammer and hit the centre of the door. A piece of steel crashed into the safe. Kharko stepped forward. 'Stop!' the sergeant yelled. 'It's hot!' But Kharko had already shoved his lantern through the hole. In the ray of light he saw glass-topped tables like those in the department of numismatics in the Pushkin Museum.

Kharko could not wait. He wriggled through the hole into the dark interior of the safe. On the shelves and along the walls were 136 glass-topped cases. Thousands of gold and silver coins, medals, and military decorations glimmered in the light of his lantern. He stumbled over something. He held down his lantern and saw that Ideal typewriters and Astra mechanical calculators were thrown around the room. Piles of bank documents were everywhere. Safe deposit boxes were open and empty. He had found what he wanted.

For the next two weeks, four Soviet officers spent their time in an unusual way: they counted money – German coins from the thirteenth century to the era of Kaiser Wilhelm II. There were 14,062 altogether, including 661 gold coins and 10,438 silver. Kharko wanted to check them against the seven-volume catalogue of the collection, but he did not have enough time. The coins were taken from the display cases, packed in boxes, and transferred to a room set aside in the commandant's office. A patrol armed with machine guns guarded the door.[7]

Kharko was now in a race with thieves in Danzig. A treasure hunt was on for hidden museum valuables, and the thieves often won. A collection of incunabula belonging to the city library was stolen from a depository in the city hall cellar, along with a glass collection from the city museum. Only the labels were left.

On 23 September Denisov, who was in charge of transport, told Kharko that they could send off their loot by air. The next day a Douglas cargo plane with seventeen boxes on board, including three big boxes filled with coins, set off for Moscow. Denisov escorted the shipment, leaving Kharko alone in Danzig. On 17 October Kharko finally received an order from Berlin to move on to Thuringia and Saxony. The three German professors were ordered to get ready for a long trip.[8] Kharko anticipated an interesting journey because his aim was to find not only the Danzig museum's numismatic collection but a legendary painting by Hans Memling. This picture, a triptych of the Last Judgement, had an exciting history. It was ordered from the artist by Angelo Tani, the representative of the Medici bank in Bruges and the most famous patron of his time, who was undeterred by its very high price. The ship he hired left the harbour with the triptych on board, but it never arrived in Italy. It was attacked by pirates from the free Hanseatic city of Danzig. They donated the painting to the city cathedral. In 1807 it was looted by the French army, delivered to Paris, and deposited in the Louvre. In 1816, after the fall of Napoleon, it was returned to the Marienkirche in Danzig.[9] Now Kharko badly wanted to ship it to Moscow as a trophy.

When everything was ready, something completely unexpected happened. For some unknown reason, the operation was cancelled. Kharko was told to prepare the Danzig treasures for shipment to Leningrad by sea, but he waited in vain for a ship. Finally, on 8 December, he went back to Moscow, leaving eighty crates full of works of art under the control of the army commandant's office.

The Danzig brigade had ended its operation, but the Arts Committee in Moscow did not want to give up the search for the hidden Danzig treasures, and they sent Alexander Zamoshkin from Berlin to organize a search for them.[10] He found the numismatic collection in Reinhardsbrunn Castle, near Gotha, in January 1946. The famous tryptich by Memling was found in April. Lieutenant General Bokov wanted to send it to Moscow in the luggage carriage of a passenger train, but there was nobody available to escort it, so it ended up in Leningrad later, along with other valuables.[11]

What happened to the other treasures of Danzig is unclear, but there is a document that may throw some light on the mystery. At the beginning of 1946 Alexander Zamoshkin wrote to Lieutenant General Dubrovsky, head of the Soviet military administration in Saxony, asking him to help organize the removal of 'unique museum valuables (silver, porcelain) from the Boesenburg cave near Halle removed by the Germans from art museums'. Perhaps the treasures of Danzig were hidden there.[12]

THURINGIA

Impressionist Masterpieces in a Cellar

In July 1945 British and American troops moved out of an area in Thuringia more than a hundred miles into the proposed Soviet zone. They had occupied this territory in violation of the London agreement of the European Advisory Council. As soon as the Red Army moved in, a group from the Special Committee on Germany, led by Colonel Andrei Belokopitov, the representative of the Arts Committee in Berlin, arrived to investigate the fate of the art shelters. They had hoped that their Allied comrades had not found all of them.

Their main goal was the Kaiserode mine near the town of Merkers, where the gold stock of the Reichsbank and the art treasures from Berlin had been hidden. There, with the help of SMERSH and the military commandant, the art experts arrested everyone who had even the slightest connection to the depositories. The manager of the mine and an official of the mining department were questioned about everything that had happened in the shelter from the time they had been told that the gold and the paintings were being sent to Kaiserode. The interrogators were extremely interested in the activity of the Americans who had removed all these treasures, but the Germans did not know much. They had been put under house arrest by the Americans so did not see what went on.[1]

Belokopitov and his colleagues were more successful when they interrogated Professor Paul Rave, a curator of the National Gallery in Berlin who had come to Merkers with the Berlin paintings.[2] Rave told the Russians that he had been questioned by the American MFAA officers Robert Posey and Lincoln Kirstein, who had assured him that 'their aim was to save German cultural valuables and to guard them, to preserve museum property for Germany'.[3] Rave said they had promised to take him and his family to Frankfurt along with the paintings. He trusted them and cooperated with them. With MFAA Lieutenant George Stout, he visited the mine in Ransbach, where the costumes of the Berlin State Theatre and Opera were stored along with some of the paintings.

Rave described for the Russians the conditions in the mine, where they had found 'traces of a shocking underground orgy that was organized there by the Russian and Polish workers and prisoners of the camps'.[4] After the German guards fled, fearing the Americans who would be in the area very soon, the prisoners left their camps and, being familiar with the underground corridors of the mines where they had worked under Nazi guard, proceeded to rob the shelters. The 'living skeletons' cast off their prison rags for the gaudy costumes of *Aïda* and *Lohengrin*. They found a huge stock of brandy and champagne, and an orgy in the torchlit mine began. When Rave and Stout discovered that six crates containing paintings by Dürer and Holbein had been prised open, they assumed that the works of art had been destroyed or stolen. To their surprise nothing was damaged or missing. Rave's explanation for this unexpected exercise of virtue: 'It seems that the paintings depicting saints stopped the Russian prisoners from stealing and damaging them. When the Ostarbeiters saw in Ransbach an unpacked Madonna by Crivelli they began to cross themselves with religious emotion.'[5]

Generals Eisenhower, Bradley and Patton had examined the Thuringian mine shelters in April and expressed concern that such valuable things were concentrated in the area where the Allied armies would meet. The Red Army was ready to begin the attack on Berlin. The speed of the Russians was well known, and the Americans did not want to risk leaving the treasures for them to find. Rave escorted the generals, and he liked and trusted Eisenhower, who, he later said, 'was nice to me'.[6] He thought his problems were over: the Americans would not only save the art treasures but would take him and his family out of the Russian zone.

On the morning of 15 April, a truck convoy loaded with 100 tons of gold had left Merkers for Frankfurt. The same day preparations to evacuate the works of art stored in Kaiserode and Ransbach began. The Germans were impressed by American efficiency. The Americans had lowered jeeps that 'moved back and forth, manoeuvring at high speed under the surface of the earth'. But the huge American trucks impressed the Germans even more. 'We had never seen such big trucks,' Rave said.[7] At six in the morning on 17 April, 400 tons of art treasures, including 393 paintings from the Berlin museums, left Kaiserode.

It had taken the Germans two weeks to unload and store the art treasures, but it took the Americans only two days to remove them.

It was at this time that information about the Nazi barbarities in Buchenwald became known. The shocked Americans told Rave that 'all Germany is responsible for this and now any talks about cooperation between Allied countries and the representatives of German science and culture are impossible'.[8] Rave waited for eight days for Robert Posey, the MFAA officer who had promised to take Rave to Frankfurt, to keep his word. On the eighth day he unpacked his bags, realizing that the American promise would not be kept.

Disappointed by their failure in Kaiserode, the Soviets examined the other mines in Thuringia and the Harz Mountains. Whenever they located a mine that had been used as a shelter and then cleaned out by the Americans, they interrogated all the participants and questioned the local people. Then they drew up detailed reports of their findings. Everything that had been left by the Western Allies – the collection of the Goethe Museum in Weimar, the libraries of the city of Kassel and Marburg University, and even forty boxes containing the private library of Bernhard Rust, the education minister of the Third Reich – was put under the control of the Soviets.

Andrei Belokopitov was convinced there was another shelter somewhere. Otto Kümmel, the director of the Berlin museums, had given him a list of objects evacuated from Berlin, and it included many that were not on Rave's list of works of art removed by the Allies. There were still treasures the Americans had not located, and Belokopitov wanted very much to find them. His last hope was the salt mine near the village of Bernterode.

The mine was on fire when the committee arrived. The village was shrouded in black smoke, and the ground shook as explosion followed explosion deep underground. It was impossible to get near the entrance to the mine. Thousands of tons of explosives had been stored there by order of the German commanders. Belokopitov was deeply disappointed. The objects on Kümmel's list – 250 paintings, forty-eight tapestries, and three boxes of treasures from the Prussian court that had been evacuated from Berlin – were gone.[9] They had been discovered by the MFAA officers Walker Hancock and Lieutenant Steve Kovalyak, who had removed them in May, together with the remains of Frederick the Great and General von Hindenburg, which had also been hidden in the mine. When it exploded, the valuables were already stored safely in Marburg and Frankfurt.[10]

The competition between the Soviet trophy brigades and the American MFAA began long before July 1945, when the Americans and the British left the Soviet zone. The Soviets knew that Hitler, Goering and other Nazi leaders had robbed the art collections of Europe, and wanted to get their hands on the loot. But they did not have concrete information. When Soviet tanks entered Vienna on 13 April, the art experts did not know that art treasures from all over Europe 'collected' for the Führer Museum in Linz were stored in the mine at Alt Aussee, only 200 kilometres from the city. The Red Army halted when it reached the border of the designated Soviet occupation zone. Stalin was not interested in the part of Austria that was turned over to the Allies because it had no large industrial installations.

On 8 May the Americans were in Alt Aussee. It was not until 14 May that the deeply distressed Belokopitov reported to his commanders: 'As a result of the questioning of Otto Kümmel, the director of the Berlin Museums ... it was learned that Hitler had a private collection for which treasures of world art were selected by someone named Voss. The collection was in Austria in the area of Salzburg ... in Aussee.' But it was too late.[11]

The Soviets did make one spectacular discovery in Thuringia and found a prize that had been overlooked by the Americans. The collection of ninety-eight paintings amassed by the industrialist Otto Krebs before the war included one of the largest and most important assemblages of Impressionist and Post-Impressionist paintings and sculpture in Europe as well as Oriental works of art and antiquities. He stored the collection in a specially equipped room in the cellar of his country estate, Gut Holzdorf, near Weimar. In 1941 Krebs died of cancer and left all his property to a cancer research foundation. The house was occupied by the Americans from April to June of 1945, but they never discovered what was hidden behind the massive iron door in the cellar. Then it sat empty for a year and was repeatedly robbed by local villagers. In the spring of 1946 General Vasily Chuikov, the commander of Soviet troops in Thuringia and head of military administration in the area, became the new master of Gut Holzdorf.

Walter Scheidig, the director of the Weimar museum, had known the Krebs Collection well before the war. He wrote to the civilian prime minister of Thuringia asking that it be removed from the cellar and turned over to the museum. Finally, in the summer of 1947, he received permission from General Kolesnichenko, Chuikov's deputy in military administration, to remove the paintings. Scheidig arrived at the house with the Russian officer who handled cultural matters for the military administration, a representative of the prime minister, and an experienced bank robber from Berlin, whose job was to open the iron door. But to Scheidig's intense disappointment, Chuikov refused to let them in.[12]

A year later, at the end of 1948, a German art historian, probably the indefatigable Scheidig, told the whole story to Major General Leonid Zorin, head of the Department of Reparations, Supplies, and Restitution of the Soviet Military Administration in Germany. Zorin had been so busy removing industrial installations and repatriating Soviet works of art that he had paid little attention to rounding up German cultural valuables. He sent two of his people to search Gut Holzdorf. The astonished Chuikov did not believe there was a secret shelter in the house, but he could not refuse to let them in. It did not take them long to find the iron door in the cellar and cut it open as Chuikov watched. They walked in and looked around, dazzled by the glowing colours. There were two Manets, ten Renoirs, four van Goghs, four Gauguins, and five Cézannes, as well as works by Signac, Matisse and Picasso. There were eighteen sculptures, ten of them by Degas. Everything was in perfect condition.[13]

But the collection was not destined for Walter Scheidig's little museum in Weimar. Almost all of it was shipped directly to the Hermitage, where it went into another storeroom and remained there, unseen and unappreciated, until 1995.[14]

LEIPZIG

Taking Only the Best

It was the energetic Alexander Voloshin who found the paintings of the Leipzig Museum of Fine Arts. On 7 July 1945 he compiled a list of the shelters to which they had been evacuated by the Germans – fourteen separate depositories ranging from bank vaults to bomb shelters, castles, country estates and quarry tunnels.[1] He apparently thought the facilities were satisfactory because he made no effort to evacuate them immediately. It was not until the end of the month, after the Dresden collections had been sent to Moscow and works of art in the Zoo tower had been transferred to the abbatoir in Berlin, that Lieutenant General Nikolai Trufanov, the commandant of Leipzig, and Colonel Belokopitov wrote a report about the art treasures of the city museums, addressed to Lieutenant General Telegin of the Military Council. A few days later Telegin replied, ordering them to 'select the most valuable and interesting for us'.[2]

On 10 September Majors Boris Alexeyev and Stepan Churakov arrived in Leipzig. They had been in Moscow for a month, not long enough to spend the 1,000 rubles each had received as payment for the Dresden operation, before they were ordered back to Germany. Churakov was promoted. Alexeyev received a new title; he was the representative of the Arts Committee in Thuringia and Saxony.

On 24 October 1945, Churakov drove up in his jeep, escorted by soldiers in a Studebaker truck, to a building on Tredlinring, and everyone jumped out. The smart Churakov was probably the only member of the trophy brigades who looked like a real officer in his uniform. With an air of authority he walked into the building, on whose wall was a sign with the words 'Commercial Bank'. Despite the early hour, the bank officials were there. They already knew the major, who had paid a visit to the bank together with representatives of the army commandant's office. A polite official led them to the vault. The soldiers followed.

The official unlocked a steel door. In the vault were ninety-seven paintings of the Dutch, German and French schools from the Leipzig

Museum of Fine Arts. Churakov checked the labels on the stretchers that he had attached during his previous visit and began to take down from the shelves the big paintings in their heavy gilded frames. 'Come here, boys,' he called to the soldiers. They came into the vault, leaving the official behind in the corridor. After half an hour of work, the last of the twenty-six chosen paintings left the vault where they had been kept since 1941.[3]

Before the eyes of surprised passers-by, Churakov, despite his officer's rank, settled the paintings himself in a specially built protective construction in the back of the truck. A few minutes later they drove off. The paintings were taken to the building at Heerstrasse 5 where the storage of trophy art was situated. As ordered by 'the special recommendation of the command', Churakov did not leave behind any documents about the confiscation of the paintings with bank officials, but they of course were afraid to complain.[4]

The truck and the escorting jeep drove through the streets of Leipzig, leaving behind the destroyed buildings of the museums. Under the ruins of one of them, Churakov knew, a superb fresco of the archangel Michael by Pintoricchio was buried for ever. In 1943 Igor Grabar had listed this masterpiece as an 'equivalent' for removal after the end of the war. Crossing the railway, they came to the depository building. At the checkpoint, Churakov showed his pass and was waved through. The vehicles stopped in front of a large, four-storey building with thick bars on the windows. A patrol guarded the doors. Churakov ordered the soldiers to take the paintings to the large lift in the lobby. They were stored in a vault like the one they had left behind, but now they had a new owner: the Arts Committee trophy brigade.[5]

Churakov's comrade in Leipzig, Boris Alexeyev, was a curator with years of experience at the Kuskovo Museum of Ceramics in Moscow. He had been appointed head of the Arts Committee Department of Sculpture. In a novel published in 1952, the defector Vladimir Yurasov described meeting Alexeyev in 1945:

People in the army didn't like 'saburovtsi' [demontageniks], because they stayed in the rear and because they had officer's shoulder boards. On every occasion they were humiliated. Once in the commandant's office Fyodor met one of these 'colonels' – small, crooked, dressed in a very long baggy soldier's uniform with a colonel's shoulder boards, he was standing near Lieutenant Kiselev, the duty officer, who was half-lying in an armchair, and was pleading with him about something. 'What do you want from me?' Kiselev asked in a terrible voice, to the amusement of the soldiers of the commandant's office, who were sitting in the same room. The 'colonel' was a professor from the Institute of Ceramics.[6]

Yurasov promoted Alexeyev and made him a professor, but the art expert is perfectly recognizable. Alexeyev's military rank was a burden to him, and he never used it when signing official documents. But the modest officer was extremely energetic and capable. He acquired an excellent building from the Leipzig military commandant and with the help of the skilful Churakov transformed it into the best collecting point in the Soviet occupation zone. Valuable objects, especially works on paper, were sent from Berlin to Leipzig to be cared for.

On 29 October Alexeyev removed thirty Dutch and German paintings belonging to the Museum of Fine Arts from the bank at Otto Schtilstrasse 30. In November he and Churakov began looking for the other Leipzig collections. On 11 November they found a shelter containing the best objects from the Leipzig University Egyptian Museum and the Grassi Museum (Museum of Applied Art). By the end of the year, the most valuable objects from those collections were stored in the collecting point at Heerstrasse 5. Fifteen soldiers and forty conscripted Germans were working day and night, packing 7th–10th century Iranian ceramics, 12th–14th century metal objects from Syria and Mesopotamia, Chinese and Japanese porcelain, 17th–18th century Italian majolica and silver, and huge quantities of European porcelain. All these treasures came from the Grassi Museum. Part of its library also went east. About 1,000 objects from the Leipzig University Egyptian Museum were packed by German women and children supervised by Churakov.[7]

Boris Alexeyev's approach to collecting was very different from that of Alexander Voloshin, who was so active in Berlin. Voloshin was indiscriminating and tried to take everything, but Alexeyev was selective and wanted only high-quality works of art. He chose only 106 of the more than 1,200 paintings in the Museum of Fine Arts in Leipzig. They included van Eyck's *Portrait of an Old Canon*, Tintoretto's *Resurrection of Lazarus*, Cranach's *Portrait of Gerhard Volk*, Frans Hals's *Mulatto* and Martin Schongauer's *Madonna Among the*

Roses. From the sculpture collection he selected only fifteen statues, including works by Rodin and Maillol.[8]

Alexeyev travelled around Germany, begging and humiliating himself but reeling in painting after painting to the vaults of the building on the Heerstrasse. At the beginning of January 1946 he went to Berlin to take part in the selection of objects from Museum Island; at the end of January he prepared the documents for the transportation of works from Malsdorf Palace, near Erfurt; in the middle of February he delivered the entire documentation of the Linz museum and other valuables from the castle of Weesenstein directly to the train in Berlin; at the end of the month he was in Leipzig again, where he selected five more pictures from the collection of the Museum of Fine Arts.

Alexeyev scoured the Dresden area for a second time, having been given permission to 'confiscate unique objects of art (paintings, sculptures, applied art, furniture, and art books) from Pillnitz and Weesenstein castles'.[9] He had good relations with the representatives of the Frunze General Staff Academy, who were also collecting trophies in the area. One of them, Lieutenant Gorbunkov, obligingly removed the art valuables from Friedenstein Palace in Gotha on 4 March 1946. This rich haul included fifty-three paintings from the Danzig and Gotha museums that had been found in the hunting castle at Reinhardsbrunn. Among them were two famous paintings by Rubens of St Basil and St Athanasius. The paintings, together with graphics, sculpture, bronzes, porcelain, and 4,206 volumes from the library of Friedenstein, were transported by Gorbunkov to Leipzig. The removal was controlled by Lieutenant Kaimakin, the operational representative of the Counterintelligence Department of SMERSH in the department of the Gotha military commandant.[10]

This was not the only Arts Committee operation in Gotha. The collections that had been accumulated over 300 years by the dukes of Coburg-Gotha in the castle of Reinhardsbrunn were also removed. Alexeyev received authorization to confiscate the castle's 'museum objects' from the Main Trophy Department of the Red Army at the end of January 1946.[11]

The Gotha collections were shared between the Committee on Cultural Educational Institutions of the Council of People's Com-missars of the Russian Federation and the Arts Committee. The Russian committee received three-quarters of the coins from the

numismatic collection; the antique and Celtic coins had been hurriedly taken to Coburg before the occupation and were found by the
Americans. The Arts Committee received the best works of art,
including five paintings by Cranach and a portrait by Frans Hals.[12]

The valuable libraries of Gotha, Leipzig, and other cities of Saxony
and Thuringia were shared by the Lenin Library and the Library of
the Academy of Sciences. The famous Gutenberg Bible and other
rare editions from the collection of the German Library and the
Museum of Books and Literature in Leipzig were removed on 22
September 1945 by Colonel Maloletkov and Lieutenant Andrei Mos-
kaletov and were deposited in the Lenin Library. The collections of
the Leipzig University Library and the Leopoldina in Halle went to
the Academy of Sciences of the USSR.

The Institute of Nuclear Researches in Dubna, which took an
active part in the creation of the Soviet nuclear bomb, received 3,332
volumes from the Department of Experimental Physics of Halle
University, and 37,000 volumes belonging to the Meiningen State
Library went to the Academy of Sciences.[13]

The collecting point on the Heerstrasse contained 50,194 works of
art. Alexeyev paid special attention to porcelain, glass and ceramics,
which were represented in the 'collection' of the brigade by 3,997
objects, including even the old moulds removed from the Meissen
porcelain factory.

It took ten days to load the train with the treasures collected by
Alexeyev and Churakov. Sixty soldiers filled nineteen carriages with
200 tons of objects and books.[14] The Frunze Academy was sending
its trophies by the same train and filled eighteen carriages with
aluminium beds, metal pots and building materials, but paintings,
sculptures and books were crammed into these carriages too. The
transportation documents listed their contents as 'art valuables and
aluminium beds'.[15] The art valuables had been selected for the
academy by Alexeyev. On some of the crates the words 'Present of
Marshal Konev' were written in big letters. Among the German
souvenirs the marshal presented to his beloved academy was a painting
of Napoleon at Fontainebleau by Paul Delaroche, from the collection
of the Leipzig Museum of Fine Arts.[16] On 11 March 1946 the train
left Leipzig, and the Arts Committee brigade in Thuringia and Saxony
ended its operations.

The group's efficiency wasn't matched in Berlin, where the competition between rival trophy brigades was threatening to get out of hand. In March the military administration showed Alexander Zamoshkin a draft order relating to trophy property found in the shelters. It assigned numerous art objects from Saxony and Thuringia to the Committee on Cultural Educational Institutions of the Russian Federation. This organization also wanted the remains of the Dresden Gallery and 1,000 paintings from the Potsdam palaces left by the Arts Committee experts. Some other valuables that Zamoshkin wanted were also listed.[17] Zamoshkin's outraged protest was effective: further looting of the remains of the Potsdam and Dresden museum collections was avoided, and the other finds were shared by the rival bodies.

Since the trophy brigade had left Thuringia, the most valuable booty received by the Arts Committee – the best paintings from the collection of the Dessau museum, works of art from private Dessau collections, and canvases from the Gotisches Haus in Wörlitz, which were hidden in the Solvayhall mine near Bernburg – were sent to Moscow via Berlin. The experts were all busy on Museum Island, and Alexeyev and Churakov had been sent to Moscow in charge of the train, so Voloshin sent Fyodor Novikov, who in civilian life was the director of the Second Travelling Theatre in Moscow and who had no idea how to treat valuable objects, to collect the things. When the two carriages filled with 149 crates arrived at the abbatoir in Berlin on 29 April, Voloshin and Sidorov were appalled. All the crates were damaged, some were open, and some had no tops. It was impossible to make out the identification numbers. Inside the crates there was complete chaos. Some crates contained frames without paintings. The packing was so bad that numerous paintings had been damaged.[18] But there was no time to sort things out. The next train to the USSR was being loaded and could not wait. The two experts put the broken boxes into larger crates and sent them to Leningrad. It was the last operation of the Arts Committee outside Berlin.

The removal of art trophies from Germany lasted until 1948. The military administration, in cooperation with the representatives of various state organizations, continued to export works of art and libraries. The army also took what it wanted. The marshals decorated the General Staff Academy in Moscow and their own headquarters in Germany with objects from German museums. On 9 March 1946 Major General Ivan Kolesnichenko, head of the military administration in Thuringia, confiscated twenty-three paintings from the Schlossmuseum in Weimar. Canvases by Salomon van Ruysdael, Simon Douw, Daniel Seghers, Adriaen van de Velde, and other Dutch and German artists were sent to Berlin to decorate Marshal Zhukov's headquarters. Kolesnichenko knew his 'modest' gift from Thuringia would please the commander.[19]

The army did not forget its own military museums. Twenty-five crates of objects from the long-suffering Dresden Historical Museum, whose collection was torn apart by the trophy brigades of the different state organizations, were confiscated from the shelter in Pfaffroda by Lieutenant Colonel Sorokin. He marked every crate with the words 'Artillery Museum of the Red Army'. Arms and armour were especially popular. Even in June 1948, when the wave of confiscations was seemingly over, 128 exhibits of arms, from medieval swords to a First World War hand grenade, were confiscated from the museum in Zeulenroda by Major Snezhkov, a representative of the commandant's office in Greiz.[20]

Major Snezhkov's confiscation was unimpressive when compared with events at the castle of Wartburg, near Eisenach. Here Lieutenant Colonel Novoselov, the Eisenach commandant, ordered the whole collection of the renowned Rustkammer, the armoury of the counts of Thuringia, loaded onto trucks. The banners that fluttered from the ceiling, the swords and sabres that decorated the walls, helmets and suits of armour, hunting trophies of the counts and dukes – 1,500 objects were all removed from Wartburg and sent east. The transport can be traced to Merseburg, but what happened to it later is unknown. The operation was organized at the order of the 'master of Thuringia', Major General Kolesnichenko.[21]

But representatives of the civilian professions were also active. From April to August 1946, one Konokotin, director of the State Corporation of Playing Cards based in Leningrad, emptied seven halls of the castle of Altenburg in Thuringia, which contained a rich collection of cards. He took not only the cards but all the documentation on them, including the inventory lists of this unique collection.[22]

HOSTAGES OF
THE COLD WAR

FREIGHT TRAINS FULL OF
TREASURES

Late in the evening of 2 February 1946, two men in civilian clothes escorted by a major nervously entered a study in the Kremlin. Three men were sitting around a table waiting for them, and another, wearing a marshal's uniform without military decorations, stood near the window. The attention of the visitors – Walter Ulbricht, leader of the German Communist Party, and Friedrich Elsner, propaganda chief – went to the fourth man. Normally it would have been impressive enough to meet Foreign Minister Vyacheslav Molotov and Politburo members Georgy Malenkov and Andrei Zhdanov, whose decisions would affect the fate of Germany. But the fourth man was Stalin himself. He shook hands with Ulbricht and then, without preliminaries, said to him, 'I hear you want to unite. Very good . . .' The fate of postwar Germany was decided. Despite the warnings of his former allies, Stalin was permitting the unification of the Communist and Social Democratic parties in the Soviet occupation zone. His new political aim was to establish East Germany as a Soviet puppet state.[1]

The Socialist Unity Party of Germany was founded on 21 April. The union between the Communists and the Social Democrats was strategically necessary for Moscow. The Social Democrats were popular, and the unification of the parties, inspired by the Soviet occupation authorities, put them under the control of the Communists. The Soviet administration believed that the same thing would happen in the Western zones as well and that the Communists would assume power in the whole country.

A few weeks earlier, Marshal Vasily Sokolovsky, deputy head of the Soviet military administration in Germany, had signed a secret order temporarily halting all dismantling and confiscations in Germany until 1 May 1946.[2] This was the first step towards nationalization of industry in the Soviet zone. On 21 May, the military administration transferred all sequestered and confiscated property of the Third Reich to the control of local governments.

The Special Committee on Germany had already begun to curtail its activities. Alexander Voloshin remembered that Sokolovsky's order reached them when they were working on Museum Island. 'The difficulty and scale of the confiscation work had seriously prolonged our presence there. Because of the order, we had no time to realize our plan on Museum Island. Of course ... we had to move the most important valuables immediately, having no time to register them.' Voloshin was worried about the numismatic collection. 'The strong-boxes containing unique pieces were removed without any control. They were covered with thick square boards like other crates and then covered with metal plates attached with staples to make theft impossible.'[3]

On 14 May 1946, Voloshin sent a telegram to Moscow informing the Arts Committee that removals from the Reichsbank had ended on 6 May. 'All necessary objects were confiscated ... According to new orders all work on confiscation is stopped.'[4]

On 18 June, the Soviet military administration issued order No. 177, concerning the return to German museums of works of art hidden in shelters and mines in the Soviet occupation zone.[5] It was a hypocritical order, since the military administration knew perfectly well that most of those works of art had already been deposited in the museums of Moscow and Leningrad and that the rest of the art trophies were being hurriedly and secretly prepared for transport to military facilities.

Over the course of the preceding year the biggest transport operation of works of art in the history of mankind had taken place. It had begun before the war ended, when the various army groups stumbled upon depositories in their areas of activity. The most important of these was the underground shelter found near Hohenwalde in March, in the area of Meseritz, where the treasures of the Kaiser Friedrich Museum in Posen had been stored.[6] They were packed up and sent back to Moscow by Major Sergei Sidorov, a member of Andrei Belokopitov's trophy brigade. The shipment was authorized by the military council of the front, as was the case with all the depositories found in Silesia, which Hitler had wrenched from Poland in 1939 and which were handed back after the war.

Some of the most important works of art came on the first transport out of Berlin, a military cargo plane that left on 30 June 1945, bound for Moscow. The crowded cabin was loaded with objects of particular importance, including new microscopes destined for the Academy of Sciences and the valuable gem collection of the Altes Museum. The escorting officers, Majors Kopas and Kulakovsky of the Fifth Shock Army Trophy Department, had orders to deliver the greatest prizes to the Arts Committee: the three crates containing the Trojan gold and other treasures from the Ethnographic Museum, and eighteen paintings from the private Gerstenberg and Koehler collections, all found in the Zoo tower. Among them were El Greco's *John the Baptist*, Goya's *Portrait of Lola Jimenez*, and Daumier's *Revolt* and *Laundry Women*.[7]

This cargo was removed from Germany in violation of the Soviets' own rules. After the German surrender, a new procedure had been adopted for the removal of trophy valuables. Permission had to be given by the State Committee of Defence in Moscow or the Special Committee on Germany. But the military council of the Fifth Shock Army had dispatched the plane full of treasures without waiting for permission.

The pictures were in excellent condition. They had been stored in Treskov Castle, a depository with a good reputation. At least it was dry, which was not always the case. The abattoir buildings, where thousands of objects from the Berlin museums were collected, were in bad shape, with leaking roofs and broken windows. In the beginning 110 soldiers and four officers had worked there, but late in 1945, when troop withdrawals began, shortage of labour became a serious problem. The harried Voloshin decided that proper record-keeping was impossible: 'If the scale of our job (about 1,000,000 objects) is kept in mind, and at the same time the small number of workers', he complained, 'it becomes clear that to observe all regulations as in a normal situation was impossible. Only the simplest registration of valuables was done.' The boxes were covered with metal sheets and camouflaged to hide their contents from the workers who loaded them onto trains – displaced persons and Vlasovites (soldiers in the army of the renegade General Vlasov). Voloshin pointed out in his report that he would not have been able to send so many objects east if he had followed all the rules.[8]

The train that left Dresden in July was authorized by a decree of the Special Committee of Defence. A few weeks later the Special Committee on Germany secretly authorized the removal of the

Pergamum Altar and the other museum valuables from the Zoo tower in Berlin. Serafim Druzhinin was in charge and would escort the train to Moscow. The loading began in mid-September. Soldiers brought the heavy reliefs of the altar to the railway station in ten trucks and crammed them into all forty carriages of the train. They were put on the floor, and 'light cargo' was loaded on top of them. The train left Berlin on 27 September.[9]

After this there was a pause that worried the brigade experts. Winter was fast approaching, and the works of art had to be sent immediately or left in Berlin until spring, in which case the depositories would have to be overhauled. Nobody would take the responsibility of sending them across Europe in unheated cars. Voloshin reported to Moscow in November:

> The art historians working in Germany think that the artworks, which are wet and react rapidly to temperature changes ... should be sent not now but in the spring. I am talking about antique sculptures, antique pottery objects, Egyptian reliefs, which were found wet in the cellar of New Mint, where they were under water for a long time.[10]

Since the distance between rails in Russia was (and is) wider than in Europe, the cargo of every train arriving at the Soviet border had to be reloaded into new carriages, and the danger of reloading the trains in Brest – particularly in bad weather – discouraged even Voloshin, an enthusiastic supporter of the immediate removal of the trophies. In mid-November Marshal Zhukov was asked to supply the brigade with ninety carriages and three cargo planes. The Arts Committee pleaded to the military administration that 'the urgent transportation of artworks is prompted on one hand by the lack of storage equipped according to museum standards and on the other by the fact that some sculptures hidden by the Germans in cellars got wet and in the course of transportation to the USSR during a period of frosty weather could be damaged.'[11] Zhukov agreed to give them one cargo plane, seven trucks and eighty goods carriages, but, as usual, the execution of the marshal's order took time. The cargo plane was not available until December, when it flew to Moscow with the greatest masterpieces of the Leipzig museums and a part of the graphics collection of the Berlin museums on board.

Despite the concerns of the art experts, the train shipments finally resumed during the coldest month. On 15 January 1946, a train containing forty-one carriages packed with art valuables left from the Lichtenberg station for Leningrad. For a month, precious prints by Dürer and Rembrandt, paintings by Rubens and Fra Filippo Lippi, along with hundreds of other masterpieces from the Berlin and Potsdam museums, travelled through the snowy landscape of Poland and Russia. The crates of antique and Egyptian sculpture were in badly maintained, unheated goods wagons. The Egyptian limestone reliefs found wet in the New Mint cellar were also on this train, along with Italian marbles and Egyptian papyri, Persian miniatures and Oriental textiles.[12]

Another train left Berlin on 18 February. For Major Yuli Sabsai, loading it was a nightmare. He did not have enough officers to supervise the simultaneous loading of eight goods wagons and when he tried to use soldiers who had worked in the abattoir to count the boxes, he discovered that 'the squad commanders were not usually literate'.[13] This trip too took a month, as the February frosts gave way to the March thaw. Finally, on 17 March seventy crates with the ill-fated objects excavated in the Friedrichshain tower, 216 crates of sculptures, and several hundred boxes of Western European paintings, prints, arms and armour, Japanese umbrellas and Chinese paintings on silk, as well as documents about the Führer Museum in Linz, reached the Kiev station in Moscow.[14]

With the beginning of spring, trains full of valuables began to arrive in Moscow one after another. In March came trains from Danzig and Leipzig. At the end of March and the beginning of April, the Committee on Cultural Educational Institutions began to receive its loot.[15] Two more trains pulled into Leningrad in the summer, bringing gifts from the Arts Committee brigade. This one hard-working brigade had sent to Russia twelve trains and three cargo planes loaded with looted art treasures.

MOSCOW

Too Much Loot

On a March morning in 1946, a man wearing a military overcoat with the shoulder boards of a first lieutenant jumped from the back of a truck into one of the goods wagons of Train No. 176/1759, which had just arrived in Moscow from Berlin. Making his way across the wagon through the piles of crates, he opened the door a crack and peeked out. The unloading of the train, carrying trophies from the Berlin museums, was in progress, and nobody had noticed the truck that had moved to the side of the tracks opposite the one the official workmen were using. Frantically, First Lieutenant Klimov and the driver began unloading crates into the back, urged on briefly by Major Yuli Sabsai, the train commander. When the last box was loaded, the truck sped off, the March mud splashing up from under its wheels.

The events that followed were described by Inspector Astafiev of the Moscow customs office. 'On 20 March 1946, First Lieutenant Klimov, who escorted the train, unloaded five boxes ... one of which he delivered to his own apartment, and the other four to the State Tretyakov Gallery. The cargo was stopped and seized.'[1] Klimov, who had worked at the museum for thirty-five years, later explained that the box he had delivered to his apartment contained nothing more than a radio, but nobody believed that he had organized such a complex operation for only a radio.

Radios were, however, a recurring problem for the trophy brigades. Customs officers found these prized symbols of Western life hidden among the works of art in almost every train sent from Germany. In answer to official questions about the source of his four Telefunkens, Lev Kharko of the Pushkin Museum wrote defensively that the radios had been 'received' before the ban on their import. 'Whole trainloads of radios were sent to various people's commissars without limits or official documents,' he added.[2]

Private looting was inevitable, from the gold and diamonds stolen by the generals to the wristwatches favoured by common soldiers because they were easy to carry. Unaccustomed to consumer goods, the Soviets happily took the humblest things. The brigade members were no exception and had better opportunities than most to export their private trophies. All the works of art in the train from Danzig were packed in blankets, quilts, pillows, and carpets, which were represented as simple packing materials.[3] All kinds of useful goods shared the goods wagons with the Pergamum Altar and the Sistine Madonna. In the wagons containing the Dresden treasures, Roto-tayev's brigade loaded not only the usual radios but also motor scooters.[4] A list of cargo confiscated from Lieutenants Rogunkov and Miasnikov, who took part in the excavations in the Danzig city hall and bank, included a bicycle, an accordion, a small lathe, an overcoat, three raincoats, spools of thread, an umbrella, seven carpets, a painting, a violin, a mandolin, and a fox fur.[5] The more intellectual Professor Ludshuveit, the 'saviour' of Potsdam, after whom a street in the city was named during the days of the German Democratic Republic, tried to appropriate two boxes of books that had come on the train from Leipzig.[6]

Some cases had a kind of pathos. Fyodor Novikov, the careless packer who escorted the last train sent by the Arts Committee from Germany, spent two months desperately looking for a vacuum cleaner that was mentioned in the cargo list. It could not be found among the things unpacked at the Hermitage, and a vigilant customs officer accused poor Novikov of stealing state property – an extremely serious charge. He stayed in Leningrad, checking box after box again and again, and sending desperate telegrams to his superiors in Moscow: 'The vacuum cleaner has not been found in the Hermitage. Please prolong my mission.' Some weeks later it became clear that a com-mittee inspector, Dmitry Vasilievsky, had decided to send his vacuum cleaner with Novikov's train and secretly put it on the list. He got frightened at the last minute and removed the vacuum cleaner but forgot to cross it off the list. When the truth was discovered the case against Novikov was quietly dropped.[7]

The first trophy shipments were not controlled at all. Boris Fil-ippov's brigade, which returned from Silesia to Moscow in May 1945, was the only one that was not accused of smuggling. Problems with the customs office began early in July, when there was a big scandal connected with the shipment sent from Berlin by plane and escorted by Majors Kopas and Kulakovsky. When the aircraft was checked, it turned out that half of the boxes were not listed in the documents. They were full of shoes, raincoats, and textiles. The whole load of cargo was then seized. Only when Lieutenant Statuyev, head of the NKVD checkpoint at Vnukovo airport, and the head of the customs office learned what was in the remaining six boxes did they agree to admit the shipment. The boxes contained the Trojan gold and other gold and silver objects as well as paintings. Irina Antonova, a young staff member who later became the director of the Pushkin Museum, was one of the officials who signed the receipt when the crates were released by customs.

A few days later, behind closed doors in the Pushkin Museum, the curators checked the cargo list and discovered to their astonishment that the boxes contained 350 gold objects not mentioned in any document.[8] They were also puzzled by the presence of Manet's portrait of Rosita Mauri, from the private Koehler Collection.[9] They never learned whether the gold and the painting had been left off the list by mistake or if they had been smuggled in.

Looters were ingenious in finding ways to get past customs officers. A former pilot recalled later that the officers in his squadron found a very successful hiding place for their private trophies: they stuffed them into the plane's empty bomb bay. But one trip ended in disaster. A pilot who was in on the scheme got so drunk that he had to be replaced at the last minute by a young officer who did not know about the illegal cargo. He playfully opened the bomb bay, and so a few minutes after takeoff a miraculous rain of pictures in gilded frames, porcelains, furs, cameras and typewriters fell on a quiet German town.[10]

Some contraband was discovered only much later. After Lev Kharko's death, in 1961, his office safe was opened and two miniatures were discovered, one of which was dated 1543 and attributed to Hans Holbein. These were given to Kharko's widow. In 1969 she gave them to the Pushkin Museum and said that they 'were found by my husband, Lev Petrovich Kharko, in 1945 in the ruins of the bombed church in Danzig and saved by him from destruction'. But Kharko had been in Danzig as a major in the Arts Committee trophy brigade and he did not save the miniatures, he stole them. Irina Antonova put them into the museum's special depository.[11]

Theft during the unloading process was another serious problem. When the first train from Germany arrived in Moscow from Meseritz on 25 April 1945, the wagons were unsealed and the sliding roofs opened, and the contents unloaded in an unsecured storage area. Nikolai Lapin, chief curator of the Pushkin Museum, later wrote that the railway officials and the soldiers who unloaded the train all knew where the objects came from. When Lapin told the soldiers not to throw the crates around because they contained works of art – 'our socialist property' – they answered that it was not socialist property but things that had been taken from Germans. Lapin was angry at Sergei Sidorov for telling everyone that even generals had stolen things from the Meseritz shelter. All of this created an 'atmosphere of theft'. Labourers were complaining that if the bosses could take trophies from Germany, why couldn't they?[12]

The situation in Leningrad was no better. In one train alone, nine thefts were discovered. A few Egyptian papyri disappeared from one car; in another, boxes of graphics were forcibly opened. The guards were absent during the unloading, and many of the cargo lists were missing, while others were completely garbled.[13] For instance, according to transportation documents, 786 crates were loaded onto Train No. 176/1759 in Berlin, but the train commander, Major Sabsai, reported that he had taken 796 crates to the Pushkin Museum. Museum officials reported that they had received 794. The Arts Committee officials who managed the operation could hardly control the confusion.[14] The Pergamum Altar arrived in Leningrad with false transport documents. The originals had been lost in Berlin, and creating new ones would have required unloading the whole train, so Major Starostin, who was in charge, decided to make up an imaginary list instead.[15]

The train that arrived from Meseritz in April 1945 was the cause of a major scandal. It turned out to contain some Nazi works of art as well as traditional art – portraits of President Hindenburg and Field Marshal von Runstedt, an oil sketch of a street decorated with Nazi banners, a bronze bust of Goering. Who had imported this rubbish into the country of socialism – and why? Was it a provocation? High-ranking people had to be told: concealing bad news was always dangerous, since there were so many informers. But before the Central Committee was notified, the Commission on Reception and Registration of Trophy Valuables decided to burn the evidence. The situation was serious and the commission was in a hurry. The Nazi artefacts were set on fire in the courtyard of the Pushkin Museum.[16]

The registration commission had been established in April 1945, when the first train carrying trophies arrived from Germany. Nikolai Lapin was appointed secretary. He was a dour man with a dry, pedantic manner, but he was ruled by a passionate love of the medieval Genoese fortress of Sudak in the Crimea. He dedicated all his free time to it, spent his summer vacations there, wrote books and articles about it. Lapin tormented Sergei Sidorov, who had escorted the train from Meseritz, with his endless questions. He refused to understand that the freight wagons had been loaded under German bombardment and that the compilation of properly detailed transport documents had been impossible. Finally he denounced Sidorov to the Arts Committee for spreading secret information and falsely accusing the generals of robbing the Meseritz shelter. The result was that Andrei Konstantinov hurriedly sent Sidorov to Berlin to suppress the scandal, which might have drawn attention to his own private trophies.

Pyotr Sisoyev, the head of the commission, had been in charge of the Arts Committee's Department of Visual Arts for only a few months but had already acquired a reputation as a very careful man. Later he became a legend of Soviet cultural officialdom. He had an outstanding career at a young age but then took the well-paid but relatively modest job of research secretary of the Academy of Arts of the USSR. Understanding the dangers of high office, he refused promotion, but he succeeded in transforming his post into one of the key positions in the cultural life of the country.

Igor Grabar and Boris Vipper were invited to play the role of connoisseurs. Vipper was a strange character even in this company. In 1921 he was arrested by Lenin's secret police during the repression of the Committee to Ease the Suffering of the Hungry. In Lubyanka prison he delivered lectures on art to his fellow prisoners. Vipper emigrated to Latvia in 1924 and settled in Riga, where he became a professor at the local university, but in 1940, after the Molotov–Ribbentrop pact, Latvia was occupied by the Red Army and Vipper found himself again in the USSR. He got a job in the Pushkin Museum, whose director, Sergei Merkurov, skilfully protected his staff. There Vipper hoped to find a niche in which to write books and stay out of trouble, but he could not refuse to take part in the trophy campaign.

The commission dealt not only with the registration of trophy works, it also decided how to distribute them. The best objects were sent to the central museums, and the rest went to the provinces. Trainloads of works of art were sent to Turkmenistan, Tadzhikistan, and Kaluga. But there were problems. A large number of works which the Germans had stolen from Riga were found in Meseritz. Ignorant of where they came from, the commission promised the objects to the museum in Nizhni Tagil, and the Riga museum had trouble reclaiming them.[17]

The commission's quiet life soon ended. They spent a leisurely three months sorting out the cargo of the first train, but on 10 August 1945 thirty goods wagons containing the treasures of the Dresden museums arrived in Moscow. That day people observed curious events on the streets of the capital. A column of trucks loaded with crates three metres high moved slowly through the streets. Soldiers with long forked poles stood on every truck. When the column came to the overhead tram wires on the Boulevard Ring Road, the soldiers lifted them with their forked poles so the trucks could pass underneath. Thus the famous Assyrian reliefs from the Dresden Albertinum were transported from the Kiev station to the Pushkin Museum. There they were unloaded with the help of cranes and then carried inside the building.[18]

Counting them was easier than transporting them. The story was different with paintings, graphics, coins and medals – in all, hundreds of thousands of objects. The Arts Committee decided to create a new system of registration and gave the Pushkin Museum the responsibility. The reception commission was disbanded, and Grabar ceased to be involved in the undertaking that had been his idea. Now it was the government, not the commission, that would decide the fate of the works of art.

The Arts Committee decided to give them permanently to the Pushkin Museum. Khrapchenko, head of the committee, reported to Molotov, secretary of the Council of People's Commissars, on 22 August 1945, informing him that the Dresden Gallery valuables had arrived in Moscow and would be given to the museum. The two collections together would 'make it possible for us to establish in Moscow a Museum of World Art similar in importance to such art museums as the Louvre in Paris, the British Museum in London, and the State Hermitage in Leningrad'.[19]

By the end of 1945 the Pushkin Museum had received more trophy works of art than any other institution: 2,991 crates of objects and one portfolio of drawings.[20] Why this portfolio was mentioned separately in all the official documents is a mystery. Apparently it was not because it was transported by the museum official Ilya Tsirlin from the Königsberg Art Academy and contained five drawings attributed to Michelangelo as well as 134 works by other masters.[21] The reason seems to have been purely bureaucratic; unlike the other objects, it had not been crated.

The registration of the works was a laborious task. As late as the end of 1946 a hundred crates were still unopened in the Pushkin Museum and nobody knew what they contained. But the main problem was where to store all these treasures and how to guarantee their safety. On 28 November 1945, Andrei Lebedev, deputy head of the Arts Committee Department of Visual Arts, accompanied by director Merkurov and Arts Committee officials, examined the storage conditions in the museum. An Academician, a People's Artist of the USSR, a Stalin Prize winner, and the recipient of numerous other prestigious awards, Sergei Merkurov was one of the best-known figures in the art world of the USSR in the Stalin era. He was a sculptor, and he had created many gigantic statues of Lenin and Stalin in granite and basalt, but he was particularly proud of a special assignment given him by the Party: he made the death mask of every prominent Soviet official from Lenin on. Stalin knew when he met Merkurov that the museum director would be the last man to touch his face. But even this very influential person was denounced by Andrei Lebedev for storing the trophies in unsatisfactory conditions. Lebedev was upset by the high humidity in the paintings and graphics storage areas, and he became even more upset when he learned that there was no inventory of the trophy objects. Neither the old German numbers nor the new Russian ones were given in registration documents. Lebedev knew very well that the museum had no fire alarm system, and he was appalled to discover in the courtyard a huge tank of petrol. But the last straw was a group of children playing in the courtyard and paying no attention to the High Commission. They were the offspring of museum employees who were housed in communal apartments in the basement of the building. Not far from the depositories containing masterpieces by Raphael and Titian, the communal dwellers were cooking on primus stoves and hanging their wet laundry on lines suspended above the kitchen.[22]

The Pushkin Museum had problems of its own and did not need

imported ones. In the first year of the war, the building had been damaged by a German bomb. The glass roof partially collapsed and was still being restored when the Dresden treasures arrived. At the end of 1944 the museum's own collection had returned from evacuation in Siberia. Museum officials were overwhelmed. Nobody was thinking about restoration of the Dresden objects, but forty-one paintings that had been rolled up and damaged in transit were judged to be in need of urgent treatment and were lightly restored by Alexander Korin.[23] His brother Pavel, the museum's chief restorer, had no time for the Dresden paintings either because he was supervising the restoration of the famous nineteenth-century panorama *The Defence of Sevastopol in 1855* by Franz Rubio, which had been partly burned. The pieces of the panorama were strewn all over the floor of the White Hall of the museum, adding to the general confusion.

Merkurov later recalled that 'the museum was so packed with trophy objects that even finding a place to put them became extremely difficult, not to mention unpacking and registration ... Everything that was humanly possible was done, and one must keep in mind the difficulties the museum had to overcome.'[24] Merkurov drafted art students to unpack and sort the trophies. Students, soldiers, and museum officials carried heavy crates, opened them, and made up lists of the contents. Although all of Moscow knew about the trophies, they were officially a secret. The lists could be typed only inside the museum, and two staff clerks wore their fingers to the bone typing the thousands of pages.

Finally, in autumn 1945, something happened that all the curators had been fearing. A painting sent by plane from the Leipzig museum disappeared from its crate. The theft was so serious that the name of the stolen painting was never mentioned in documents. There exist two versions of events. According to one of them, it was van Eyck's *Portrait of an Old Canon* that was stolen; according to another, it was a little painting by Adriaen Brouwer. When the first panic was over, an investigation began. Museum officials decided not to inform the authorities because the dreaded NKVD would have been called in and discovered immediately that security had been seriously compromised for the sake of speed. The participants in the unloading were questioned again and again. Finally the curator of the special depository, Andrei Chegodayev, worked out that a student of the Moscow Art Institute who had spent a few minutes alone near the crate had probably stolen the painting, but he had no proof. Chegodayev visited the student at home and in the presence of his parents gave him a choice. If he returned the painting, Chegodayev promised not to inform the authorities. If he refused to return the painting, Chegodayev promised to pay a visit to the NKVD immediately. It would have meant the end of his own career, because he had supervised the department in which the theft had taken place, but the consequences for the student would have been much worse. The discussion was difficult, but a few hours later the student returned the painting. Chegodayev kept his word. The thief was never named, even ten years later, when someone notified the Central Committee of the theft.[25]

On 2 March 1946, the usual groups of tourists in Red Square were waiting for the changing of the guard in front of the Lenin Mausoleum when suddenly a convoy of trucks appeared. People stared in astonishment. Only state military parades, such as those on May Day and Revolution Day, were allowed on the square. The column stopped near a large red building in pseudo-Russian style, chains were put up around the trucks, and soldiers jumped out. Huge crates were quickly unloaded and carried into the building. Trophies arriving from Germany were being delivered to the State Historical Museum.

The State Historical Museum was run by the Committee on Cultural Educational Institutions of the Russian Federation, which controlled almost all of the museums of Russia, including the famous palaces outside Leningrad. Only the main museums – the Hermitage, the Tretyakov Gallery, and the Pushkin – were controlled by the Arts Committee of the USSR Council of People's Commissars. The Institute of Museology and Regional Studies, which had taken part in preparing the list of equivalents, was controlled by the Russian committee, and there, in one of the halls of the Historical Museum, on 22 November 1943, institute officials had discussed the lists with the art experts. There Topornin had fought for his idea to create a museum of world history after the war.

Now the trophies were arriving. They had been selected in Berlin by Alexei Manevsky, head of the museum department of the Cultural Educational Institutions Committee, who arrived in the capital of the fallen Reich with the rank of lieutenant colonel at the beginning of May and was appointed the committee's representative on the staff of the Special Committee on Germany. In operational questions, Manevsky, like Arts Committee representative Belokopitov, was under the command of Major General Pyotr Zernov, the representative of the Special Committee in Berlin.

Aside from his own searches in the Russian zone, Manevsky took objects already collected by the army trophy department. In July 1945 the Sixth Special Trophy Department turned over to him 6,000 crates of books and museum objects. In total, he and his group collected 12,500 crates, 3,500 of which contained museum objects. The others held books and museum equipment. The official documents said that 'these cultural valuables were found in various places in the Soviet Zone of Occupation in Germany, in libraries, museums, depositories, shelters, in the storages of the commandants' offices and trophy departments, private castles and mansions of Nazis'.[26]

Manevsky's base in Berlin was in Packhaus No. 16, at the Stettiner railway station. He called his group Bureau No. 2 of the Committee of Culture to avoid confusion with the brigade of the Arts Committee. The two brigades were in competition. Manevsky tried to gain control of 1,000 paintings and other valuables from Potsdam, but Alexander Zamoshkin, head of the Arts Committee brigade, used his influence to prevent the threat to his authority. Despite this defeat, Manevsky soon began to send trophies to Moscow. Books were sent directly from the railway station to the Historical Library and the Library of Foreign Literature. A large load of museum property was delivered to the Museum of the Revolution, the Literature Museum, the Darwin Museum, and the Polytechnic Museum. But most of the trophy objects – 2,587 crates – were delivered to the Historical Museum on Red Square. The stream of cargo seemed to go on for ever. (In comparison, the museum's own collections had filled only 1,012 crates when they were packed for evacuation.)

The museum staff worked feverishly. Nikolai Sobolyev, head of the department of arms and armour, received 15th–18th century arms, 16th–17th century armour, and an impressive collection of 16th–18th century pistols. Pyotr Neznamov, a specialist in domestic history, received crates containing a rich collection of costumes. Tamara Goldberg, head of the precious metals cabinet, registered silver objects that had belonged to Count von Zieten, the famous hussar and favourite general of Frederick the Great, and a precious silver vase that had belonged to Prince Henry of Saxony. More than half of

82,000 coins were either gold or silver, but there was no time for careful examination. There were thousands of graphics works depicting the cities of Europe, old furniture, medieval maps, textiles, ceramics, Greek papyri of the Alexandrian period, and many other treasures. The archaeological department received 512 crates of objects from excavations.[27]

Unlike the cargoes sent to the Pushkin Museum, the trophies arrived at the Historical Museum during a brief period when secrecy was not imposed. On 16 March, Zuyeva, head of the Committee on Cultural Educational Institutions, issued an order concerning the distribution of trophy works. Two museums shared 445 crates of ethnographical material from the Völkerkundemuseum in Berlin, the objects connected with the Slavs, Central Asia, and the Caucasus going to the Museum of the Peoples of the USSR and a rich collection of African, Far Eastern, South American, and Indian objects going to the Museum of Ethnography. The order gave special mention to the military decorations of Napoleon, which had been taken as trophies by Field Marshal Gobhard von Blücher after the Battle of Waterloo, and to Blücher's own military decorations. They were to be shown in the permanent exhibition dedicated to the War of 1812. (In fact, they were never exhibited.)

Many objects were taken by the Academy of Sciences of the USSR. Materials on the history of religion and a collection of documents on Freemasonry assembled by Heinrich Himmler were deposited in the Anti-Religious Museum of the Academy, situated in Kazan Cathedral in Leningrad and headed by Lenin's comrade Vladimir Bonch-Bruyevich.[28] Some of the objects that were left over after the distribution were sold in state shops. For 366 porcelain objects, 33 paintings, and 24 pieces of furniture, 19,868 rubles were received.[29]

LENINGRAD

The Hermitage Adds to Its Collection

Lieutenant Colonel Vyacheslav Moskvin was not looking for treasure when he arrived in the little town of Kynau, near Waldenburg, about sixty-five kilometres southwest of Breslau (Wroclaw). He was head of the road engineers of the 21st Army of the First Ukrainian Front, and had come to Kynau at the end of May 1945 to check on one of his units, which was securing the crossroad. Noticing that the attic window was open in an attractive two-storey building, he decided to investigate. The house, which belonged to General Hans Robert von Seydlitz, was empty, and the door to the attic was locked. Moskvin ordered his soldiers to break in. The attic was also empty. Moskvin and the men took a quick look around and saw nothing unusual. Then, just as they were leaving, a soldier noticed rolled-up paintings in one corner. Another joked, 'The general took the tables and chairs but forgot the paintings.'[1]

The German general had not forgotten the paintings, because they did not belong to him. They had been taken by the Germans from the National Museum in Warsaw and hidden for safekeeping in his attic. Two months later, on 31 July 1945, Moskvin was standing in front of the portico of Alexander's Palace at Tsarskoe Selo as the crates containing the paintings were being unloaded. The Central Depository of Museum Valuables of the Palaces on the Outskirts of Leningrad was situated in the palace, and the vigilant lieutenant colonel was delivering 196 crates of paintings belonging to the Polish museum and seventy crates containing a thousand books from the Klein öls castle of Count Yorck von Warkenburg. Moskvin had badgered the commanders of the Twenty-First Army to send the valuables to Leningrad, his home town, and he and his soldiers had driven the six trucks filled with paintings through Poland, Ukraine and Belorussia. Anatoly Kuchumov, director of the depository, counted 212 canvases by European masters and 290 by Polish painters, including the famous *Joker Stanchik* by Jan Mataika.[2]

Two days later, in the Leningrad Department of Culture, Moskvin received a letter of gratitude signed by the city fathers. 'We thank you for the zeal you demonstrated in saving and delivering to Leningrad the valuable artworks you found in the den of the enemy, which had been stolen from our land,' it said. In fact, of course, they were Polish pictures that had been stolen from Warsaw.[3]

On the morning of 7 October 1945, Joseph Orbeli, the director of the Hermitage, received a telegram from the city of Sverdlovsk informing him that two freight trains loaded with things that had been evacuated from Leningrad were now on their way back. Each train had twenty-three carriages, including an armoured carriage for especially valuable objects. Orbeli was relieved that everything was going well in Sverdlovsk, but he was worried about the fate of another train that had disappeared somewhere in Eastern Europe two weeks earlier, on its way from Berlin to Moscow. That train had no armoured carriage, only an old refrigerated carriage that was used for particularly valuable objects.[4] The carriages were in bad condition, but their contents were as valuable as those carried in the trains from Sverdlovsk.

Special train No. 176/2284 was escorted by Serafim Druzhinin. On 27 September he had been ordered to deliver a shipment to Moscow,[5] but the train never arrived. A few hours after it left Berlin, Alexander Voloshin received an urgent telegram to reroute it to Leningrad, but it was too late.[6] The trouble was that Pushkin Museum officials were refusing to accept any more shipments because they had too much work dealing with the Dresden objects they had already received. The special train was not located until 8 October.

Three days later, the Hermitage collection came home from Sverdlovsk. The newspaper *Leningradskaya Pravda* reported: 'Yesterday all valuables of the Hermitage evacuated at the beginning of the war to Sverdlovsk arrived in Leningrad in two trains ... The trains were escorted by officials of the Hermitage led by Vladimir Levinson-Lessing ... They were met by the officials of the Hermitage led by Academician Joseph Orbeli.'

In their book *The Heroic Feat of the Hermitage*, Sergei Varshavsky and Yuli Rest described the unloading of the trains from Sverdlovsk: 'Trucks loaded with sealed crates leave Leningrad October Station. The cargo is escorted by soldiers armed with rifles ... The trucks turn into Nevsky Prospekt. It's true, nothing is better than Nevsky Prospekt! ... And finally Palace Square and the Winter Palace! ... Six portals are open. Museum curators are standing nearby and

The Palace of Soviets – an immense skyscraper topped by a colossal statue of Lenin – was to be built near the Pushkin Museum in Moscow. It was to have included a museum of world art, which would house the artworks sent from the Axis countries as compensation for Soviet art stolen or destroyed by the Germans.

Marshal Kliment Voroshilov, the Politburo member in charge of culture in 1945, not only came to see the newly arrived trophies in the Pushkin Museum, he gave the museum his own loot: five French and Flemish tapestries. Director Sergei Merkurov (left) and deputy director Boris Vipper (right) showed him around.

By the end of 1945 the Pushkin Museum was bursting with more trophy artworks than any other Soviet institution. Every available space in the building was used to house them.

Many of the objects excavated from the ashes in the Friedrichshain control tower were transported to the Soviet Union in unheated trucks and trains in very cold weather. Before these things were returned to Germany in the late 1950s, restorers had to perform miracles of repair because officials were afraid that their bad condition would be seized on as 'enemy propaganda'. The relief by Andrea della Robia (above) and Donatello's *Madonna and Child with Angels* (below) were victims of the Friedrichshain fire that ended up in the Hermitage.

Soviet leaders enjoying the May Day parade from the top of the Lenin Mausoleum in the late 1940s (above): Khrushchev, Stalin, Foreign Minister Vyacheslav Molotov, and Presidium head Nikolai Shvernik. The space between Molotov and Shvernik was once occupied by NKVD chief Lavrenty Beria, but after his fall in 1953, Soviet censors cut him out of official photos. The sinister Alexander Poskrebishev (left), Stalin's personal secretary and one of his few confidants. Total secrecy about trophy artworks was imposed soon after Poksrebishev visited the Pushkin Museum in late 1948 or early 1949.

Stalin kitsch: in December 1949 the Pushkin Museum ceased to exist. The pictures were taken off the walls and replaced by the 'Exhibition of Gifts to Stalin', in honour of the 70th birthday of the 'leader and teacher of the world proletariat'. Many interesting objects of applied art as well as boxes of chocolate and bottles of wine were presented to the beloved chief – but, contrary to Moscow gossip, no talking salami.

Pavel Korin, a restorer, copied the Sistine Madonna before its return to the GDR in 1955. Soviet cultural officials of the 1950s still believed in the aesthetic value of copies. During the period of Sistine Madonna mania, reproductions of the painting flooded the country.

After the victory of Socialist Realism as the only approved art style in the Soviet Union, the Sistine Madonna became the standard of beauty for Russians. Dmitry Nalbandyan, court painter to Soviet officialdom from Stalin to Brezhnev, produced a large picture of Lenin admiring the picture, which he had never seen.

The return of the Dresden Gallery to East Germany in 1955 was the source of inspiration not only for painters, poets and composers, but for cartoonists as well. Kukrinsky's *Return of the Dresden Gallery* (above) became the source of inspiration for contemporary conceptual artist Yuri Albert in 1993.

The Painting is Saved, by the East German artist Hermann Kohlmann, shows Natalia Sokolova admiring a canvas by Rembrandt rescued from a damp cave. GDR officials used the story of the 'twice-saved' masterpieces as one of the most striking examples of Soviet–German friendship.

comparing the codes and numbers of unloaded crates with those on their lists and documents.'[7]

About the arrival of the train from Berlin – the one that had been temporarily lost – on 13 October, the Leningrad newspapers said nothing. But Hermitage officials remembered the event for a long time. The route of the trucks from the station was the same, and the six portals were open, but otherwise things were different. There was no armed escort and no list of what was in the 1,154 crates that made up the shipment, only a description of the contents, half of it false.[8] It was a nightmare for the Hermitage, which was later described by Orbeli:

> The unloading of the first special train arriving in Leningrad took place on the day when the work of unloading the returned valuables of the Hermitage was finished. The unloading was very fast. The crates transported to the Hermitage blocked all portals and the nearest halls. It was necessary to open the crates to understand to which departments they belonged ... The codes in most cases gave no information about the contents of the crates ... many had no codes or numbers at all.[9]

When the huge crates coded 'AS' for antique sculpture were opened, they were discovered to contain Egyptian sculpture and had to be moved to the Ancient Near East Department. There, boxes thought to contain papyri were found to be filled with archaeological collections from another part of the world. At the same time, the museum's own immense collection was being unpacked. To forty-six freight carriages of their own exhibits, thirty-four carriages of trophies were added.

Immediately after the unloading of the crates from Sverdlovsk, the curators began to prepare an exhibition. Everyone was in a holiday mood. The treasures were back and the galleries were swarming with journalists and important guests who wanted to see them. But behind the scenes another part of museum life was hidden – what official documents called the 'conspiracy' side. The Pergamum Altar reliefs and Degas' *Place de la Concorde* from the private Gerstenberg Collection, Botticelli's illustrations to the *Divine Comedy* and paintings by Kokoschka from Berlin – all these treasures were being unpacked and registered. The journalists and guests had no idea of what was happening in the depositories, but museum officials were astonished at the 'new acquisitions' Druzhinin had brought them.[10]

On 19 October 1945, Boris Piotrovsky, the future director of the Hermitage (and father of the present director, Mikhail Piotrovsky), opened a box with 'Saal VIII' written on its side and then the number 7.6. It contained gold and silver jewellery from ancient Egypt. There were forty-nine wide gold rings. The fiftieth was missing from its nest. Many years later the German-born American Egyptologist Bernard V. Bothmer remembered that when he was a young assistant curator at the Boston Museum of Fine Arts he was visited by a man who wanted to sell him an Egyptian gold ring. Bothmer, whose career began in the Aegyptisches Museum in Berlin, recognized the ring and told his visitor that it had probably been stolen from the Berlin collection. The man told Bothmer that in 1945 he had been in the American army in Berlin and worked in a DP camp in the Zoo. One of the DPs had given him the ring. He said he had found it in the Flakturm. This was very possibly the fiftieth ring.[11]

Under the gold rings were two other boxes of Egyptian jewellery and statuettes. All these objects were packed in crate No. 445 [AG 35]. It was the code of the Aegyptisches Abteilung. These objects from the Berlin Egyptian collection had been taken from the Zoo Flakturm.[12]

Druzhinin's train was the first bearing trophy works to Leningrad. During the following months museum officials spent all their time dealing with trophies from Germany. On 22 February 1946, they were still busy with this work while their director, Orbeli, was giving a speech at the Nuremberg trials of high-ranking Nazis on the destruction and robbery of cultural and scientific valuables. That was the day his staff was unpacking works of Andrea della Robbia and other Italian and French sculptors that had arrived on the second special train from Berlin, escorted by Major Boris Kaptsov.[13]

It was one of the 'winter trains' that made the trip from Berlin to Leningrad in bitterly cold weather. Only the car in which the guards travelled was heated. Etchings by Rembrandt, prints by Dürer and Goltzius, and old master drawings remained damp for a long time.[14] But even in a summer train escorted by Sergei Sidorov a painting by Zoppo of the *Enthroned Madonna with Four Saints* arrived literally soaking in its wet packing materials.[15] On 20 August 1946, the curators unpacked stained glass, some of it broken into fragments. They wrote that 102 stained-glass sections and fragments of glass 'of rude German work' dated to the late fourteenth and early fifteenth centuries all belonged to the same church. This glass was made in 1395 by an unknown German master for the Marienkirche in Frankfurt an der Oder in eastern Germany. Since there were no transportation documents, it was impossible to say when the glass had been broken. Describing it, the Hermitage curators made a curious error, mistaking the story of the Antichrist as a depiction of the life of Jesus.[16]

In total, the Hermitage received the contents of four special trains, which contained three times as many carriages as the museum had needed for the evacuation of its own collection. The unloading of only one train, the one escorted by Kaptsov, cost the Hermitage the immense sum of 960,000 rubles (about £120,000).[17]

MOSCOW

The Plot Against Zhukov

Rumours about the misdeeds of the *demontageniks*, the dismantlers of German industrial sites, finally reached Moscow, and in October 1945 a special commission of the Central Committee started to investigate the activity of all the trophy brigades. The commission was headed by Alexander Porivayev, a high-ranking Central Committee official, and included two experts who were not Party members, Andrei Chegodayev from the Pushkin Museum and Pyotr Zayonchkovsky, a well-known historian and professor at Moscow State University. They travelled around the Soviet occupation zone, visiting Magdeburg, Leipzig, Dresden, Halle, and Berlin, and discovered that the rumours were true, but the brigades that dealt with cultural valuables were not punished. Their misdeeds were nothing in comparison with the transgressions of the representatives of the industrial commissariats.[1]

The commission also had to decide what to do with the works of art and cultural valuables that had been found during the summer in the stone mines near Magdeburg, one of the major discoveries made in the Soviet zone. Here were the objects and the library from the Berlin Armoury, the collections from the Ethnographic Museum, the archaeological riches of the Preussischer Kulturbesitz, and an immense quantity of books and archival materials, including the Lübeck city archives and the library of the Prussian Academy of Sciences. All of these were made the responsibility of the Committee of Cultural Educational Institutions. Alexei Manevsky and his brigade removed the hoard to Berlin, and eventually most of the books and archives, including the Lübeck archives and the Prussian Academy library, were delivered to the Academy of Sciences and other institutions in the USSR.[2]

Andrei Chegodayev did not forget the interests of his museum, the Pushkin. In Magdeburg, in the cellar of a ruined bank, he found a superb triptych by Hans von Marées depicting three nude boys. The military commandant of the city liked the painting so much he supplied a special plane to carry it to Moscow. At Marshal Zhukov's order, General Bokov asked Chegodayev and Zayonchkovsky to search the ruins of the Reich Chancellery for the archive of phonograph records of Nazi leaders' speeches. They found it. Later Chegodayev recalled that they had

> climbed down into the half-ruined cellar and took out of it an unbelievable quantity of records and tapes of the speeches of Hitler, Goebbels, Goering, Ribbentrop, Bormann – everybody. We received a cargo plane which we loaded to the top, packing nothing. Zayonchkovsky sat in the pilot's cockpit and I climbed on top of this mound. We delivered the stuff to Moscow and later part of it was used during the Nuremberg trials.[3]

After the commission's departure, the first danger to the trophy brigades was over. But the real problems were in the future, especially for the Arts Committee, which had been so active in the removal of cultural valuables. Reception and registration of trophy property was controlled by the Special Trophy Group, part of the main Department of Supply of the Arts Committee. Pyotr Zubtsov was the first head of this group, established at the beginning of 1945. But endless scandals with the customs office, the complete mess in documentation, and numerous thefts ended with his replacement at the end of January 1946. The position was taken by Elizaveta Alexandrova, who began to establish order. The deputy head of the Arts Committee, Andrei Konstantinov, whose responsibility was the trophy question, was accustomed to the easy-going Zubtsov. The tough new head of the group was not to his taste, but she received the enthusiastic support of many Arts Committee officials. Konstantinov's trips to Germany and his opportunities to collect private trophies had aroused the jealousy of his colleagues who had been tied to their desks in Moscow.

Finally, in March 1946, Konstantinov was caught. The customs office checked a train from Berlin much more thoroughly than usual, examining the whole shipment, not just a few boxes. They discovered that one goods wagon had no connection with museum valuables and was not documented. It contained carpets, a concert piano, a mechanical piano with a collection of discs, crystal, and many other interesting objects. The cargo was seized and stored in the Pushkin Museum's Italian Garden. Konstantinov had to explain this incident to the head of the Moscow customs office. He tried desperately to save his loot, insisting that part of it had 'museum character' – meaning that it was possible to use carpets and crystal chandeliers in museums – and that part had been bought legally in Germany.[4] But a scandal was inevitable. According to Chegodayev, the depressed Konstantinov came to the museum one day with his wife and they looked over all the desirables they had lost.

On 3 May Konstantinov signed an order requiring complete checks of all arriving trophies and investigation of the activities of all trophy brigades. Everyone who was connected with trophy property had to write a report. But Konstantinov himself was not named to the investigative commission.[5] On 15 May he sent an hysterical telegram to Voloshin in Berlin, asking him to send to Moscow as soon as possible all papers connected with the activity of the Arts Committee brigade in Germany. It was the last official paper he signed. The next day the Council of Ministers issued an order concerning the Arts Committee. Konstantinov was not even mentioned. That was how he discovered he had been fired.[6]

The Ministry of State Control finally began an investigation. On 16 July 1946 Minister Lev Mekhlis signed the order 'On the Inspection of the All Union Arts Committee'. Mekhlis was known as a man without mercy. Before the war he had headed not only the People's Commissariat of State Control but the Main Political Department of the Red Army, thus controlling both civil and military institutions. The only person he feared – and worshipped – was Stalin, who called him 'my Jew' and skilfully played him against Lavrenty Beria.

Mekhlis had lost his influence in 1942, when, as a result of his mistakes, Soviet armies were destroyed in the Crimea. On his knees, he begged Stalin's pardon. He lost his rank and would never again play so crucial a role, but he was forgiven and remained head of the ministry. A fanatical Communist, he was ascetic and incorruptible. Knowing full well the appetites of his colleagues, he investigated the misdeeds of the various agencies involved with removing trophies from occupied Europe, hoping to regain Stalin's favour by providing him with evidence against the victorious marshals and generals. The Arts Committee investigation was only a link in this chain of intrigue. Mekhlis uncovered a number of cases of smuggling, theft and mis-management.[7] Accused of such serious misdeeds, Arts Committee officials saw only one way to save themselves: to shift the blame elsewhere.

The investigation of the brigade lasted five months. Andrei Belokopitov and Alexander Voloshin, who had worked so hard removing as many works of art as possible from Berlin, were chosen as scapegoats. The contraband on the plane that had transported the Schliemann gold was brought up again, and both men were accused of using their positions 'to send their personal belongings by plane'.

They were both fired. This pleased Alexander Rototayev, who had built his career on his participation in the removal of the Dresden Gallery, which had brought him to Stalin's personal attention. He wanted to be the only hero of the trophy crusade and preferred to be rid of competitors like Belokopitov and Voloshin, who had sent home more valuable works than he. Voloshin tried to find an excuse for himself: 'We were guided by the idea of not leaving the valuables to the Germans but sending them to the USSR as soon as possible. In a critical situation we made decisions that were dictated to us by our duty as Soviet citizens and, in my case, my duty as a Communist.'[8]

The investigation might have ended with immediate serious consequences for all those accused, but Stalin decided otherwise. He wanted to keep the information Mekhlis had collected for later use. In his postwar campaigns against rivals from Zhukov to Voznesensky, Stalin often used the 'trophy card'. But Mekhlis received little benefit from this blackmail of high-ranking officials he had masterminded. Never completely pardoned or ever again promoted, he died a month earlier than his master. The middle-ranking officials who had been repressed during the investigation were not rehabilitated; all of them lost their positions.

Andrei Belokopitov was a man of spirit and had no intention of surrendering without a fight. He looked around for allies and learned that Lieutenant General Konstantin Telegin had returned to Moscow. Telegin, a former official of the NKVD during the war, had taken part in the battle for Moscow and in the storming of Berlin. He had been sent to Marshal Zhukov as a political commissar − clearly an attempt by Beria, head of the NKVD, to control the rebellious marshal. But Telegin and Zhukov unexpectedly became close friends. During the occupation Telegin had signed some documents on transportation of trophy art valuables and had been informed about the activity of the trophy brigade. Belokopitov decided to ask him for support.

'I learned from my friends that the general lived in his dacha near Moscow,' he later wrote.

In the late evening, two days before New Year, I went there. The snow was very deep. The house was guarded. After a long argument an adjutant agreed to let me in.

Telegin listened to my story and said: 'I agree, I can understand that you were humiliated, but what do you want from me?'

'I want you to give me a document that those domestic things that were found in the plane were presented to us by the military admin- istration. Aside from that, I want to ask you to confirm that we had no chance to organize registration of the trophies in Berlin because train after train was sent to Moscow urgently.'

Telegin silently sat down and typed the document. Then he handed it to me to read and asked: 'Is this enough?'

'Very good,' I answered.

He signed the paper, returned it to me, and said: 'I will ask Fyodor Bokov to support you too. He is in Moscow now. He had a good opinion of you. We often remembered how you visited Zhukov and tricked the Americans.'

The next day I ran to the Arts Committee with this letter in my possession ... 'Let's see who'll win now,' I thought. I went directly to Khrapchenko's office, but he wasn't there. While waiting for him I decided to pay a visit to one of my friends who was a committee official. I found him in his office and proudly showed him the paper. 'Here's the document. Now everything will be all right,' I said.

He looked at me silently for a few seconds and then asked in a quiet voice, 'Do you know what happened? Telegin was arrested last night.'

It was the beginning of a plot directed against Marshal Zhukov. Numer- ous people in his circle were arrested in those days. What could I do? Of course I didn't return to Khrapchenko's office.

After many troubles, Belokopitov finally found a job a few years later with his beloved Moscow Art Theatre, but his career was ruined.[9]

Stalin was afraid of Zhukov, who had become very popular during the war and was particularly well liked by the army. At a dramatic meeting of the Military Council in 1946 Stalin accused him of taking the credit for all the Red Army victories. Zhukov was fired and sent into virtual exile in Odessa as commander of the unimportant Odessa Military District. But for his rivals Beria and Abakumov it was not enough. They wanted to compromise him completely in Stalin's eyes.

The trophies issue was useful in the plot against Zhukov, who had done more than his share of looting. On 23 August 1946, Stalin was informed that the customs office had seized seven railway carriages of furniture sent by Zhukov from Germany.[10] The MGB immediately began to investigate. At the end of 1947 his adjutant was arrested and questioned about the marshal's private trophies. That was only the beginning. On the night of 8 January 1948, in the village of Rublevo, near Moscow, Zhukov's dacha was searched secretly at Stalin's order.

Even experienced MGB officers were astonished by the luxury of the marshal's house. Crates with silverware, porcelain, crystal, 4,000 metres of expensive cloth, hundreds of furs of various animals from mink to monkey, forty-four carpets and tapestries from the Potsdam palaces, fifty-five paintings, eight richly decorated accordions, and twenty expensive hunting rifles were discovered there.[11] Abakumov reported:

> Aside from this, in all the rooms of the dacha there were many bronze and porcelain vases and statuettes and various knick-knacks of foreign origin, on windowsills, shelves, tables, and whatnots . . .
>
> Zhukov's dacha is like an antique shop or a museum, decorated with various valuable paintings, and there are so many of them that four paintings are hung in the kitchen. It is shocking to say, but in Zhukov's bedroom a huge painting depicting two naked women is situated over his bed! Among the paintings there are really valuable canvases that should not be in a private apartment but should be given to state foundations and placed in a museum.
>
> All domestic items beginning with furniture, carpets, dishes, decorations, and ending with window curtains are of foreign origin, mainly German. There is nothing of Soviet origin in the dacha. We didn't find even one Soviet book. But on the book shelves there are many expensively bound books . . . in the German language only . . . When you enter this house it is hard to imagine that you are not in Germany but close to Moscow.[12]

In the marshal's Moscow apartment on Granovsky Street, the secret policemen found a box of jewellery, but the suitcase full of gold and diamonds their spies had told them about was not there. The marshal's wife usually took it with her whenever she travelled.[13] Stalin gave the order to confiscate all Zhukov's valuables, and on 3 February

Lieutenant General Blinov, deputy minister of the MGB, personally confiscated 2,000 items, most of them art objects. All the seized property was handed over to Yakov Chadayev, the head of the Management Department of the Council of Ministers.[14]

What happened to Zhukov's treasures later is unknown. The marshal was ruined. He tried hard to justify himself, insisting that he was a 'loyal servant of the great Stalin', but it did no good. From Odessa he was sent to the distant Urals.[15]

Telegin was not so lucky. Under torture, he confessed to numerous crimes and was sentenced to twenty-five years' imprisonment. He was accused of slandering the Red Army and toadying to the West: he had remarked that Soviet soldiers looked like tramps compared to Allied troops. He was also accused of looting in Poland and Germany, and a search of his apartment turned up 'more than 16 kilos of objects made of silver', along with porcelains, furs, French and Flemish tapestries, antiquities, and other valuables. Only Stalin's death released him from the gulag. The fate of his confiscated property is unknown.[16]

Trophies played a large role in another power struggle between two ruthless men. Viktor Abakumov had been the head of SMERSH and then the MGB. General Ivan Serov had been in charge of the NKVD operation in Germany that confiscated gold, precious stones, and hard currency. Both men had been close to Zhukov, and when he fell from power they hastened to convince Stalin of their loyalty by denouncing each other. In 1948 the MGB arrested a man who had worked with Serov, Major General Alexei Sidnev. He admitted under torture that he had been involved in looting. He had stolen five Flemish and French tapestries in the cellar of the New Mint in Berlin and he had 'confiscated' from various German banks fifteen gold watches, forty-two gold pendants, fifteen gold rings, three gold bracelets with diamonds, and a lady's purse made of pure gold. He had also stolen 600 silver spoons and forks but could not explain why he needed so many. Furs and furniture, expensive clothes, pianos and film projection equipment had all been sent to the general's Leningrad apartment on military planes as well as a Serov's private plane.

Abakumov's real interest was not in Sidnev's loot but in information that could be used against Serov. Finally Sidnev confessed that he had appropriated about 80 million Reichsmarks found in various banks and shared the loot with Serov. He said that Serov, who had been responsible for removing gold and jewels to the Soviet Union, had kept the most valuable for himself and sent them home on his private plane. Sidnev admitted that he personally had given Serov about thirty kilograms of jewellery made of gold and precious stones.

Serov's abuses of power were sometimes quite original, according to Sidnev. He told the interrogators that Serov had found a German engineer who made him some excellent radios encased in oak panels taken from the walls of Hitler's study in the Reich Chancellery. He ordered Sidnev to find him 'two little English dogs with beards' (terriers presumably) 'that he probably needed to present to someone. It was a very difficult task, but thanks to my efforts the dogs with beards were bought for 15,000 marks each.'

The other NKVD bosses were not very different. Bezhanov, head of the NKVD operational department in Thuringia, filled his mansion there with looted luxuries, and even confiscated a brewery to produce beer for himself and his guests. Klepov, his counterpart in Saxony, stole a whole depository full of furs his men found in Leipzig. The facilities of the NKVD, which had its own workshops and artisans, were used by all the high-ranking commanders. Sidnev said that Marshal Zhukov had given his NKVD colleagues a crown that he said had belonged to 'the wife of the German emperor' and asked them to find a jeweller who could melt it down and use the gold to make his daughter a riding crop.[17]

Abakumov presented all of the information against Serov to Stalin. The equally ruthless Serov fought back. He did not have the power to arrest Abakumov's people, but he wrote a letter to Stalin relating all of Abakumov's sins. Looting figured among them as well.

> It seems that Abakumov has already forgotten that when soldiers and officers of the Soviet Army were still dying in the Crimea liberating Sevastopol, his adjutant Kuznetsov flew to the headquarters of SMERSH counterintelligence and loaded the whole plane with trophy property. The commanders of the air force refused to fuel Abakumov's plane for the flight back because they didn't have enough fuel for the planes that were in battle with the Germans.[18]

Every time Abakumov wanted to remove loot from Germany, Serov told Stalin, he sent a plane for 'transportation of arrested persons'. The plane, filled with loot, was always met in Moscow by armed MGB soldiers who kept customs officers at a distance. Once, when

SMERSH officers sent Abakumov a goods wagon full of 'presents' from Germany, they wrote his name in big letters on the sides. That was enough to scare away thieves as well as customs officers.[19]

Serov prevailed. Abakumov was arrested and executed. His treasures and those of other high-level secret police officers who were arrested were confiscated by the state. All those who had taken the opportunity to enrich themselves in Germany were terrified by Abakumov's downfall. Rumours about his treasures spread rapidly, and suddenly nobody – not generals or high-ranking Party officials – wanted to be caught in possession of loot. It was not unreasonable to fear that the secret police chief's fall was the prelude to a new purge. Trophies, sold in a panic, gave a strong boost to the Moscow art market.

Serov went on to become the head of the KGB during the Khrushchev years and planned the suppression of the Hungarian revolt. He eventually became the head of Soviet military intelligence. But his good luck did not last. In 1962 his world collapsed when his best friend and boon companion, Colonel Oleg Penkovsky, was arrested and unmasked as an American spy. The merciless Serov, who had destroyed the lives of thousands, had to resign. He began to drink heavily and finally shot himself. His trophies were never confiscated.

THE RETURN TO SECRECY

Andrei Guber, chief curator of the Pushkin Museum from 1945, read the name on the pass, 'Nikita Khrushchev, First Secretary of the Central Committee of Ukraine', and invited the high-ranking guest into the museum. A group of generals in parade uniforms followed the leader. Their names were also on passes signed by Kliment Voroshilov, at that time the Politburo member in charge of culture. Only the bearers of such passes had the right to visit the two galleries of the Pushkin Museum situated in the southwest corner of the first floor. These two locked galleries were full of paintings hung from floor to ceiling: more than 200 pieces belonging to the German museums were on exhibit here. Valentina Tikhanova, the curator of the exhibition, waited for the visitors beside Ribera's *St Agnes*. As she talked about the paintings they were looking at, the good-natured Khrushchev slapped his thighs and from time to time exclaimed enthusiastically, 'Ah!' The generals kept a respectful silence. They particularly admired Frans Hals's *Mulatto* from the Leipzig Museum and Giorgione's *Sleeping Venus* from the Dresden Gallery. But the supreme excitement was called forth by the Sistine Madonna, placed at the very end of the second gallery.

Khrushchev did not know that his guide, Valentina Tikhanova, was the adopted daughter of one of the leaders of the October Revolution, Anton Antonov-Ovseyenko. In 1938 Khrushchev, then secretary of the Moscow Party organization, had signed Antonov-Ovseyenko's arrest warrant, and soon the unfortunate man and his wife, whose only crime was that they were Old Bolsheviks – followers of Lenin from before the Revolution – were executed by Stalin's order. Tikhanova was sent to an orphanage. Such children of 'enemies of the people' left the orphanage at eighteen for prison, but Tikhanova's natural father rescued her and she took back her original family name. Under this disguise she graduated from Moscow University and got a job at the Pushkin Museum. Unexpectedly she was named curator of this strange secret museum within the museum.[1]

The special exhibition was organized in the autumn of 1946 as the result of curious events. Late in the summer, Sergei Merkurov had received an order from the Arts Committee to prepare the new display before September, when the reopening of the museum was planned. To his delight, he received permission to include the best trophy paintings. Andrei Chegodayev, chief curator of the trophy depositories, supervised the hanging of the Sistine Madonna, Vermeer's *Girl Reading a Letter*, Giorgione's *Sleeping Venus*, and other Dresden masterpieces along with those from the museum's own collection. Invitations to the opening were sent out. Impatient art lovers began to line up hours before the time specified.

They were destined to be disappointed, because the museum did not open. Instead, a notice appeared on the locked door stating curtly that the new exhibition would be delayed until 3 October for technical reasons. But the reasons were not technical, they were political. At the last moment the Arts Committee decided not to open the show, and on 3 October, when visitors were finally allowed into the museum, they did not see any of the masterpieces looted from Germany. All of those pictures had been hastily moved to the two galleries later visited by Khrushchev, where admission was restricted.[2]

Valentina Tikhanova often guided high-ranking visitors through the 'secret museum'. Members of the Politburo, scientists, artists, ballet dancers – everybody of importance in the capital wanted to visit this exhibition. Its popularity was equal to that of the Armoury of the Moscow Kremlin, which was also closed in those days except to the elite.[3]

An attempt to 'legalize' the trophies was aborted in Leningrad as well, where preparations to reconstruct the Pergamum Altar in the Hermitage were in progress. Andrei Sivkov, the chief architect of the museum, had estimated the cost at 369,630 rubles (about £50,000). The restoration of fifteen damaged reliefs was estimated at 45,000 rubles only. But Sivkov's plan was never realized.[4] Goya's *Maypole* and Degas' *Place de la Concorde* were on view briefly and then disappeared.[5]

The return to secrecy ruined the initiative of Ivan Anisimov, the deputy head of the Arts Committee, to share the trophies with provincial museums. The Pushkin curators had already selected fifty-two first-class paintings and 238 prints for the Museum of Fine Arts of Georgia. Rembrandt's *Old Woman Weighing Gold* and Van Dyck's *Apostle Matthew* from the Dresden Gallery, Paris Bordone's *Woman with a Rose* from Berlin, and the School of Cranach *Presentation in the Temple* from Leipzig, all scheduled for the museum in Tbilisi, stayed in Moscow.[6]

On 12 November Elizaveta Alexandrova, head of the Arts Committee trophy group, wrote: 'According to the order of Mikhail Khrapchenko, trophy property temporarily will not be distributed until special orders.' But the special orders were never issued.[7]

In late 1948 or early 1949 Khrapchenko brought two unexpected guests to the museum who did not need special passes. Since Merkurov was absent, Chegodayev had to take them around the secret exhibition. The more striking of the two was a short man dressed in a paramilitary outfit whose shaved head seemed to grow directly from his shoulders. He ignored Chegodayev's greeting. The other man, who wore a well-tailored suit, tried to compensate for this rudeness and greeted Chegodayev warmly. He was Vasily Kuznetsov, the head of the All-Union Central Council of Trade Unions. The short man was Alexander Poskrebishev, Stalin's personal secretary and one of his few confidants. According to rumour, Poskrebishev had a seal with a facsimile of Stalin's signature.

Later Chegodayev remembered: 'He was the most frightening man I met in my life ... He didn't utter a word. Luckily Khrapchenko escorted him. I walked behind them with Kuznetsov. From time to time Khrapchenko called me when he couldn't explain something to Poskrebishev, who never asked questions but simply stopped near a painting. He was a real monster.' Poskrebishev left the museum without a word of farewell. Everybody understood that his visit had not been motivated by curiosity; it was clear that he had no interest in art. Poskrebishev had been sent by Stalin.[8]

Momentous political changes were taking place in Germany, and it was time to decide the fate of the trophy art. The decision was made very soon after Poskrebishev's visit. Chegodayev was ordered to stop all tours of the special depositories. From now on, only restorers had the right to visit them. Total secrecy was the new order of the day.[9] But museum officials who had dreamed of mixing the trophy masterpieces with their permanent collections had a bigger shock in store. Soon their permanent collections would share the fate of the trophy pictures.

Nineteen forty-eight was the year of the campaign against 'cosmopolitanism'. Jews, people with pro-Western sympathies, writers, artists, and scientists were all under attack. The great poet Anna Akhmatova, the writer Mikhail Zoshchenko, the composers Dimitri Shostakovich and Sergei Prokofiev were all viciously reviled in the press. Literary magazines were shut down. The famous Tairov Theatre was closed. The Museum of Modern Western Art, which housed the great Impressionist pictures seized after the Revolution from the Shchukin and Morozov collections, was also closed. The famous Socialist Realist artist Alexander Gerasimov, the president of the Academy of Arts, proposed that the pictures – masterpieces by van Gogh, Matisse and Picasso – should be burned, an idea enthusiastically supported by Kliment Voroshilov, who had the reputation of an art expert among his Politburo colleagues. At his order, the museum building was given to the academy, but fortunately the paintings survived. They went into the Pushkin Museum secret depositories. Later they were divided between the Pushkin and the Hermitage.[10]

MOSCOW

Presents for Stalin

It seemed that nothing could be worse than 1948, but for museum people the next year brought a bigger blow. On 9 December 1949, at 11.20 in the morning, the closing bell suddenly rang in the Pushkin Museum. Panic spread among the staff. Within moments the news spread like wildfire: the Central Committee had just ordered the museum to be closed immediately. A column of military trucks suddenly filled the courtyard, soldiers jumped out, and the sharp commands of the officers echoed in the galleries. Museum curators and guides were ordered to supervise the soldiers who moved the paintings. The curators themselves gently removed the smaller canvases from the walls, and groups of soldiers shifted the huge sculptures. Carpenters built plywood walls to block the entrances to galleries that were turned into storage areas.

The 'leader and teacher of the world proletariat' would celebrate his seventieth birthday on 21 December, and presents from his admirers had been pouring in from all over the world. What better place to show them off than the Pushkin Museum, whose galleries were filled with alien Western art? Even the museum's highest officials had no warning of what was in store for it. Chegodayev remembered that on his way to work that morning he met the artist Romas on the steps of the building. The artist was in a very cheerful mood. 'What are you doing here?' he asked Chegodayev. 'Why are you asking?' replied Chegodayev. 'I'm going to work.' 'But the museum doesn't exist any more. There's going to be an exhibition and I'm going to design it,' Romas said. That was how Chegodayev found out about the 'Exhibition of Presents to Stalin'.[1]

The next morning, when staff members came to work, they saw that the courtyard was full of trucks. Heavy crates were being unloaded. Hundreds of people were working outdoors despite the freezing weather, and hundreds more were labouring in the galleries. More than 2,000 people worked day and night to open the exhibition on time. The museum guides were drafted to organize tours, and political instructors lectured them on exactly what to say to visitors. Thirty 'suspicious' people were ordered to be fired from the staff: Jews, people who had relatives missing in action, and people whose relatives had been in territories occupied by the Nazis were among those let go. Valentina Tikhanova was fired because she was known to be a member of the family of an 'enemy of the people'. Chegodayev resigned in protest against the closing of the museum. Fortunately for him, people were too busy to notice his risky political gesture.[2]

The museum was dismantled. In the department of Western European art, which included the huge trophy collections, only four people remained. One person, the curator Maria Drozdova, was left to take care of 23,000 objects of decorative art, from Chinese porcelains to medieval suits of armour. Furniture was stored in the Greek Yard, and antique sculptures from Dresden and Berlin were crammed into the White Hall. The Dresden paintings were in two halls on the ground floor, and the so-called Michelangelo Hall was transformed into a depository for masterpieces from Berlin, Leipzig and Gotha.[3]

In the emptied galleries there was a frenzy of activity, and finally, on 22 December, only two weeks after work began, the exhibition opened. People waited breathlessly for Stalin. But he did not come. Nikolai Shvernik, head of the Presidium of the Supreme Soviet, opened the exhibition instead. This was the same Shvernik who, as head of the Extraordinary Commission, had started the planning for the trophy operation in 1943. Now he delivered his speech in a museum filled with trophy works of art, although they were all squirreled away. After the ceremony he led high officials and honourable guests into the special exhibition.

Among the foreign visitors that day were Palmiro Togliatti of Italy and Maurice Thorez of France, *La Pasionaria* Dolores Ibaruri of Spain, General Ludwig Svoboda of Czechoslovakia, and other chiefs of the 'fraternal parties'. Each of them represented a gallery filled with gifts from his party to 'the greatest genius of all times and peoples'. There was a private room where officials greeted the representatives of the illegal Communist parties of capitalist countries. These people had come to the USSR secretly to deliver presents and congratulate the Great Proletarian.

The halls were full of objects created by 'people's industry' from the 'people's democracies'. There were paintings by the well-known Italian Communist artist Renato Guttuso along with coal and salt sculptures made by miners. There was a belt woven by a Hungarian woman who had lost her hands during the war and who had created the gift with her feet. Swedish Communists presented an ultramodern desk of Constructivist design. There were many interesting objects of applied art and boxes of chocolate and bottles of wine presented to the beloved chief. When a museum guard broke a bottle by accident, a meeting of the museum staff was called immediately. The poor woman was accused of sabotage and terrified out of her wits, but finally pardoned.

After the exhibition ended, in 1953, the wines disappeared and the uncounted boxes of chocolate spoiled. Stalin never visited the exhibition, but a full set of photographs, including every wine bottle and every box of bonbons, was sent to him. His daughter, Svetlana, came once to see her father's gifts.

The exhibition was wildly popular. People queued up for hours to see Stalin's presents and then filed through the galleries in respectful silence. One visitor ostentatiously stated as he left: 'It is impossible to compare this to the Hermitage. I have visited the Hermitage. This is better. What beauty! It is a genuine manifestation of human creativity!' Fantastic rumours about the show circulated in Moscow. One of the exhibition guides visited a barber shop, situated opposite the museum, to be shaved. The barber told him about the many wonders that were said to be in the show, including a talking salami that had been presented to Comrade Stalin. It was too much for the guide; he revealed that he worked in the museum and insisted that there was no talking salami nor any other sausage of any sort in the museum. The barber became furious; he thought the man was making fun of the glorious exhibition and kicked him out of the shop half-shaved.[4]

Conditions in the museum became more and more ominous. An atmosphere of suspicion and vigilance was pervasive. Anastasia Tolstikhina, a relative of Stalin's wife and the director of the Museum of the Revolution, moonlighted as the director of the exhibition. An arrogant woman, she tormented the remaining Pushkin staff. Merkurov had left, and Nikolai Slonevsky, the new director, had no power at all. Museum officials remembered Tolstikhina shouting at him: 'You are nobody here!' Secret policemen were on duty in every gallery and patrolled with dogs all night long. A former gulag camp commandant was made special commandant of the exhibition. Museum officials tried to hide when they encountered this terrifying man in the galleries. The secret police were especially suspicious of the remaining members of the Pushkin staff. The demoralized curators had lost their offices and worked in the crowded depositories. They knew that the rulers of the country were seriously discussing the possibility of liquidating the Pushkin as a museum of Western European art.

The museum was saved by the Ministry of State Control, which sent people to check the condition of the trophy depositories. The idea behind this may have been to close the museum and transfer its collection to the Hermitage, leaving the Stalin presents on view more or less permanently. But the inspectors were appalled by the deplorable condition of the thousands of extremely valuable works of art. Most of them were not even registered. Gold and silver treasures, including the Trojan gold, were kept in wooden crates on the balconies of the White Hall. The parts of the Pergamum Altar that had been sent to Moscow were outdoors, in the portico. The staff were simply incapable of registering the objects because most of the qualified curators had been fired.[5]

The Ministry of State Control was angry. Andrei Guber received a reproof, but the inspectors did not want to liquidate the museum. They recognized that all this extremely valuable property had to be cared for. Instead, they gave the order to hire new curators and to begin registration of the trophies immediately. Alarmed, they decided to examine the situation in the Hermitage as well. It was no better than in Moscow. The inspectors learned that a painting by Van Dyck from the permanent collection had gone missing during the evacuation. The treasury had been robbed by a museum official, who stole some gold objects.[6] Registration of the trophies had begun but was far from complete. Neither museum, nor any other Soviet museum, had been issued instructions on the preservation and registration of works of art. After the scandal in Moscow and Leningrad, these instructions were finally composed.[7]

In March 1953 Stalin died. Tolstikhina immediately wrote a syrupy letter to the Central Committee pleading with them to make the exhibition permanent. But in May it was closed and all the gifts from the world's proletarians were moved to the cellars of the Museum of the Revolution, where they remain to this day. The long nightmare of the Pushkin Museum was over. It reopened in late 1953. By that time the trophy collections had been registered in the museum's 'special inventory'.[8]

THE RETURN OF THE DRESDEN GALLERY

On 3 March 1955, Vyacheslav Molotov wrote a note to the Central Committee about the Dresden Gallery. 'There are two possible ways to resolve this problem,' he said. The Soviets could either publicly announce that the 'cultural treasures of the Dresden Gallery' belonged to the Soviet people as their trophies, or they could return them to the German people 'as their heritage'. The phrase 'cultural valuables of the GDR temporarily kept in the USSR' was used for the first time in this note.[1] The war loot had previously been known only as 'trophies'.[2]

On 31 March, Soviet newspapers published a statement from the Council of Ministers about the return of the Dresden Gallery. 'In the course of the Great Patriotic War, during battles on German territory, the Soviet Army saved and removed to the Soviet Union masterpieces of classical painting from the collection of the Dresden Gallery, which are of great international value,' the statement said.

> The Council of Ministers of the USSR has decided to return to the Government of the German Democratic Republic all paintings of the Dresden Gallery that are kept in the Soviet Union, for the purpose of further strengthening and developing friendly relations between Soviet and German people and because the Government of the German Democratic Republic is loyal to the policy of peace and friendship between peoples and struggle for the reunification of Germany on the basis of peace-loving and democratic intentions . . . There are about 750 paintings belonging to the Dresden Gallery in the Soviet Union . . .[3]

Although the Council of Ministers issued the statement, the decision had actually been made in secret by the Secretariat of the Central Committee.

The figure of 750 paintings came from the Ministry of Culture, which two days earlier had informed the Central Committee that there were 738 paintings, ten tapestries, and seven miniatures from the Dresden Gallery in the Pushkin Museum and eleven paintings in the Hermitage. But the day the statement was issued, a special commission sent to the Ukraine reported from Kiev that they had found an 'extra' 501 paintings and two pastels belonging to the Dresden Gallery.

The Kiev loot, which included such masterpieces as Dürer's Dresden Triptych and Rubens' *Old Woman with Brazier*, had been completely forgotten in Moscow. The activity of the Ukrainian trophy brigade was not well known because it did not arrive in Dresden until the autumn of 1945, when the Moscow brigade had already left. The Ukrainians were in no hurry to inform the Ministry of Culture about their treasures, and Moscow had learned about them mainly from rumours and informers. The irony of the situation was that the Ukrainian trophy brigade had been dispatched to the Soviet occupation zone by Nikita Khrushchev, head of the Ukrainian government at the time. In 1955 the same Khrushchev made the decision to return the Dresden paintings but forgot about the Ukrainian trophies that had been sent from Germany directly to the Council of People's Commissars of the Ukraine.

It was most likely Georgy Alexandrov who initiated the return of the Dresden Gallery. The minister of culture of the USSR in 1955, he was a man who had made an impressive career at an unusually young age. A philosopher, he had already published books on Marxism and a monograph on Aristotle by the time he was thirty-two. Noticed by Stalin, he was appointed head of the Department of Propaganda and Agitation of the Central Committee and for seven years was one of the most influential figures in the cultural life of the country: everything from theatre repertoires to museum budgets had to be approved by the Central Committee. The heads of all the trophy brigades sent Alexandrov reports from Berlin about their activities.

Alexandrov was known as a liberal. At the beginning of 1945 he published an article that made a deep impression on many soldiers and officers, urging humane treatment of the population of occupied Germany. He wrote that the time for the slogan 'Kill a German' was over. Germany was the motherland of Beethoven and Marx. Mistreating the civilian population would disgrace the victorious army.

In 1946 Alexandrov became an Academician, a very high honour. During the campaign against 'cosmopolitanism' of the late 1940s he kept a low profile. He was at the time director of the prestigious

Institute of Philosophy, but neither exalted position nor high honours protected people in those days. He had written a history of Western European philosophy, and his pro-Western sentiments were well known. All this made him vulnerable. But at the beginning of the Khrushchev era, during the so-called Thaw, when the first stirrings of free thinking enlivened the country's cultural life, Alexandrov's career took a new turn. In 1954 he was appointed minister of culture, the only Academician ever to hold the position.

Official thinking about the trophy problem began to change too at this time. Works of art of Polish origin were returned to Poland by the Pushkin Museum. At the same time, discussions began about returning the Dresden Gallery. Official interest in the matter had been stirred up by publications in the Western press claiming that the paintings had been seriously damaged in transit to the Soviet Union.

If it was Alexandrov who initiated the return of the Dresden masterpieces to Germany, he did not have time to complete the job. He had spent only a year at the Ministry of Culture when his career took another turn. It became clear that he was too popular – in elections to the Supreme Soviet of the Russian Federation he received more votes than Khrushchev – and his liberalism alarmed the old guard. At the beginning of 1955 the Central Committee sent a secret letter to all party organizations about the 'immoral actions of comrade Alexandrov'. He was accused of participating in 'drunken orgies' in which young actors, artists, and poets took part. The implication that he was homosexual was clear, although the word was not used. This was an extremely serious offence for an official. The attack on Alexandrov was the first attempt to create an image of the amoral intellectual that was used later in the struggle with the dissident movement. Alexandrov was expelled from Moscow to Belorussia and given a job in a provincial research institute. He died there in 1961.[4]

Alexandrov's successor as minister of culture in 1955 was Nikolai Mikhailov, a former Komsomol leader. Mikhailov was officially credited with organizing the return of German cultural valuables. Immediately after it was announced that the return would take place, a large-scale campaign was begun in the Soviet press glorifying this 'wise, humanitarian decision'. In the weekly *Ogonyok*, the most popular illustrated magazine in the country, five articles dedicated to the return of the Dresden Gallery were published from May to July of 1955. The first reaction to the official announcement appeared in

Literaturnaya Gazeta on 28 April. The article, entitled 'How It Was', was signed by the writer Leonid Volinsky (Leonid Rabinovich, who actually wrote it) and Vladimir Perevozchikov, an important official of the Ukrainian Communist Party who had been Rabinovich's commanding officer in the 164th Trophy Battalion.

Rabinovich retold some stories he had told the Arts Committee brigade in 1945 about his 'discovery' of the Dresden works of art, but he shaped them more artfully. The theme of the article was a comparison between the barbarians – the Americans, who had mercilessly bombed the palaces and museums of Dresden, and the Nazis, who had callously planned to destroy all the masterpieces of the gallery – and the humanitarian Red Army, which had saved the art treasures. The article also offered an exciting plot with the kind of Indiana Jones twists that Rabinovich liked. He related how he had learned about the hidden treasures from a curator of the Albertinum, who confessed to him a secret plan to destroy the treasures worked out personally by Joseph Goebbels. Despite the danger – the courageous lieutenant and the heroic curator were surrounded by Nazi spies – she agreed to cooperate to save the masterpieces. Thanks to the information she gave him, Rabinovich found a secret map that was the key to the hidden caves full of treasures.

The article was rich in picturesque details: a camouflaged tunnel given away by a patch of fresh plaster on the wall, immense quantities of landmines and armies of saboteurs. Near the Gross Cotta hiding place of the Sistine Madonna, in a half-ruined house, Rabinovich claimed to have arrested a 'saboteur'. (This man was in fact a well-known museum curator in the German Democratic Republic.) Rabinovich also claimed to have arrested two people in Weesenstein Castle: one, Arthur G., was a friend of Goebbels and the centre of an evil plot to destroy the paintings. The other was Wilhelm V., the director of the Dresden Gallery, Hermann Voss.

But the main element of the myth created by Rabinovich was the terrible condition of the paintings found in the damp caves. He likened them to wounded soldiers and compared Churakov's restoration workshop to a military hospital. Rabinovich had no doubt that the paintings had been placed in the shelters not to protect them from Allied bombardment but to destroy them, but he did not explain why the Germans had chosen such a complicated way of doing this.

The article published in *Literaturnaya Gazeta* was the opening

skirmish in a war over who 'saved' the Dresden Gallery that would
end only with the deaths of the participants. A week later Khrushchev
received a letter signed by the members of the Arts Committee
brigade that had operated in Dresden. Only Natalia Sokolova had
refused to sign, since the letter was initiated by her enemy and rival,
Rototayev. It was directed against Rabinovich, who, to Rototayev's
fury, had appropriated the glory of discovering the hidden masterpieces. Rototayev and his supporters accused Rabinovich of numerous fabrications. There had never been a secret map of the depositories. As for Frau Ragna, the 'heroic' curator who had saved the
paintings, she had in reality tried to obstruct the brigade in every way
and had hidden the files of the museum from them. Insisting that half
the article was made up of lies, Rototayev and the other signatories
demanded justice.[5]

On 2 May 1955 an exhibition of Dresden's 'rescued' masterpieces
was opened at the Pushkin Museum by Nikolai Mikhailov and Hans
Loch, deputy prime minister of the GDR. The opening was a gala
event, with a joint delegation of East and West German workers in
attendance. The date, the day after May Day, was chosen so the
celebrations could merge into a festival of solidarity. The numerous
guests – representatives of the international Communist movement –
watched the parade of tanks on Red Square on the first day and, on
the next, enjoyed the pictures in the Pushkin Museum.[6]

In his speech at the opening, Mikhailov boasted that the masterpieces had been saved twice: first, from the damp caves by the heroic
Red Army and second, by museum officials and restorers.[7]

The exhibition was extremely popular. More than 1,200,000 people
stood in line day and night to see the rescued masterpieces. Seventy-
five thousand copies of the catalogue were sold so quickly that an
extra 50,000 had to be hurriedly printed.[8] The propaganda machine
worked overtime, with a plethora of articles in the press. Most
followed the useful model proposed by Rabinovich: damp caves were
featured in every one of them. The paintings were half ruined and
saved only by the efforts of the Soviet restorers. The Germans were
accused of various sins, from attempting to blow up the paintings to
letting them rot. *Ogonyok*, along with the standard article, published
a letter to the Soviet people from Otto Nagel, president of the
Academy of Art of the GDR, and Professor Bernhard Kretschmar.
Called 'The Great Act of Friendship', the letter claimed that 'real

friendship gives more than it takes'. With profuse declarations of thanks to the Soviet government and accusations against the imperialists and warmongers in the West, Nagel and Kretschmar wrote: 'Today in the Berlin Museums only reproductions of the great masterpieces that formerly filled their galleries are exhibited. But like all valuable masterpieces they were removed by the Americans and sold to private collectors.'[9]

The German authors stressed the propaganda role of the show: 'We will exhibit the collection in the Berlin Museum and the inhabitants of the Western sector of Berlin will visit the exhibition. They can see with their own eyes the true nature of the friendship of the great Soviet people. They can see how stupid and crazy are the rumours spread in the West that copies, not originals, will be returned to Germany.' Like the invitation to the joint delegation of German workers, the show in Berlin was aimed more towards the West Germans than the GDR. Khrushchev wanted to show what a good friend he was to them.[10]

The exhibition gave birth to the strange phenomenon of Sistine Madonna-mania. Reproductions of the painting flooded the country, and countless articles about the Madonna appeared in newspapers and magazines. Naturally, the admiration for this unequivocally religious figure had to be expressed in ideologically acceptable terms. In an essay written by the famous poet Pavel Antakolsky and published in *Ogonyok*, the Madonna was called a 'contemporary of Copernicus' and the poet expressed his admiration for 'the art that helped this living, very earthy and healthy woman to overcome gravity and fly freely in the air'.[11] Another poet, Alexander Kovalenkov, wrote a poem called 'Madonna' about a barefoot peasant girl who models for Raphael:

> She flew away, she escaped from monks, priests, and Magi . . . It happened that they met each other [Raphael and his model], and I hope to be excused for my guess that they knew happiness and the sorrow of loss, being both happy and melancholy together . . . The hearts of the heroines of the Leningrad blockade and the daughters of the soldiers of Stalingrad are full of friendly feeling toward her.[12]

A joke made by the famous actress Faina Ranevskaya became extremely popular. To a friend who had visited the exhibition and said that he did not like the Madonna, Ranevskaya was reported to have retorted, 'The Madonna has been admired by so many men that now *she* has the right to choose.'[13] And it seemed that she did make her choice. Museum officials noticed that a strange thing was happening to one of the young curators of the department of Western European paintings. He was spending a lot of time in the gallery where the Sistine Madonna was exhibited. His colleagues joked that he was falling in love with the picture. One day, when the museum closed, he refused to leave the gallery. Nobody could persuade him to go, and when the guards tried to remove him by force he resisted violently. He had to be taken to a mental hospital.[14]

Behind the scenes of this feast of friendship, relations were not quite so amiable. Soviet cultural officials wanted very much to keep at least some of the Dresden pictures as an 'answering gesture' from the German side. The echoes of the oratory about German–Soviet solidarity had hardly died away before Mikhailov was busily scheming to get his hands on some of the gems of the collection. He wrote to the Central Committee:

> The Ministry of Culture of the USSR wants ... to discuss with our German friends that it would be acceptable if the government of the GDR proposed in gratitude for the saving and return of the internationally known treasures of the Dresden Gallery ... to present two paintings to Soviet museums.[15]

Mikhailov told the Central Committee exactly which ones he wanted: Giorgione's *Sleeping Venus* and Vermeer's *Girl Reading a Letter*. But the Central Committee apparently did not support the idea, and the 'gesture' was never made.

After the exhibition closed, the collection went back to Germany and was shown at the Pergamum Museum, which was conveniently empty because the Pergamum Altar was still in the USSR. Despite the relentless propaganda campaign in both the Soviet and the East German press, Western countries did not express admiration for the return of the collection. On the contrary. In January 1956 Mikhailov wrote to Foreign Minister Molotov that 'a short time ago in some American and Russian émigré newspapers in New York there were slanderous articles stating that the collection of paintings of the Dresden Gallery was damaged during its stay in the USSR from 1945 to 1955'. The 'slanderous' articles were the result of the trip of Alfred

Frankfurter, an editor of *ARTnews* magazine, to Berlin, where he was allowed to examine the Dresden pictures. Frankfurter was shocked by the bad condition of some of them and the complete absence of any equipment, from humidifying devices to restoration materials, in the East Berlin museum.[16]

He did not accuse the Soviets of damaging the paintings; on the contrary, he praised the Moscow restorers highly for cleaning some of them. But he was puzzled by some of the restoration work. Titian's *The Tribute Money* had been restored by the famous painter Pavel Korin and widely used in Soviet propaganda as an example of the 'second rescue of the masterpieces'. But Frankfurter thought it had been restored so badly that he asked if it had been done in Germany during the war, when equipment and materials were unavailable. Extremely alarmed, he addressed an appeal to the international community to provide help for the masterpieces. He thought the United Nations should finance restoration. Art treasures, he said, should be removed from the context of political struggle.

The Soviets were seriously disturbed both by Frankfurter's opinion of the paintings' condition and by the questions of Western journalists during a press conference in Berlin about the location of the Pergamum Altar and the collection of the Dresden Grünes Gewölbe, which of course remained unanswered. The Ministry of Culture decided to counterattack, and the furious Mikhailov asked Foreign Minister Molotov for permission to publish a protest. 'It is unnecessary to answer such slanderous accusations,' he wrote, advising 'interested people to visit the National Gallery in Berlin and see how superb the paintings look'. Then yet again he told the story of the rescue of the masterpieces from the damp caves and their second salvation by Soviet restorers. 'The accusations of American newspaper reporters who never saw the paintings but judge their bad condition are false and of a provocational character,' he concluded.[17]

The controversy gave a new impulse to the creation of the myth about the rescued masterpieces, which had an ideological role beyond the immediate needs of propaganda. It was an important component in revising the interpretation of the Second World War as an historical event. In the first few years after the war, the major war hero was Stalin, thanks to whose genius the Soviet people had been able to crush the enemy. At the beginning of the Khrushchev era, a new hero was required. It was at this time that the cult of the simple soldier as the saviour of mankind was introduced. The story about the rescue of the Dresden Gallery treasures, which were saved for the 'new Germany', was the first brick of this new conception.

While articles in the newspapers extolled the heroic deeds of the simple soldiers of the Red Army, the real heroes of the Dresden affair were sitting in the Ministry of Culture answering questions about what actually had happened ten years earlier and who exactly had 'saved' the Dresden Gallery. When Mikhailov received the letter signed by the brigade members from Khrushchev's office, he ordered his deputy to find out the truth. It was almost impossible. Every participant in the event had a different story. The members of the trophy brigade of the Arts Committee who had worked in Dresden belatedly wrote a collective report of their activity, and could not resist some enhancement of their role.[18] In hindsight they renamed their brigade, calling it the Brigade to Save the Dresden Gallery.

The rivalry was not diminished by the generosity of the East Germans, who handed out decorations to all who had participated. Rototayev continued his crusade against Rabinovich, but the hack Kiev writer did not give up easily. In 1957 he published a book, *Seven Days*, about the saving of the Dresden Gallery and his role in the historic deed. It combined his usual detective story plot, full of secret shelters that he called 'concentration camps for works of art', and Nazi saboteurs, with what used to be called 'vulgar Marxist' art history. Bloodcurdling stories about masterpieces languishing in damp, mined caves were mixed with biographies of the painters who had created them and who of course had fought against the Church and the social elite to create truly realistic works of art. The words of Karl Marx, 'Rembrandt painted the Madonna as a Dutch peasant girl', were used as the epigraph to one chapter. The book was illustrated with colour reproductions of Dresden paintings, many of which had nothing to do with the activity of Rabinovich or the Arts Committee brigade. They had been removed to the USSR by SMERSH officers working for Gokhran.

Rabinovich falsified events not only in Dresden but in Berlin as well. About the Zoo tower, he said that 'on the eve of the surrender, SS soldiers exploded a bunker that contained the antiquities collection of the Berlin Museum'. Of the Friedrichshain tower, he reported that the Germans had burned it, destroying '411 paintings – according to our information, masterpieces by Rubens, van Dyck, Murillo . . . and other paintings of the Berlin Gallery were there. Two famous paintings by Menzel, *Breakfast in Sans Souci* and *Rolling Metal*, were destroyed there too.' And he stated that a fire started by an explosion set off by saboteurs in the area of Humbolthain had destroyed 'priceless sketches by Michelangelo for the tomb of Pope Julius II and preparatory works for the Isenheim Altar by the famous German artist Mathias Grünewald were destroyed. Five portfolios ... of illustrations to the *Divine Comedy* by Botticelli were burned out ... Now the fate awaiting the Dresden paintings became clear to us.'[19] A year after the publication of *Seven Days*, the drawings of Michelangelo, Grünewald, and Botticelli that Rabinovich claimed had been barbarously destroyed by the Nazis were exhibited in the Hermitage as part of an exhibition of masterpieces 'saved' by the Red Army. Menzel's *Rolling Metal* had been presented to the East German delegation by Mikhailov during the opening of the exhibition of the 'rescued' masterpieces in the Pushkin Museum.[20]

Despite these 'mistakes', the book was broadcast by state radio and reprinted twice. The members of the Rototayev brigade protested to the publishing house and to the Central Committee, stating that 'Everything connected to the saving of the paintings of the Dresden Gallery in Volinsky's book *Seven Days* is a fabrication.'[21] But their protests were ignored. They continued to protest until the end of their days. The last angry letter, signed by Volodin and Churakov, was sent to the head of the Committee on Radio and Television in 1984. Rabinovich, Rototayev, and Sokolova were already dead. The two surviving participants protested against the committee's plans to show the film *5 Days, 5 Nights*, based on Rabinovich's book, because 'the film misrepresents that great event and is a falsification'.[22]

Rabinovich's rivals not only denounced him, they wrote their own memoirs in an attempt to set the record straight, or at least to skew it in a different direction. Volodin painted a huge canvas depicting six soldiers carrying the framed Sistine Madonna upright from the dark tunnel (which would have been impossible). Natalia Sokolova published excerpts from her memoirs at the end of the 1960s, dedicated to Marshal Konev. Finally, in 1977, a book called *Saved Masterpieces* appeared. This strange volume published for propaganda purposes brought together all the memoirs of participants, but despite heavy censorship and editing, a single consistent version of events was not created. The editors could not reconcile the various accounts and finally wrote: 'The history of the discovery of the hiding places that contained the treasures of the Dresden Gallery has various versions in the literature dedicated to this question. And each of them has its portion of truth.'[23]

But Andrei Chegodayev, the first curator of the Dresden Gallery in the Pushkin Museum, remembered it differently: 'Nobody talked about the "saving" of the Dresden Gallery,' he said.

> It was taken as trophy. But soon after its return, the story about the saving of the collection was widely circulated ... It was a blatant lie, but the officials found it useful, and even the Germans were hypnotized by it. Shostakovich even wrote a cantata on the 'saving' of the Dresden Gallery ... But it was a lie, a barefaced lie.[24]

IS RECIPROCITY POSSIBLE?

The silvery TU-104 taxied down the runway of Vnukovo airport and slowly rolled to a stop. A group of officials dressed in grey overcoats and fur hats made their way towards the plane. When the door opened, Chou En-lai stepped out, smiling. The prime minister of the People's Republic of China was in Moscow on a state visit. Among the greeters were Otto Grotewohl, prime minister of the GDR, and other East German leaders.[1] It was 7 January 1957, and that morning in the Kremlin the Soviet and East German delegations had completed their negotiations and signed a protocol.

A few weeks earlier, Soviet tanks had rolled into Budapest and crushed the resistance of the capital's defenders. The legal government of Hungary, which had attempted reforms not welcomed by Moscow, was arrested. While the East German and Chinese leaders were embracing at Vnukovo, KGB officers were torturing the Hungarian prime minister, Imre Nagy, and his colleagues. Two members of the Hungarian government died as a result of torture, and secret trials followed by execution awaited the survivors.[2] General Ivan Serov, head of the KGB and organizer of the invasion, was at the airport to welcome the Chinese visitor. Delegations from the 'friendly socialist countries' of Europe and Asia had been following one another to Moscow to express their support. The meeting at Vnukovo was intended to demonstrate the unity of the socialist camp.

Otto Grotewohl was satisfied. The East Germans had used the occasion profitably. They had been paid well for their support. The statement of the Soviet and East German delegations praised the Red Army's 'suppression of counterrevolution ... in the interest of the Hungarian working people and all peace-loving peoples of Europe, because it halted the white terror and prevented the creation of a launching pad for aggression in Europe'. The statement declared that there was 'a plan prepared by reactionary forces to destroy the people's power in Hungary and restore the rule of the Horthy–fascist regime'. Only a few words at the end of the long statement dealt with another matter. 'Both sides affirmed their readiness to discuss questions connected with the return on a mutual basis of cultural valuables (artworks, archival materials, etc.).'[3]

At the time this statement was published, more than two million works of art removed from Germany were still hidden in Soviet special depositories. The Soviet participants in the negotiations – Marshal Konev, Nikolai Shvernik, Maxim Saburov, and Khrushchev – knew all about the cultural trophies. But at that moment, support for the Soviet invasion was more important to Khrushchev than works of art.

Museum officials had always suspected that the return of the Dresden Gallery would be followed by another return of works of art, and they were determined to do what they could to prevent it. A few days before the end of the Dresden treasures exhibition of 1955, they asked the Ministry of Culture for permission to include in the main inventory of the Pushkin Museum 353 paintings and 92 portfolios of drawings from the museums of Berlin, Leipzig and Gotha. This would have been tantamount to taking permanent possession of the objects. The ministry agreed to the proposal but wanted the list revised. Deputy Director Boris Vipper reduced it to 266 artworks and 7 portfolios,[4] but the ministry waffled all through 1956. In that year works of art that had been looted by the Nazis from Poland were returned to the Poles, including the famous *Last Judgement* by Hans Memling, which was kept in the Hermitage. Communist Romania received art collections that had been sent to Russia for safekeeping during the First World War and had been kept in the Armoury of the Moscow Kremlin ever since. But the Ministry of Culture still could not decide what to do with the German trophies.

Events in Hungary finally determined their fate. In January 1957 the East Germans decided that the USSR was ready for compromise and acted boldly. Foreign Minister Lothar Bolz took to Moscow a list of claims of the Berlin and Dresden museums. At the end of May, the GDR Embassy in Moscow sent a note to the Ministry of Foreign Affairs that included lists of other museum objects removed from East Germany.[5]

On 21 May the Presidium of the Central Committee adopted the decree 'Concerning Cultural Valuables of the GDR that Are in the Soviet Union for Temporary Storage'. It was decided to establish a commission that would include both museum curators and officials from various state agencies and would be headed by the minister of culture, Nikolai Mikhailov. The commission's task was to prepare a proposal for the return to the GDR of the cultural valuables taken by the Soviets and the return to the USSR of cultural valuables taken to Germany. The proposals were to be delivered to the Central Committee.[6]

The Soviet government did not know where the objects removed from East Germany were. The Ministry of Culture sent out a request to all cultural institutions to inspect their depositories and send back information about their art trophies. In the Pushkin Museum and the Hermitage, the curators compared the lists of German claims with the treasures hidden in their storerooms. They noted that the claims were composed very diplomatically, with the East Germans parroting the Soviet myth about the 'saving' of the works of art. The objects missing from the Völkerkundemuseum were said to have been 'rescued by the Red Army to Karlshorst'. In the case of the impressive library of scientific books and documents belonging to the Department of Experimental Physics of Halle-Wittenberg University, which had been removed to the very secret Institute of Nuclear Research in Dubna, the East Germans were afraid to admit that they knew of its location, so they wrote: 'If these collections are needed, they must remain here and not be returned.'[7]

Nora Eliasberg, head registrar of the Pushkin Museum, sent a list of the most valuable works of art in the museum's special depository to the ministry. It included 'unique objects from the Great Trojan Treasure', along with paintings from private collections by El Greco, Goya, Daumier and Manet. Kapitolina Butenko, the ministry official, crossed out the paintings from the Kohler and Gerstenberg collections because it had been decided at the very beginning not to return works of art from private collections, but the Trojan treasure remained on the list until the last moment.[8]

Chief curator Andrei Guber made a more complete accounting of the art trophies. The Pushkin Museum's depositories contained 536,357 looted objects (363,903 transported to Moscow by special trains, 165,720 given to the museum by Gokhran). Ninety-four of the 1,051 paintings came from private collections and 480 were of unknown provenance.[9]

The Hermitage depositories were richer, with 829,561 works. There were also historical archives: of the electors of Brandenburg, of the German Archaeological Institute, and of the Cemeteries of Greater Berlin, which for some unknown reason had been removed to Leningrad. There were 2,724 paintings, including 180 from private collections, and 26,214 objects of unknown origin. More than 20,000 of the trophies were urgently in need of restoration.[10]

The state ministries also sent information about their loot. The Ministry of Railway Transport had the archive of the German railways. The Ministry of Geology admitted that it had a large mineral collection. The treasury of the electors of Saxony, from the Grünes Gewölbe, was hidden in Gokhran, which was under the control of the Ministry of Finance. The Ministry of Defence kept silence longer than the other state agencies, but finally the generals admitted that they had 'marine paintings' in the Central Naval Museum in Leningrad, a large quantity of arms and armour in the Museum of the History of Artillery, and numerous objects spread around various military institutions.

When Ministry of Culture officials added it all up, they discovered that a total of 2,614,874 objects and 534 crates of archaeological materials had been reported. There were 108,338 art objects from private collections, including 915 paintings. More than 50,000 objects were of unknown provenance. Most of the objects were in institutions that were under the control of the ministry, but other state agencies also had valuable loot, the Ministry of Defence in particular.[11] Some works of art were in the Interior Ministry. The KGB did not reveal any information about their trophies, but apparently nobody asked them.

The biggest problem now was to restore the trophies so they could be returned. Because nobody knew what would be sent back to Germany, the ministry's first decision was to restore everything. The museums, especially the provincial museums, could not organize a total restoration of the hundreds of thousands of works of art on their own, so the ministry drafted the Central Restoration Workshop in Moscow. It was headed by Sergei Sidorov, the former trophy brigade officer in Berlin, who knew from experience that the condition of many of the trophy works was very bad. From the spring of 1957 through to the summer of 1958 the best restorers in the country were busy working on the trophy objects.

Guidelines came from Vera Karaseva, the workshop's chief restorer, who led a restoration commission to the Hermitage. She specified that paintings to be returned must have no damage that could be attributed to careless packing or transportation or inadequate care. Paintings with punctures or holes were to be repaired. Paintings selected for exhibition when the return took place were to be brought to exhibition standards. The myth of the rescued masterpieces had to be maintained.

But the amount of work was immense. Karaseva was in despair over the condition of the trophy paintings kept in the Hermitage: scratches, holes, and other damage to canvases as the result of transportation; paint flaking off wood panels; everything dusty and dirty.[12] Mikhail Alexandrovsky, who took part in the same commission, noted that 125 sculptures made of marble, limestone and terracotta had been damaged by fire and recommended that Greek vases not be glued together since it was safer to transport the fragments. Another big problem was cleaning rust from the arms and armour. Alexandrovsky wrote that they had survived removal to the USSR but looked 'very bad'.[13]

Since it was impossible to transport the thousands of damaged works of art, all the restoration was done in the Hermitage. A shed equipped with huge tubs was set up in the courtyard, and sculptures burned in the Friedrichshain explosion were cleaned in them. Brigades of restorers were sent from Moscow, but there were severe shortages of materials and a desperate lack of space. One group of Moscow restorers worked on a cramped and drafty landing, with a single hotplate to heat their materials and without any lamps at all.

Despite the heroic attempts of the restorers, 561 trophy objects were considered beyond restoration and therefore impossible to return. Among them were Italian plaster sculptures of the fifteenth century, Etruscan tomb urns, and Chinese frescos. An Egyptian relief depicting an Ethiopian king and the god Anubis was impossible to restore because 'before arrival in the Hermitage it was kept in a wet place'.[14] Professor Blavatsky had been right when he opposed the transport of the reliefs found in the New Mint cellar.

In the Pushkin Museum the quantity of irretrievable works of art was even higher. There were 1,277, about half of which were antique sculptures.[15] The situation in the Historical Museum was no better: 213 Egyptian papyri were in such bad condition that museum officials decided to destroy them, and sixty-eight 17th–19th century paintings were considered impossible to exhibit.[16]

Finally the Ministry of Culture decided that badly damaged works had to be returned to Germany as they were because restoring them would delay necessary restorations to 'our own museum exhibits for some years'. But some of the works were in such bad condition they had 'lost both exhibition and historical value. The return of such materials makes no sense and could provoke the attacks of enemy propaganda ... Because of this, all materials of this type must be destroyed immediately.'[17]

It was not only Moscow restorers who worked in the Hermitage. A special brigade of the Directorate of Exhibitions and Panoramas came to produce plaster copies of the Pergamum Altar and more than a hundred other masterpieces of antique sculpture. The famous head of Queen Nefertiti from Berlin was copied in stone. Hermitage officials pulled new prints from the plates of Altdorfer, Cranach and Dürer. In 1958 the brigade returned to the Hermitage with a list of forty-five objects selected by ministry officials and made five copies of each of them.[18] Copies were made in the Pushkin Museum too. Some of the objects in the Trojan treasure were reproduced because it was widely believed that the objects would soon be returned to Berlin.[19]

When the information about the trophy works in Soviet museums had been collected, the ministry prepared a proposal for their future and sent it to the Department of Culture of the Central Committee. The document was written by Andrei Guber. The first part of the proposal was dedicated to Soviet works of art removed by the Germans during the war. Guber recommended that the list of losses composed by the Extraordinary State Commission in 1945 simply be retyped and given to the Germans as the Soviet claim.

Guber and Butenko also proposed to create a Special Archive under the command of the Main Archival Department of the Ministry of the Interior. This new archive would bring together all of the 274,450 documents removed from the Soviet occupation zone. A commission with representatives of all the interested agencies, from the KGB to the Institute of Marxism–Leninism, would sort out the documents and choose for 'further storage in the USSR those materials that have scientific, operational, and political interest for the boards and organizations of the USSR'.

German library collections would not be returned because the books and periodicals had been divided among scientific libraries.

The German seals had been obliterated and pages and sometimes whole chapters of questionable political content had been cut out by the censors. Guber and Butenko recommended that only some unique editions be returned.

But the most interesting part of the document was the fourth point. It recommended that 'cultural valuables from private collections, objects and collections whose provenance was unknown, and objects stolen by the Nazis in occupied countries' should not be returned. And of course objects belonging to the museums and institutions of West Germany had to remain in Soviet secret depositories. In other words, the only objects that would be returned were those from public institutions located in the GDR – and not all of those.[20]

The mechanism of return Guber proposed was very simple: it had to be an exchange of works found in the depositories of state institutions in both countries. In the joint Russian–East German statement, the return of cultural valuables had been described as 'mutual', without further elucidation. Ministry of Culture officials were assuming that their East German counterparts were also busy collecting information about Soviet works of art in German museums and preparing to return them in massive quantities. After minor changes, the document composed by Guber was signed and sent by Mikhailov on 30 July to the Presidium.[21]

But the Soviets were dumbfounded by the East German response. On 19 October 1957 the GDR Embassy in Moscow sent a note to Soviet officials along with the list of German claims: 'After a careful search organized by German state organizations, it was learned that there are no cultural valuables from the USSR in the German Democratic Republic.'[22]

Although nobody had seriously researched the fate of the works that had disappeared during the war from the occupied territories of the USSR, it was assumed that most of them were in the depositories of German museums. The experts who had been involved in the search for looted Soviet works of art in Germany in 1947 – Georgy Antipin of the Historical Museum in Moscow, Anatoly Kuchumov of the Pavlovsk Museum, and David Marchukov of the Committee on Cultural Educational Institutions – had not been invited to participate in the preparations for the second return of trophies. Almost no one knew that they had supervised the removal of twenty-one goods wagons from occupied Germany filled with works of art taken by the Germans from the museums of Russia, Belorussia and Ukraine. For over two years these objects – a huge mound of unpacked works of art belonging to Soviet museums – had sat in the Derutra depository in Berlin. Occupation officials were busy removing German trophies and simply forgot about the Soviet things. They 'discovered' their own works of art only later, after the transport of the German trophies was accomplished.[23] These objects had been found in various occupation zones, but most had been found and returned to the Russians by the Americans.

Mikhailov's commission informed the Presidium that 'until this moment, only a minimal quantity of objects that were removed from the USSR have been returned'. But the Department of Reparations, Supplies, and Restitution of the Soviet Military Administration in Germany, headed by Major General Leonid Zorin, had received 534,120 objects from the Americans between 1945 and 1948, belonging to the museums of Kiev, Minsk, Smolensk, Pskov and Novgorod, and the palaces outside Leningrad. The problem was that records of the department were classified and unavailable to the commission.[24]

The Committee on Cultural Educational Institutions, which had organized the search for looted Soviet works of art in Germany, was closed in 1953, and its archives were distributed to various agencies. By 1957 the events of ten years earlier had been forgotten, and reality had been supplanted by a myth about hundreds of thousands of looted Soviet masterpieces hidden in Germany.

Soviet art historians were opposed to returning anything to Germany unless they received something in return. In January 1958 three well-known museum officials – Boris Vipper and Andrei Guber of the Pushkin Museum and Vladimir Levinson-Lessing of the Hermitage – sent a letter of protest to Minister of Culture Mikhailov. They urged the government not to send anything back to Germany without getting something in exchange. They speculated that the objects removed from the USSR by the Nazis were probably in West German territory. If the works of art were returned to Germany and nothing remained in the USSR, 'we will have no incentive later to offer the other side, to search for and return our valuables' – presumably after the unification of East and West Germany, which it was widely believed would take place very soon, when the West Germans understood the advantages of socialism.

At the very least, the writers suggested, the return should be limited. The Pergamum Altar frieze, the antique sculpture collection of the Dresden Albertinum, the collection of the Dresden Historical Museum, the works of nineteenth- and twentieth-century German artists from the National Gallery in Berlin, and the archival collections could be returned. But all other trophy works should remain in the Soviet Union as compensation for Soviet losses from the museums of Russia, Belorussia and Ukraine.

The art historians pointed out that the museum buildings of the GDR had not been rebuilt, which meant that 'not all of the returned valuables could be kept in normal conditions'. Furthermore, they complained, there were in the USSR parts of divided collections whose other parts were in West Germany, as in the case of the former Kaiser Friedrich Museum in Berlin. It made sense to return such collections only after the reunification of the country.[25]

This letter was an open revolt. The curators were accusing the government of a short-sighted policy and proposing to delay the return of art trophies until the reunification of Germany. The Ministry of Culture had a problem: it was impossible to ignore a letter signed by such influential figures, but nobody wanted to argue with the unpredictable Nikita Khrushchev.

THE SECOND RETURN

In June 1957 Khrushchev finally destroyed the 'old guard' in the Politburo. At a meeting of the Presidium of the Central Committee, Kaganovich, Molotov, Saburov and their supporters demanded his expulsion and were supported by a majority of the Presidium, including, surprisingly, Minister of Foreign Affairs Alexander Shepilov, who belonged to the young generation of Soviet politicians. It was proposed to Khrushchev that he become minister of agriculture. One of the major accusations against him was his unpredictable foreign policy.

Khrushchev prevailed, and his enemies lost their positions. In October the last one went: Marshal Zhukov, who had been recalled from exile to become defence minister after Stalin's death but who had displayed too much independence for Khrushchev, was dismissed. Under the circumstances, Nikolai Mikhailov, the minister of culture, had no desire to begin another discussion about the wisdom of Khrushchev's foreign policy. He apparently sympathized with Kaganovich and Molotov, believing that his fortunes were more likely to thrive if they prevailed. But after their defeat, his position in the Soviet hierarchy became weaker and he had to protect even his relatively modest rank. To complain against an important part of the Khrushchev reformist foreign policy – the return of trophy art – was risky, if not political suicide.

Support came from an unexpected quarter. In December 1957 Viktor Zorin, the deputy minister of foreign affairs, sent his thoughts about the trophy problem to the Central Committee. Zorin did not want the trophy works of art exhibited before their return to Germany. He considered it 'not politically advisable' to let the Soviet people know what they were giving up, since they were getting nothing in exchange. Unexpectedly, the Department of Culture of the Central Committee supported this idea.[1]

In February 1958 Mikhailov took a risk. He proposed the return to East Germany of only 1,375,000 of the 1,990,000 objects that had been found. Both this proposal and Zorin's recommendation were supported by Central Committee officials. But the angry Khrushchev sent the matter back to the Secretariat.[2]

Under these circumstances, the only thing Mikhailov could safely do was to remind everybody about the losses of the USSR during the war and to encourage the German side to keep on looking for lost Soviet works of art. In a letter to the Central Committee, Mikhailov reminded them that 'in the statement the mutual return of valuables removed during the war was mentioned, and this fact is well known to the Soviet public, which is awaiting the results of this exchange'.[3]

But the GDR could not return valuables removed from Soviet territory because they had already been returned to the USSR in 1947. And for the Soviets to halt the restitution of the German works of art was already impossible. On 13 May 1958, during a session of the Secretariat of the Central Committee, Khrushchev had insisted on the return of German cultural property according to the plan proposed by Guber and Butenko in the summer of 1957, but without waiting for the mutual gesture. The protest of the art historians was not heeded. The return had to begin on 15 October and had to be finished on 1 January 1959. About 400,000 objects, mainly numismatic collections, were cut from the list of objects to be returned, but most of the treasures claimed by the East Germans had to be sent back. Mikhailov was responsible for the execution of the Party order.

He issued a secret order on 24 May describing in great detail the duties of all organizations involved in the preparation of the return. The Pushkin and the Historical Museum in Moscow, the Hermitage in Leningrad, and the Museum of Western and Oriental Art in Kiev were named as the collecting points. Trophy objects housed in various state agencies and institutions were to be delivered to these museums. There would be exhibitions of 'rescued masterpieces' in Moscow and Leningrad. The minister warned everyone that 'because of the exceptional political importance' of the planned return, everything must be done on time.[4]

Nikolai Danilov, deputy culture minister, was at Vnukovo airport on 25 June to meet a delegation from the East German culture ministry that came to negotiate the return of the German works of art. Fyodor Petrov, deputy head of the department of the visual arts of the ministry, was also there; he had been the last head of the Arts

Committee trophy brigade in Berlin. Andrei Guber, who had been protesting so violently against the return of works of art, was also present. He informed his German colleagues about the objects on their list of claims that had been found in the secret depositories of Soviet museums. The Central Committee had made the decision to give the trophies back and protests were a waste of time.

The protocol that determined the fate of hundreds of thousands of works of art was signed on 30 June. The Germans agreed to pay the expenses of packing and transporting the returning objects. It was not a very big price. The 'mutual' aspect of the return was forgotten. And of course ritual words about 'German cultural valuables saved during military operations by the Soviet Army' were attached to the protocol.[5]

But the East Germans knew the rules of the game. When Irina Kuznetsova, a curator at the Pushkin Museum, showed German colleagues the paintings selected for return, they stated that some of the canvases should be left in the USSR because they were from the collections of Charlottenburg, in West Berlin. Kuznetsova wrote on the list of trophy paintings the words 'British zone of occupation'. Thanks to this exchange, Pietro da Cortona's *Venus and Cupid*, canvases by Antoine Pesne and Droohsloot, and *Portrait of a Noble* by the famous eighteenth-century Russian painter Fyodor Rokotov remained in the secret depository of the Pushkin.[6]

To clear up such confusion, Nikolai Danilov sent a secret message to the Soviet Embassy in Berlin asking the diplomats to explain which museums were in the 'democratic sector' of the city. On 19 July Kochumasov, a counsellor in the embassy, reported back to Moscow with the list. His message, which he read over the telephone, ended with the mysterious phrase: 'According to the information of our friends, a castle named Fabaar doesn't exist in either East or West Germany.' Who the mysterious friends were and why the Ministry of Culture was looking for a castle named Fabaar is unknown.[7]

On 7 July the Pushkin Museum was closed and the permanent collection was once more placed in storage to make room for the show of the most important masterpieces that had been hidden in the secret depositories for thirteen years. Paintings from van Eyck to Edvard Munch, drawings from Bruegel to Picasso, antique marbles and sculptures by Rodin and Maillol, and priceless works of decorative art filled eleven galleries. In the twelfth, under the eyes of special guards, the treasures of the Dresden Grünes Gewölbe were displayed. The decision to return these beautiful objects made of precious metal and studded with gems had been taken at the last minute. In the museum's auditorium, the joint Soviet–German commission was meeting, but it was impossible to let the Germans into the depositories because hundreds of trophy objects that had not come from East Germany were hidden there.

The Central Committee hurried the cultural officials and brought forward the date of the openings to 7 August. To celebrate the return, Mikhailov presented the German delegation with Adolf Menzel's *Rolling Metal*, which had been chosen to play the role of symbol and was urgently sent from Leningrad to Moscow.[8] The Pushkin show was larger, but the Hermitage's was more impressive, with the Pergamum Altar and the famous head of Nefertiti on display.

A few weeks before the opening, the editors of the main Soviet newspapers were invited to the Ministry of Culture and told what to write about the event. On 30 July a strange document with the name 'Timing of Publications in the Soviet Press Concerning the Return of German Cultural Valuables to the GDR' was signed by Nikolai Danilov. The timetable of the future publications, including articles that had to be written by Grotewohl and Ulbricht, covered the period from the opening of the exhibitions to the beginning of January 1959.[9] But despite the careful planning, the press campaign was not as enthusiastic as it had been for the Dresden masterpieces. The problem was that it was difficult to explain how and by whom a million works of art had been 'saved'.

Some of the participants in the trophy crusade took an active part in the preparation of the second return. Fyodor Petrov, the last head of the Berlin brigade, was a ministry official. Stepan Churakov spent a year in the Pushkin Museum restoring trophies. Alexander Zamoshkin had become the director of the Pushkin and prepared the exhibition. Sergei Sidorov, the director of the Restoration Workshop, was frantically busy trying to patch up damaged canvases and crumbling sculptures.

Igor Grabar, who first proposed the idea of equivalents, and Viktor Lazarev, who played an important role in the looting of Berlin, were not involved in the return and, it seems, tried to keep their distance.

Some of the brigade experts came to sad ends. The energetic Alexander Manevsky was fired during the campaign against cosmopolitanism because of his Czech origin and died soon after, forgotten by his colleagues. Belokopitov and Voloshin, whose careers were ruined as a result of their trophy activities, tried to forget about everything connected with their stay in Berlin. Belokopitov confessed that he had refused to visit the exhibition in the Pushkin because he was afraid of being overcome with emotion.[10]

Ilya Tsirlin, an art historian who had worked in the Zoo tower and visited Königsberg, became one of the main figures of the Soviet artistic underground. He was a close friend of the poet Genrikh Sapgir, organized the first apartment exhibitions of dissident art, and finally was accused of various crimes, including homosexuality. He lost his official position and the possibility of publishing in the Soviet press. He died in mysterious circumstances, aged forty, soon after the second return.[11]

Mikhailov did not manage to keep his job as minister of culture. The year after the second return, Khrushchev sent him into honourable exile Soviet style: he appointed him ambassador to Indonesia.

Three hundred freight wagons full of trophies were sent to the GDR. The works of art that had travelled east fourteen years earlier were returning. By the middle of January 1959, 1,569,176 trophy objects and 121 boxes of books and photographs from the secret depositories of the museums of Moscow, Leningrad and Kiev had been returned to the GDR.[12]

In May 1960 the Secretariat of the Central Committee turned again to the problem of trophy art. It was decided that the 'return ... of cultural valuables temporarily kept in the territory of the Soviet Union is completed'. Mikhail Pervukhin, the Soviet ambassador to the GDR, was ordered to sign the final protocol. No notice of this event was published in the Soviet press.[13]

After the fall of Khrushchev, the problem of trophy art was almost forgotten, although about one million trophy objects remained hidden in the USSR. Works of art from West German museums, objects removed by the Nazis from at least three countries, books, archives, photographs and other materials were buried in cellars, used as decorations in state dachas, and stored in depositories closed to the public.

The official loot collected by the trophy brigades was hidden, but 'unofficial' plunder was another matter entirely. Thousands of paintings, drawings and *objets d'art* privately looted from Germany circulated on the art market, both legal and illegal, in Moscow, Leningrad, Kiev and other Soviet cities. The prices were low, and sometimes looted masterpieces sold for almost nothing. Trophy paintings and drawings still bearing the seals and labels of German museums were on sale in official state-run antique shops and in the hands of black market dealers.

The well-known collector Viktor Magits recalls that at the beginning of the 1960s, when most postwar private collections were established, he discovered in a state-run shop on the Arbat a set of bisque reliefs depicting Napoleon and Josephine. When he removed the frames, he found on the back of one a paper label written in German with the words: 'The end of 1940. Our Fatherland and Führer Adolf Hitler won the great war with France. I took these portraits of Emperor Napoleon and Empress Josephine as souvenirs from a French castle . . .' Looted from France, the reliefs had been looted again from Germany.[14]

Magits was accosted one day outside an antique shop by an old man who noticed him looking with interest at the paintings in the window. The old man had an old painting he wanted to sell. It was a panel by Andrea del Brescianino, a follower of Raphael. The old man explained that he had looted it during the war. It was broken because he and his comrades had used it as a camp table.[15]

Museums also bought looted works of art, but quietly. The owners often did not know that their attempts to sell 'souvenirs' taken from Germany by their fathers or grandfathers were not exactly legal. The museums would sternly inform them that their treasures had been stolen from foreign museums and then offer to buy them for very little. In this way many paintings with German museum labels joined the other works already stored in the special depositories.

Most Western European works of art in Soviet private collections are of trophy origin. Almost every serious collector who was interested in German, French or Dutch art had some objects that appeared in the USSR after 1945. Feliks Vishnevsky, probably the most important private collector of the postwar period, vastly enlarged his collection during the 1950s and early 1960s, when the possibilities for the connoisseur were unlimited. A curator at the Historical Museum, Vishnevsky was called the 'dustbin man', not only because he always wore a dirty old suit but because he literally found treasures in dustbins. He began to collect at the end of the 1920s and was arrested twice for 'illegal dealings in antiques' – private collecting was not prohibited, but it was not entirely legal either. During the early 1950s, when Moscow was flooded with private trophies whose owners had no idea of their value, he began to pay special attention to Western European art. He owned twenty-five prints and drawings from the Bremen Kunsthalle, including works by Rembrandt and Dürer; panels from the Dresden Gallery's famous Torgau Altar by Lucas Cranach; and paintings by Luca Giordano, Karl Schinkel and Max Klinger from the National Gallery in Berlin.[16]

THE ART GULAG

One spring night in 1962 a thief climbed through a window of the Water Tower of the Troitse-Sergeyevsky Monastery in Zagorsk, seventy kilometres north of Moscow.[1] He spent a very short time there. Perhaps he was a nervous amateur, or perhaps he heard a noise that alarmed him. At any rate, he stayed just long enough to open a cupboard that stood right inside the window and grab the first things he saw. Six trophy objects included in the 'special inventory' of the Pushkin Museum disappeared for ever.

At the end of 1961 the museum's secret depository had been temporarily moved to the Water Tower. After the return of hundreds of thousands of works of art, books and archives to the GDR, museum officials had decided to clean up the Greek Yard, which was packed with trophy furniture from the seventeenth and eighteenth centuries. The museum desperately needed storage space, and early in 1959 the Ministry of Culture had proposed as a depository the monastery in Pereslavl Zalessky, a little town 200 kilometres north of Moscow.[1] Those were the years of Khrushchev's anti-church campaign. Dozens of churches were closed and many were destroyed. By converting the Pereslavl Zalessky Monastery into a depository, the ministry thought it would resolve the Pushkin's space problem and at the same time save a monument of old Russian architecture from town authorities who might very well have destroyed it in their anti-religious zeal. A truck convoy set off for the old town, which was situated near the picturesque Pleshcheyevo Lake. The trophy furniture was stored in the monastery's huge empty cathedral. Finally the Greek Yard could be opened to visitors.

But a year and a half later it became clear that the objects were deteriorating in the unheated building, which had holes in the roof. The restorers found it very difficult to travel so far from town, so there was no control at all over conditions there. The furniture was cracked and covered with mould. It was obvious that a new depository had to be found. Andrei Guber remembered the so-called Special

Archive of the Ministry of Culture, situated in the Troitse-Sergeyevsky Monastery in Zagorsk, and he went there to negotiate the possibility of moving the ill-fated furniture.[2]

Troitse-Sergeyevsky was founded in the fourteenth century by Russia's most revered saint, Sergei Radonezhsky, beside a miraculous spring. It became the country's pre-eminent monastery, drawing pilgrims of all classes, from czars to beggars, to pray to the saint's relics, drink the miraculous waters, and kneel in wonder before Andrei Rublev's *Holy Trinity*, the most beautiful of all Russian icons. In 1918 Lenin turned out the monks, and in 1920 the monastery became a museum. The great icon was deposited in the Tretyakov Gallery. In 1946 Stalin returned some property to the Russian Orthodox Church in thanks for its support during the war, including some of the monastery buildings, and in 1953 the Moscow Theological Academy and the church's oldest seminary were installed here. One of the church patriarch's residences is in the monastery complex, as well as the graves of two patriarchs, whom the government would not allow to be buried in the Kremlin, their traditional resting place.[3]

The Special Archive was unusual. Established in 1951, when officials decided to purge the museums of the 'degenerate art' of the late nineteenth and early twentieth centuries, it was a kind of political prison for works of art. Museum curators had been hiding 'ideologically harmful' masterpieces since the first campaign against formalism in the 1930s, and in the 1950s cultural officials decided to get rid of these dangerous works. They were taken from the Tretyakov Gallery and other museums, delivered to Zagorsk, and placed in the empty buildings of the monastery, where church officials coexisted with the monastery museum personnel.

Olga Yesipova, the curator of the Special Archive, was a well-educated art historian and experienced museum curator. She was interested in modern Russian art and agreed immediately to become the director of this art gulag, realizing that she could use the position to protect the masterpieces she loved. Yesipova not only created more or less normal museum conditions in the building in which the exiled canvases were kept, but transformed it into a kind of museum by appointment only, quietly showing the prohibited works to interested people. Very soon the monastery became a place of pilgrimage not only for believers but for art lovers who wanted to see the productions of the Russian *avant-garde*.

Sometimes Yesipova showed guests the big portrait of Marshal Zhukov by Vasily Yakovlev. When the marshal was exiled to the Urals, his portrait was imprisoned in the monastery. Alexander Gerasimov's portrait of a group of Red Army commanders was also hidden there. Most of them had been executed by order of Stalin in 1937.

The Zagorsk Archive should have had the words 'Sic Transit Gloria Mundi' inscribed above the door. Through ironies of fate the images of the persecutors often joined the images of those they had persecuted. Portraits of Lavrenty Beria, and all paintings in which he was a character, were sent to Zagorsk after the arrest of the powerful secret police chief in 1953. After Khrushchev's famous speech at the 20th Party Congress in 1956 attacking the 'cult of personality' of Stalin, which began an abortive attempt at de-Stalinization, convoys of trucks loaded with paintings and statues glorifying the late dictator began to arrive at Troitse-Sergeyevsky. Stalin's death mask and casts of his hands, made by Sergei Merkurov, finally appeared there as well. Later, when Khrushchev overcame the 'anti-Party' group of Molotov, Kaganovich, and Malenkov, the portraits of his enemies were exiled to the Zagorsk Archive. But the same fate awaited the images of the Kremlin reformer. After his fall in 1964 all paintings and portraits depicting Khrushchev were seized from museums and state institutions and hidden in the monastery. Images of the smiling Khrushchev embracing Fidel Castro in a Russian birch forest, painted during the Cuban missile crisis, joined portraits of Stalin working in his Kremlin study. Later the Zagorsk Archive housed portraits of Khrushchev's victorious rival Leonid Brezhnev dressed in his clownish marshal's uniform. Even today many heroic images of former leaders of the USSR rest, covered with dust, in the Carpenters Tower of the Troitse-Sergeyevsky Monastery.

When Guber presented his plan to remove trophy works of art to the Zagorsk Archive, Yesipova was alarmed. The Pushkin Museum wanted to resolve the problem of the trophies for ever. Guber wanted to move to Zagorsk not only the furniture in Pereslavl Zalessky but hundreds of thousands of trophy art objects stored in the museum. Yesipova agreed to this plan only after the Ministry of Culture promised to enlarge the staff of the archive and to equip one of the empty towers as a depository. The Beer Tower (named for the commodity that had been stored there in earlier days), which had been renovated not long before by the architect Viktor Baldin, was chosen. While it was being prepared, some of the objects arrived from the Pushkin Museum and had to be stored temporarily in the Water Tower, where the theft took place.

The huge space of the Beer Tower was divided into three levels. A heating system was installed, and the trophies began to arrive in the spring of 1962.[4] The paintings were housed on the second level, along with 5,957 graphics and two cases of pottery. Among the paintings were canvases by Lucas Cranach, van Dyck, Guido Reni, Murillo, and Corot. The graphics included works by Dürer, Michelangelo and Poussin, as well as 1,157 Oriental prints. The furniture from Pereslavl Zalessky was stored on the first level. Here too were arms and armour and 674 sculptures, 215 of them Italian sculptures of the Renaissance, including works by Donatello, Verrocchio, and Nicola Pisano.

The first level of the Beer Tower gave rise to rumours about appalling storage conditions in the Zagorsk Special Archive. The rare visitor was shocked by the sight of the huge below-ground space packed with dozens of sculptures in deplorable condition. Most of them had been damaged in Germany or in transit to the USSR. Wood sculptures were losing their paint and gilding; heads and fingers were broken off. The furniture from Pereslavl Zalessky was unrestored. Many of the sculptures had been badly damaged by the fire in the Friedrichshain Leitturm. Museum restorers needed help to cope with all this destruction, but a wide-scale effort using various specialists was not possible because of the demand for secrecy. It was not even possible to organize regular conservation. The restorers could only record the new 'illnesses' of the works of art but could not help them.

The depositories situated on the second and third levels looked much better. Most of the 7,142 objects of applied art were stored on the third level. The collections of trophy textiles, tapestries, porcelain, and Oriental arms are still stored in their original German crates and cupboards.[5]

The Pushkin curators spent a year and a half in Zagorsk arranging the depository, an exhausting job. The work was completed at the beginning of 1963, and the depository was transferred officially to the supervision of Olga Yesipova, but the curators of the Pushkin continued to control it as well and to send restorers at intervals. Since then nothing has changed in the Beer Tower of the Troitse-Sergeyevsky

Monastery. Restorers visit the depository in Zagorsk (now called Sergiev Posad) every three months for one day, but they can examine and provide emergency treatment for only about ten pictures during each visit. To treat the whole collection would take five to seven years.

The curators of the Pushkin Museum visit it more often, but the main responsibility belongs to three curators of the Special Archive. Day after day, year after year, they check the climate-control equipment and close the tower in the evening. Only once, in 1986, a fire in the monastery disturbed the established routine. Fortunately, neither saints nor trophies were damaged, but the alarm was so great that even Boris Yeltsin, at the time head of the Moscow Communist Party organization, drove out to Zagorsk. Then everything returned to normal.

The exiled 'degenerate' art long ago returned to the halls of the Tretyakov Gallery and the Russian Museum in Leningrad. Socialist Realism has become fashionable, and paintings depicting the 'prohibited' leaders of the country from Stalin to Brezhnev are seen today in museum exhibitions. Only the trophy works from German, French, Polish and Austrian collections continue to languish in exile, although Moscow has finally admitted the existence of the depositories.

In addition to the works in the Beer Tower, there are more than 200,000 trophy objects in the Pushkin Museum itself. The most valuable trophy paintings are stored in the basement; graphics, including the famous Koenigs Collection from Rotterdam, are in the mansion next to the museum that houses the department of graphics; and tens of thousands of books from German libraries, their seals cut out, are in the library. Until late in 1994, when the museum grudgingly admitted that it held the Trojan gold, the treasure was hidden in an unexpected place. In the tour guides' office is an iron door, hidden behind a curtain. Staff members call it 'Pinocchio's door' (because in the Russian version of the story, a magic door hidden by a painting of a fireplace gives entry to an enchanted paradise, rather like the Communist ideal society). The iron door leads to a two-room depository. The first room is where all the documents connected with trophy works of art are kept, including the inventories of the collections that were returned. In the second room are safes full of objects made of precious metals. It was in one of these safes that the Trojan treasure, as well as gold objects from Cottbus, Eberswalde and

Holm, was kept for almost fifty years. After the official admission that the Trojan gold was in the museum, it was taken upstairs to the department of archaeology to be studied and prepared for exhibition in 1996.

The trophies are shared among different departments in the Historical Museum as well. In the numismatics department the curators have organized a small private exhibition of the military decorations of Napoleon and Field Marshals von Moltke and Blücher. The Spanish Order of the Holy Spirit and the Danish Order of the White Elephant are especially impressive.

In the Hermitage also the trophies are divided among different departments. Among the riches here are seventy-eight paintings, including works by Manet, Signac, van Gogh, Renoir, Cézanne, Matisse, and Picasso, that belonged to the Krebs Collection. The great canvas by Degas, *Place de la Concorde*, from the Gerstenberg Collection, is here too, along with silver from Dessau. In 1994 the director of the Hermitage, Mikhail Piotrovsky, finally admitted that the trophies were in the museum, and in April 1995, seventy-four of the paintings were put on exhibition.

In the Kiev Museum of Western and Oriental Art are stored the graphics collection of the Berlin Art Academy and prints from the Dresden Gallery. Paintings by Franz Marc and Oskar Kokoschka from German private collections are also hidden in this museum's depositories.

Trophy works were distributed to other institutions as well. Many dachas of the Council of Ministers and the Central Committee were decorated with 'secondary' objects of trophy origin. In the sanatorium of the Academy of Sciences in the Moscow suburb of Uzkoe, there are more than a dozen trophy paintings from the museums of Potsdam and Charlottenburg.

'What's that?' the sculptor Viktor Goncharov asked the barber who was shaving him. He pointed to the sculpture used as a hat rack that stood in the hall of the shop on Pushkin Street.

'I brought it from Germany, but I don't know what to do with it,' the barber answered. 'We don't have enough space at home, and my wife is mad because she thinks it's immoral to keep a sculpture of a naked woman at home.'

'Sell it to me,' the sculptor proposed. 'I'll give you three rubles for it.' The barber agreed.

The hat rack was a marble torso of Diana wearing a quiver. It was made by the French sculptor Houdon in 1777 for the Polish king Stanislaw II Poniatowski. It was in the Dresden collection, and in all monographs on Houdon it is said to have disappeared during the war. The sculpture was spotted by Goncharov at the end of the 1960s, when the trophy topic had been forgotten.[6]

On 6 December 1967, Vladimir Popov, the deputy minister of culture, gave his East German counterpart, Horst Brasch, four paintings and three drawings from the Dresden Gallery 'found recently on the territory of the USSR'.[7] The most valuable was a painting by Lucas Cranach, *Portrait of the Elector Johann des Bestundigen*. It had been offered to the Pushkin Museum by a private individual and purchased in 1953, but it was not returned either in 1955 or in 1959. In 1967 officials decided to organize a mini-return of trophy works to the GDR. Andrei Guber received an order to compose a short but impressive list of trophy canvases. The old curator included in this list an oil sketch by Rubens, *Monument to the Emperor Albrecht the Second*, from the Aachen Museum and some nineteenth-century pictures from Berlin, but officials decided to give back only works of art of Dresden origin.[8] The return was not mentioned in the press; it was a quiet deal between governments.

Goncharov decided at the end of the 1960s to show his treasure to the experts. He could not believe he had bought a genuine masterpiece of French art in a barber shop for only three rubles. When experts in the Pushkin assured him that the piece was a genuine Houdon, he offered to donate it to the museum, but the curators recommended that he present it to a provincial museum instead. Their reason was simple: they knew the sculpture belonged to Dresden and were afraid that it would be returned there sooner or later. Goncharov followed their advice and donated the piece to the museum in his native city of Krasnodar.[9]

During the 1970s, quiet returns continued. In 1972 the Soviet government returned to Hungary some paintings by the famous Hungarian artist Munkacsy.[10] In 1975 the collections of the Ethnographic Institute in Berlin-Dahlem and some ethnographic objects from Hamburg were sent to the Ethnographic Museum in Leipzig and quietly stored there.[11]

The last known return took place in 1986, when an investigator of the Kuntsevo department of the Moscow militia presented to Krista Teschner, cultural attaché of the East German Embassy in Moscow, a painting attributed to the School of Rubens, *Landscape with the Christ Child and John the Baptist*. The transfer took place in the presence of two German art historians and Ksenia Yegorova, a curator of the Pushkin Museum. How the canvas came into the hands of the militia and why it was given directly to the embassy is not known. It was the last scene in the long story of the return of cultural trophies to the GDR.[12]

In 1989 the Berlin Wall collapsed and 'the first state of German workers and peasants' ceased to exist. The problem of trophy art became the problem of the united German state.

REVELATIONS

THE PAPER TRAIL

In 1984, after his graduation from Moscow State University, Konstantin Akinsha returned to Kiev, his native city, and shortly thereafter began to work at the Museum of Western and Oriental Art. The museum had been familiar to him since his childhood. Visiting it with his grandfather, Akinsha had particularly admired the Japanese swords and the dark Flemish canvases depicting the ancient gods he had read about in his book on Greek mythology. The magnificent collection had been assembled by the Ukrainian nobleman Bogdan Khanenko, who donated it to the city of Kiev in 1917, along with the building he had constructed for it.

By 1984, when Akinsha arrived, the beautiful old building was literally falling apart. The staff included very few knowledgeable people, and no serious research was undertaken. Akinsha soon realized that many paintings belonging to the collection and published in old catalogues had disappeared. Research into the matter showed that most of them had been removed by the Nazis during the occupation in 1943. But there was no catalogue of the missing works.

In the library, which was disorderly and lacked even an inventory, Akinsha found numerous rare editions and even manuscripts that bore the seals and stamps of German libraries; most of them were from the Berlin Academy of Arts. When he asked where these books came from, he was told that they were war trophies. His curiosity disturbed the museum administration, and Akinsha noticed that the secretary of the Party organization was watching him with suspicion. Some of his colleagues told him that she was asking what Akinsha talked about with them, but he did not pay serious attention to this disagreeable fact.

The director of the museum was an elderly woman with bright red hair and an emotional disposition. She was known as the author of a propaganda book directed against Western contemporary art called *Bourgeois Art: The Destruction of the Image*. Her large, pleasant office was well furnished: there was a monumental German Baroque cupboard, a nineteenth-century set of shelves in Rococo Revival style, a solid safe that contained the museum seal, and ugly polished desks and chairs in the style of the 'softened brutalism' of the early 1970s. On the wall behind her chair was the usual portrait of Lenin, whose kindly smile was in sharp contrast to her own habitual expression of dissatisfaction. On the opposite wall there were two Flemish paintings: a landscape by Vinckeboons and a large panel painting by the Master of the Prodigal Son depicting Susanna and the Elders. Neither picture was listed in the museum catalogue. Akinsha learned from his colleagues that they had come from Berlin collections after the war. Eventually he discovered that the paintings in the director's study were not the only ones in the museum that the staff preferred not to talk about.

The curator of graphics told Akinsha that some months before his appearance in the museum her department had been significantly enriched in an unusual way. A truck loaded with dusty portfolios and albums had arrived at the museum from the library of one of the ministries, which was moving to a new building. In the process of removal, ministry personnel had discovered a rich collection of trophy works in the basement, where they had been deposited at the end of the war and then forgotten. The ministry had decided to send them to the museum. One day when the director and other high-ranking officials were absent, the curator invited Akinsha into the depository, situated in a room that was closed to the public. It was completely occupied by shelves piled with portfolios, heavy albums and files. Grey portfolios bound in canvas contained drawings by Rubens and gouaches by Emil Nolde, etchings by Chagall and Archipenko. There were complete sets of Piranesi prints. One portfolio contained drawings by Goethe and letters written by his sisters. Most of the seals were from the Berlin Academy of Art and the Dresden Kupferstichkabinett.

For forty years the collection had been forgotten, but almost nothing had disappeared. In one big album containing seventeenth-century Italian drawings of nudes, a couple of the drawings had been barbarously cut out with scissors. Probably a technical worker in the library had stolen them, and not for their aesthetic qualities. Otherwise the treasures were intact.

Akinsha left the museum in 1986 and began postgraduate work at the Research Institute of Art History in Moscow. Perestroika was flourishing, Andrei Sakharov was giving speeches in Parliament, and the intelligentsia was in a state of euphoria. Everyone was reading books that had been prohibited only a short time before, and every issue of *Ogonyok* magazine, with its exposés of the abuses of the past, was snapped up as soon as it appeared. The real history of the Soviet Union was being uncovered. It seemed to Akinsha that the time had come to discuss openly the problem of the secret trophies.

In 1987 a new cultural organization was founded in Moscow – the first independent public organization since the Revolution – whose main aim was to support cultural initiatives. It was called the Culture Fund, and its head was the respected scholar Dmitry Likhachev, a specialist in Old Russian literature. Likhachev was known as a person who opposed the regime, although he was not a dissident. Akinsha paid the fund a visit and convinced an official there that the new organization should address the problem of trophy works. When the official decided that Akinsha was not a madman but a postgraduate student at the prestigious Research Institute, he promptly made him a member of the Commission on the Return of Cultural Heritage.

By the time the commission met, the Fund had moved from its shabby building to a luxurious mansion on Gogolevsky Boulevard that had belonged before the Revolution to Sergei Tretyakov, the brother of the famous collector. The car park in front was filled with new black Volga limousines, and the doorkeeper looked like a typical retired KGB man. The bearded intellectuals who had filled the old house were gone. Instead, a well-dressed man appeared and asked Akinsha who he was.

Among the bureaucrats at the Fund's new headquarters, Akinsha met a man who looked more like an Old Testament prophet with his thick, unruly hair and grey beard. The badge of the Union of Journalists was pinned to the lapel of his rumpled jacket. He was Yevgeny Levit, a correspondent for *Komsomolskaya Pravda*, the newspaper of the Central Committee of the Komsomol, the Communist youth organization. Like many Soviet journalists of his generation, Levit managed to combine complete loyalty to the regime with very mild liberalism. In the mid-1970s he had published the only Soviet book dedicated to the problem of works of art that had disappeared from the USSR during the war. It was called *Only the Photographs Remain* and was published by APN, the Agency of Press and News, which was reputedly run by the KGB. Levit had collected interesting information, but the final result was quite strange. Aside from valuable photographs of works from Soviet museums removed by the Nazis and reproductions of interesting historical documents, it included typical propaganda texts, one of which, for some unknown reason, dealt with the 'crimes against humanity' committed by Israeli soldiers against Arabs. Later Levit told Akinsha interesting stories about his experiences collecting materials. At the beginning of the 1970s it was an extremely difficult task. Many cultural officials had concluded that information not only about the trophy depositories but also about Russian works of art looted during the war had to be kept secret. When Levit went to Kiev to collect information about Nazi looting, he was immediately arrested by the KGB and released only after phone calls to his newspaper in Moscow.

The Commission on the Return of Cultural Heritage met around a huge conference table covered with green felt in a vast room decorated with massive arches of dark oak and an impressive Gothic Revival fireplace. Akinsha had the strange feeling that he had stumbled into a meeting of a district Party committee in Dracula's castle. The commission's head described its ambitious aims. He wanted just about everything of significance returned to Russia: not just objects but the archives of Russian writers, artists and composers who had died abroad and even their bodily remains buried in the cemeteries of France, Germany and America. Akinsha listened attentively to his speech about 'mutual' restitution. It was necessary not only to compile a catalogue of works of art missing from Soviet museums but to find the paintings exported from German museums by the Soviets. The commission head stressed that restitution had to be a 'two-way street', perhaps because Gorbachev in a recent speech had referred to Soviet foreign policy in the same terms.

The commission met a number of times over the next six months and talked a great deal, but the art historians who were invited decided they were wasting their time and stopped visiting the luxurious mansion on Gogolevsky Boulevard. Dmitry Likhachev published many articles about the need for a spiritual renaissance in Russia, and Raisa Gorbachev, the patron saint of the organization, no doubt enjoyed thinking of herself as an enlightened empress of the order of Catherine the Great. But the bureaucrats who ran the Culture Fund did not have a deep understanding of cultural problems. The real power of the organization was Georgy Myasnikov, who had been secretary of the district Party committee in Penza and had become famous for his cultural undertakings. At the beginning of the 1980s he had created in Penza an institution called the Museum of One Painting. Myasnikov had chairs installed in a hall and a single painting, borrowed from one of the city's museums, hung on the wall like a cinema screen. Each day a group of people were admitted to sit and contemplate the painting in complete silence. The fame of this surrealistic institution got Myasnikov his appointment as Likhachev's deputy.

When it became clear to him that the Culture Fund was not going to resolve the trophy question, Akinsha tried to publish an article in the Soviet press. His first attempt was so heavily censored that it made no sense at all. Then Akinsha tried *Ogonyok* magazine, the most liberal in the country, but its editor, Vitaly Korotich, was not interested.

'Why do you want to return all those works of art to the Germans?' he asked impatiently. 'The topic is interesting, but the right moment hasn't come.'

If the liberal Korotich would not publish an article about the secret depositories, Akinsha realized, then nobody would.

Akinsha had met Grigorii Kozlov at Moscow State University in the late 1970s, where they were both studying art history. They shared an interest in Russian and Soviet private collections and had heard stories from elderly collectors about the works of art that had turned up in the Soviet Union after the war. Just as Akinsha had learned about the trophy works in the Kiev museum, Kozlov had discovered that there were secret depositories in the Pushkin, including the one behind Pinocchio's Door.

His office was in the Church of Saint Antipii, which stood beside the Pushkin. It had been used for a long time as a depository, and now it also housed the new Museum of Private Collections, which was being organized as a branch of the Pushkin. The former rectory was filled with broken plaster copies of sculptures of Greek and Roman gods that had lost their arms and noses during their long museum life and finally found themselves under the vaults of a Russian Orthodox church.

It was here that the Pushkin Museum's specialists offered their expertise every Thursday. Anyone could bring in a work of art or an *objet d'art*, and for three rubles the specialists would examine it and tell the owner who had made it and where it came from. Kozlov often saw the heirs of officers and soldiers who came to the museum with trophy paintings. It became clear to him that trophies had been taken from Germany not only by state agencies but by private individuals: everyone – soldiers, officers and generals – had looted.

In the autumn of 1987, when Kozlov discovered the piles of documents being shredded in the basement of the Ministry of Culture, he brought what he was able to salvage to his office in the church. The next day he called Akinsha, and they began in earnest their investigation into the secret depositories of trophy art.

In 1990 Chancellor Helmut Kohl of Germany and President Mikhail Gorbachev of the USSR signed the Treaty on Good-Neighbourliness, Partnership and Cooperation. Article 16 seemed to apply directly to war loot, with both sides agreeing that 'lost or unlawfully transferred art treasures which are located in their territory will be returned to their owners or their successors'. At the time the Germans did not know that vast quantities of trophy objects actually existed in the Soviet Union. But the secret was about to be broken. The following year Akinsha and Kozlov began publishing their findings in *ARTnews*. They wrote several articles describing the trophy brigades and the official campaign to remove works of art from Germany, and they listed some of the works that were still hidden in the Soviet Union. The news was quickly picked up in *Izvestia* and other Russian newspapers, and Moscow journalists besieged the Ministry of Culture for more information. The government's first response was silence. As pressure mounted during the summer and early autumn of 1991, ministry officials simply refused to answer questions, pleading that they had no information on the subject. But in the cultural establishment, people were taking sides.

After she read the *Izvestia* article, Irina Antonova, the museum official who had signed a receipt for trophy objects in 1946 and who was now head of the museum, called Kozlov into her office. Seated behind her large nineteenth-century oak desk, she immediately began to berate him. 'How did you dare to write about trophy art works when you have nothing to do with them – and in a foreign magazine?' she asked. 'You know the state importance of this problem and your responsibility not to spread information about it.'

Kozlov had put the museum, and Antonova personally, in a difficult position. According to the code of the International Council of Museums, it is unethical for a museum knowingly to keep objects

The Trinity St Sergius monastery in Zagorsk (now called Sergeyev Posad) was restored in the 1950s by Viktor Baldin to become a prison for trophy artworks. The Beer Tower (left of photograph) is the largest secret depository in Russia, with works from German, French, Polish and Austrian collections.

Stalin's death mask, made by Sergei Merkurov, shared the fate of the trophy masterpieces. After Khrushchev's attack on the 'cult personality' of the dead leader, the mask was hidden in Zagorsk.

In March 1993, a few hours before presenting 101 Bremen drawings to the German Embassy in Moscow, Konstantin Akinsha and Grigorii Kozlov (opposite, top) drew up a list in Akinsha's Moscow apartment. The cache included Dürer's watercolour *Landscape with a Castle Near a River* (opposite, below), Toulouse-Lautrec's lithograph *La Goulu* (right), and Adrian von Ostade's *Tavern Scene* (below). They had been kept under a sofa for half a century.

(Opposite) A shipping document for the Trojan gold. This 'Short Description of Museum Valuables Sent by Plane to Moscow' describes three crates that had been loaded onto the plane: 'These boxes were confiscated from a military installation – the anti-aircraft tower in the Zoo. The valuables packed in them belonged to the Museum for Pre- and Early History. The crates contain gold, silver, and other objects ... The most ancient objects are the Treasures from Troy (excavated by Schliemann) ...' The signature is that of Major Serafim Druzhinin, a member of the Berlin trophy brigade.

Two Heads, red and black chalk on paper, by Hans Baldung Grien (above), and *King David*, red chalk on paper, by Jacob Jordaens (right). Both drawings were part of the cache of Bremen drawings discovered by Akinsha and Kozlov under a sofa in a provincial city.

Приложение № 1

к отношению 83

83.

КРАТКАЯ ХАРАКТЕРИСТИКА МУЗЕЙНЫХ ЦЕННОСТЕЙ,
ОТПРАВЛЯЕМЫХ САМОЛЕТОМ В МОСКВУ.

Ящики №№ 1 - 3

Данные ящики из"яты из военного об"екта - из Зенитной Башни Зоологического сада. Находящиеся в них ценности принадлежали До-и-Древне-Историческому музею / *Museum für Vor- und Frühgeschichte* /. Ящики содержат в себе золотые, серебряные и др.предметы /ящик № 1 - золото и др.предметы, ящики № 2 и 3 - серебро и др.предметы/, относящиеся к различным эпохам, начиная с нового каменного века /две тысячи лет до нашей эры/ и кончая ранним средневековьем /до ХII века нашей эры/.

В основном это - предметы женских украшений и небольшие чаши и вазочки. Все эти ценности были найдены во время раскопок. Древнейшими произведениями являются сокровища из Трои /раскопки Шлимана, затем из Эберсвальде /УI-й век до нашей эры/, из Коттбуса /У век нашей эры/, и, наконец, из Хольма около Дризена /ХI век нашей эры/.

Шкаф № 1

Шкаф из"ят из того-же военного об"екта. В шкафу находится собрание гемм /резные камни-печатки, перстни и пр./.

Данная музейная коллекция / *Altes Museum* / является уникальной и представляет собой исключительную ценность, ибо содержит образцы гемм различных времен и народов, начиная с древнейших эпох.

При вскрытии шкафа в Зенитной башне Зоологического сада и беглом ознакомлении с его содержанием было установлено, что не все ячейки ящиков шкафа содержат в себе геммы.

    П.п. Майор   -   С.ДРУЖИНИН

17.УI-45 г.

    В е р н о -

    Майор -   /Волошин/

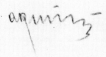

Manet's *Portrait of Rosetta Mauri*, from the Koehler collection, travelled to Moscow in 1945 on the same plane as the Trojan gold but wasn't mentioned in the shipping documents. It may have been carelessness – or a smuggling attempt.

Trophy artworks were distributed not only to museums but to sanatoria and government dachas. The Academy of Sciences sanatorium in Mozzhinka, near Moscow, is decorated with landscapes by the German 19th-century artist Wilhelm Schirmer. They belonged to the National Gallery in Berlin before the war.

Klaus Goldmann (centre of photograph, with magnifying glass), chief curator of the Museum for Pre- and Early History in Berlin, finally held the Trojan gold treasure in his hands in the Pushkin Museum, 26 October 1994.

Daumier's *Revolt*, from the Gersternberg collection of Berlin. It was sequestered in the Pushkin Museum for half a century after the collection was divided between the Pushkin and the Hermitage. The painting was finally exhibited in 1995.

illegally removed from another country. If such works are discovered in the collection, the museum is supposed to notify the legal owner.

'It's none of your business,' Antonova said. 'It's the responsibility of the museum administration. What did you think you would accomplish with your article?'

'I wanted to tell the truth,' Kozlov answered.

'There are different truths,' she said.

'I believe there is only one truth.'

'There are foolish truths and wise truths, and your truth is foolish. There is also justice. You are young and inexperienced, you didn't see Peterhof burned down, but I saw it. The Germans committed terrible crimes in our country, and the highest justice is on our side. We don't need to justify ourselves; we can dictate our conditions.'

'Among the trophy art works are masterpieces of world culture that are hidden, stolen from world civilization. And we are lying when we say those things are not in the USSR.'

'It's demagoguery,' Antonova shouted. She talked about the victims of the war whose blood had paid for the trophy works and whom Kozlov had betrayed, about the responsibility of the Germans, about morals and honour. She was looking not at Kozlov but through the open door of her office into the conference room, whose wall was decorated with a huge seventeenth-century tapestry of the Four Seasons. It was a trophy, as were the other two tapestries in the room. The many foreign visitors Antonova greeted here did not know that the room's decorations had been looted from Germany in 1945.

Antonova claimed that the trophy problem was already close to resolution and that the publication in an American magazine had done damage. 'You could provoke a situation where they' – she pointed at the ceiling, as if Gorbachev's office was on the floor above – 'will become afraid and return everything to the Germans free of charge!'

She was becoming more and more disturbed. Finally Kozlov offered to write a letter of resignation immediately, which she rejected. A few days later she held a meeting of department heads to discuss the question of his future. Some of his colleagues made angry speeches and asked for his blood. Others preferred neutrality and silence. Antonova told the accusers that it was impossible to fire Kozlov because the minister of culture, Nikolai Gubenko, had forbidden it. He was afraid of the reaction in the Western press. So Kozlov continued to work at the Museum of Private Collections. Some of his colleagues were afraid to talk to him, but others made a point of their friendliness.

There were three of them. They flashed their KGB identification cards so quickly that Kozlov could not read their names. They looked around the church with interest as they sat down at the table. Then the dark-haired one unexpectedly said, 'Please tell us about yourself.'

It was clear immediately that the silent grey-haired man in his forties was in charge. The man with dark hair and moustache did all the talking. The third was very young and seemed to be a trainee; he said nothing but watched the other two attentively.

'Where were you born, where did you graduate, what are you doing now?'

'Why do you need such information?' Kozlov asked. 'If you need my advice as an expert, let's discuss your problem. If you're interested in my biography, you can easily read my personal file in the museum.'

'Why are you reacting like this? We simply wanted to make your acquaintance,' the dark-haired one said in an aggrieved voice.

'With the help of private conversation,' the young one added, then looked to the older man for approval.

'That's right,' the dark-haired one continued pleasantly. 'We're not just chatting. We can make decisions that influence people's fate.'

'I'm an art historian,' Kozlov replied. 'If I know anything, it's about art. I can help with attributions or provenances, but I have no intention of influencing anyone's fate except my own.'

'It's no mistake,' the grey-haired one finally spoke. 'But don't be in such a hurry to refuse to talk to us about other people's fates and your own fate. Who knows, your life may change after this discussion.'

Kozlov was irritated by all these allusions. 'Be serious or find someone else to talk to,' he said impatiently. 'I'm busy.'

'We would like to know your opinion of your work, your colleagues, the situation in the art market. We're interested to know what you're thinking, what your values are.'

'I think this conversation is senseless. I can't understand what you want. We have more experienced experts in the museum. You should probably talk to them. I'll call the purchasing committee. Maybe they can help you.' Kozlov began to dial the number.

The dark-haired one shouted nervously: 'No, we want to talk to you.' But Kozlov was already speaking to a representative of the purchasing committee, telling her that three KGB men needed her help. She was not surprised because the KGB and the police often asked for expert advice. But the three men were in no hurry to leave. The dark-haired one kept on talking about 'the need to cooperate' and 'the importance of our meeting'. Finally Kozlov just stood up and said, 'I'll show you the way. The purchasing committee representative is waiting for you.'

The dark-haired man finally shut up. The grey-haired man said, 'Let's go, comrades.' On the threshold he turned back to Kozlov and asked, 'By the way, Grigorii Alexandrovich, why did you leave the Ministry of Culture?'

'I wanted a more interesting job,' Kozlov said.

'It seems that you're not bored now,' he smiled as they walked out.

At the beginning of June 1991, not long after the KGB visited Kozlov, Soviet museum directors met in Ivanovo, near Moscow. The problem of trophy art had become a major issue, and Gubenko gave a speech dedicated to it. He said that he and Antonova believed that trophy works should be returned only on a mutual basis: the contents of the special depositories should be returned to Germany only if the Germans sent back all the works that had disappeared from the USSR during the war. The museum directors were ordered not to reveal the contents of their special depositories until the Germans did the same – although there are no secret depositories in Germany. Gubenko condemned Kozlov and Akinsha, but he rejected any attempt at repression in the old style because it would be picked up by the Western press.

After the meeting, more of Kozlov's colleagues were afraid to talk to him, and his every step in the museum was watched, but he still managed to make some curious discoveries. He was ordered to collect some frames from the frame depository, which was located in a little nineteenth-century mansion not far from the museum's main building. It was packed from floor to ceiling with frames, stacked all over the floor, piled on shelves made of plywood and pipes, and hanging on the walls. The old house was in poor shape: patches of plaster had fallen off the walls, the floor was rotten, and the ceiling was supported by thick logs. There was dust everywhere and a pungent smell of mould. The curator, Olga Postnikova, was afraid to turn on the light because the wiring was so old and there was a petrol station nearby. In semi-darkness Kozlov was choosing frames when he noticed a paper label stuck to the back of an old one. It was so dirty that he had trouble making out the words: '828 H Rembrandt. *Joseph und Potifar's Frau*'. The seal was from the Picture Gallery of the Berlin museums.

Kozlov realized that many of the frames had come from trophy pictures. One of them had held Lorenzo Lotto's *St Sebastian* and another, Gerard David's *Crucifixion* from the same museum. Some of the frames came from the Weimar Museum. A big tondo frame on a shelf had a label with the Berlin seal and a handwritten inscription: '102 ... Botticelli. *Lilien Madonna*'. It had once been the frame for the famous *Virgin with a Choir of Angels* that is exhibited today in Berlin-Dahlem. How had these frames come to Moscow?

It did not take long to work out what had happened. The paintings had been hidden in Thuringia along with the gold of the Reichsbank and were found by the Americans. The frames were left behind and found by the Soviets. They were considered valuable, shipped home, and distributed to various museums. One old frame, according to its label, had belonged to Salviati's *Two Musicians* in Berlin before the war. A piece of paper with the words 'To Vladivostok' was stuck to it. It had travelled from Berlin to Moscow, and was now on its way to the Far East, where it would probably contain a Socialist Realist painting, and visitors to the Vladivostok museum would never know that the frame's history was so much more interesting than the picture's.

Kozlov made another important discovery in the church. A pile of boxes had been sitting in the rectory since the end of the 1960s. Everyone thought they contained reproductions of works of art and paid no attention to them, except to move them to a dry corner when the roof leaked. Finally, in the summer of 1991, a new place was found for the boxes, and workmen came to pick them up. When the tarpaulin that covered them was removed, Kozlov noticed that they were old and had German inscriptions on the sides. Interested in their possible German origin, he watched the staff of the reproductions department sort out their contents onto a large table. There were several copper plates, all relatively large. He picked one up and saw the image of a classical Roman-style stadium. A signature was engraved in the corner: Albert Speer.

It was a design for the gigantic stadium Hitler planned to erect for Nazi party rallies in Nuremberg, the 'ideological capital of the Reich'. It would seat 400,000 people and be three times as large as the Great Pyramid. A gigantic pit for the foundation was excavated, tons of granite were ordered, but the stadium was never built. Instead it became what Speer later called 'a picturesque lake'. The copper plates for his other projects covered the table. Looking at the designs for these grandiose, inhuman structures that were supposed to impress the world with the greatness of the Third Reich, Kozlov could not help thinking of Boris Iofan and his House of Soviets, which Stalin wanted to build on the site of the Cathedral of Christ the Saviour.

As the Ministry of Culture continued to do nothing about the trophy problem, members of the art community began to exert some pressure. The influential Soviet branch of the International Association of Art Critics asked the ministry to open the depositories, and five of the country's most prominent art historians wrote a letter to Culture Minister Gubenko urging him to resolve the fate of the hidden works. But a group of major museum directors produced a statement condemning the revelations as 'untimely'.

Finally, at a crowded and contentious press conference in October, Gubenko made the first official admission that secret depositories filled with looted art existed in Soviet museums and announced that a Commission on Restitution would be established on President Gorbachev's order to consider what to do with them. But, he added, the government had already decided to return cultural trophies only if it received in return objects of equivalent 'artistic quality' stolen from the USSR by the Germans. Gubenko made it clear that the Soviet government was in no hurry to solve the problem, warning that it would take years to find a solution. 'After this,' he concluded, 'it will be possible to say that the Second World War is over.'

The minister insisted that he did not know where the Trojan gold was and implied that the Western Allies had taken it. He gave an emotional speech about the destruction of Soviet museums by the Nazis, bitterly lamenting the masterpieces of Titian, Rubens and Jordaens that had been stolen from the museum in Rostov-on-Don. It was an unfortunate example because all of those pictures were nineteenth-century copies sent to Rostov-on-Don from the Hermitage in the 1930s. The museum director who received them fired off an angry letter to the Hermitage complaining that he had been sent such rubbish, but after the war the copies were included in the museum's list of losses as originals.

Two weeks later, the Association of Art Historians organized its own press conference – still a very unusual thing for a non-governmental body to do in the USSR, although no longer a dangerous one. Alexander Morozov, Dmitry Sarabianov, and Alexander Kamensky – three of the most prominent art historians in the USSR and signatories of the letter to Gubenko – wanted not only to criticize publicly the ministry's position but to support their former students Akinsha, Kozlov and Alexei Rastorguyev, a lecturer at Moscow State University who had been publishing articles about the secret depositories in the Soviet and Russian émigré press.

The Akinsha–Kozlov archive on trophy art had grown to an impressive size. Aside from the original documents found in the basement of the Ministry of Culture, they had many copies of archival material, video and audio tapes of interviews, books, and press clippings. After the publication of their first article in *ARTnews*, they decided to hide everything. Although the documents were forty years old, it was impossible to say what might happen if they were discovered – the laws regarding state secrets in the Soviet Union were also secret. The archive was broken up and stored with various friends and friends of friends. One batch was kept by an officer of the Afghan war veterans' association, and another batch was hidden in a greenhouse outside town, where some friends of friends were growing lilies for sale in the Moscow markets.

They were getting tired of carrying bags of documents from place to place. And they tended to forget where things were, which made research difficult. When they decided to write a second article and publish some of the documents, they needed a place to work, and a friend who was going abroad offered them a dacha in a little village on the outskirts of the city. One morning Kozlov taxied from place to place all around the city collecting the farflung archive and lugged it out to the dacha. He opened the door of the veranda and stopped, shocked. The house door was open; someone had chopped through it with an axe. In the entrance hall everything was upside down. A window was broken and there were spots of blood on the floor. His first thought was that the KGB had been there, but he was still alive and at large, so that did not seem likely. Fortunately, the owner of the dacha believed in good security. To reach the living quarters you had to get through four doors. Three of them had been crushed with the axe, but the fourth survived. The broken axe lay nearby.

Kozlov had to do something. If it was a genuine robbery attempt, he had to inform the police immediately. He and Akinsha were, after all, responsible for the house. But if it was a provocation, Kozlov would be better off escaping as quickly as possible. He grabbed the suitcases full of documents and ran to the railway station, took a suburban train to the Kiev Station in Moscow, deposited the suitcases in left luggage, and put the tickets in a safe-deposit box. Then he went back to the dacha. The police were already there. The mysterious intrusion had been a robbery attempt by a local drunkard. Fighting with the fourth door, he wounded himself and bled on the floor, broke the axe, and fled on a bicycle he stole from the entrance hall. It was kept as evidence and never returned.

After this, they got on with their work, with the help of friends. All documents on restitution had been deposited in the Central Archive of Literature and Art, but Kozlov and Akinsha suspected that they would not be allowed access to them, so they recruited friends who knew how to do archival work. The results exceeded their hopes. One of their helpers found all the documents connected to the Trojan treasure: they could trace it from Berlin to Moscow, from the list of works of art found in the Zoo tower through transport documents to the inventory of trophy works compiled in the Pushkin Museum in 1945, when the crates arrived there. These papers were accessible to anyone, but they were filed haphazardly, with lists of furniture bought for provincial libraries or equipment purchased for various cultural organizations. The filing system was more effective than secrecy. They published some of the documents in *ARTnews* and for the next two years they listened with amusement as cultural officials claimed that they did not know where the Trojan treasure was. Throughout the next year the new Minister of Culture, Yevgeny Sidorov, insisted that he was bound by state secrecy not to reveal information about the secret depositories and, in a show of liberalism, publicly asked the government and the president to declassify it. But it was there all the time, accessible to anyone who looked for it hard enough.

THE BREMEN DRAWINGS

Observing the parade of people who came every Thursday bringing objects to show to the Pushkin Museum's experts, Kozlov had been amazed at how much private plunder had made its way back to the Soviet Union from Germany. The most important loot in private hands was the collection of the Bremen Kunsthalle, which had disappeared from its hiding place in the cellar of a German castle a few months after the end of the war. In 1989, a Moscow architect and museum director named Viktor Baldin visited Germany and told the director of the Kunsthalle that he had placed a good part of the collection in the depository of the Shchusev Museum of Architecture in Moscow: 362 drawings and two paintings, a *Salvator Mundi* by Dürer and a portrait by Goya. Baldin had been trying to return them to Bremen ever since the end of the war. He had written to every Soviet ruler from Brezhnev to Gorbachev about the collection, but he never received an answer.[1]

Baldin's last letter was addressed to Russian Federation President Boris Yeltsin, who was preparing to pay his first state visit to Germany in 1990. Baldin pleaded, 'Don't lose the chance to use this situation and don't listen to those people who are trying to prevent this step. I am an old soldier and a museum curator. Before the end of my days I want to be sure that the unique drawings I saved during the war are returned to the real owner – the museum in the city of Bremen – and become accessible to the public and to researchers, and are returned to world culture.'

Yeltsin scrawled his decision on Baldin's letter: 'It would be just right and politically beneficial to return them.'

But the Ministry of Culture did not want to give up the collection. Alarmed by news reports about Yeltsin's intentions, Nikolai Gubenko, accompanied by KGB officers, appeared at the Shchusev Museum one day and confiscated the drawings. They were sent to the Hermitage to keep them as far away as possible from the impulsive and unpredictable Yeltsin. At the same time a Soviet-style defamation campaign was launched against Baldin with the clear backing of the Ministry of Culture. In numerous newspaper articles, he was branded as nothing more than an art thief.[2]

At the end of November Yeltsin arrived in Germany empty-handed. Perhaps he was trying to compensate for the absence of the drawings when he stated that he knew where the Amber Room was hidden. His information on this subject came from the GRU – Soviet Military Intelligence – which had told him that the famous room was hidden underground, beneath the Soviet military base near Ohrdruf. Why the GRU had waited until the unification of Germany to reveal this information was unclear, but the revelation drew hundreds of people armed with spades to the site. Needless to say, they did not unearth the Amber Room.[3]

Viktor Baldin had been a captain in the 38th Field Engineers Brigade of the Red Army. On 5 May 1945, the brigade was ordered to move from Berlin to the town of Kiritz, about sixty-five kilometres north of the capital, and Baldin was ordered to find them suitable quarters. He had completed his architectural training just before the war. Reconnoitring the area, he was struck by Karnzow Castle, which was set picturesquely on the shore of a small lake surrounded by a forest. The castle's owner, Count Königsmark, was at home when Baldin drove up. The young officer told him that the Red Army would be taking over the building and offered him a truck to transport him and his family wherever they wanted to go. Königsmark interrupted brusquely that he would not take anything from the Russians. A few hours later he and his mistress rowed out to the middle of the lake and slashed their wrists. She survived, but the count fell overboard and died.

The senior officers moved into the castle. Baldin and the other junior officers were camped out in tents and huts in the forest. On the morning of 30 July, as the brigade was preparing to leave Kiritz, an officer came over from Karnzow to tell Baldin that something interesting had happened. A Russian Ostarbeiter who had been working in the castle had revealed that there was a secret storeroom in the cellar, concealed behind a false wall. The officers had broken in and found hundreds of drawings, prints, and paintings. Baldin had a reputation as an expert in the fine arts, and they wanted him to come and look at their find.

Baldin hurried to the castle and down the stone stairs. The cellar floor was covered by drawings mounted on cardboard backings, and a glance was enough for him to understand what kind of treasure was lying under his feet. On the mounts familiar names were printed: Titian, Rembrandt, van Gogh, Goya, Cézanne. They had stumbled on one of the four storage depositories for the collection of the Bremen Kunsthalle. Altogether there were 50 paintings, 1,715 drawings, and about 3,000 prints hidden in Karnzow Castle.[4]

Baldin hurried to the commanding officer's quarters. As he later told the story, he insisted to his commander that the works had to be treated carefully and taken to a safe place. The commander listened in surprise and then asked him, 'How old are you?' Baldin answered that he was twenty-five. The commander drew him to the window and pointed to the brigade's few trucks lined up outside. All of them were overloaded with senior officers' loot. 'And now,' he snapped, 'get out of here.' Baldin realized that nobody cared about safeguarding the works of art.

By the time he got back to the cellar, most of the drawings were already gone, but there were still hundreds strewn over the floor. He began to sort them out by candlelight. The heavy Bristol cardboard mounts made them bulky, and it was impossible to carry more than ten at a time. He carefully cut out the thin leaves of paper from their mounts and wrote the name of the artist on the back of each drawing. It was after midnight and his candle was burning low. Baldin could not take them all. He left behind the ones he thought were less important, but it worried him because he was afraid everything left in the cellar would be destroyed. He carried an armful of drawings to his hut in the forest and placed them gently in a suitcase.

The brigade began its long journey home. On the way Baldin added to his collection whenever he could. The soldiers had decorated the trucks with nudes – drawn by Tiepolo, Rodin and other masters. Baldin traded wristwatches, belts and minor trophies for these pin-ups. He sacrificed a fine pair of German boots for Dürer's priceless *Salvator Mundi*. 'They were really good boots,' he remembered with feeling fifty years later. Altogether, he came home with 362 drawings and two paintings: the Dürer and a portrait by Goya.

After the war Baldin worked as an architect, taking part in the restoration of the Troitse-Sergeyevsky Monastery in Zagorsk. He designed the restoration of the Beer Tower as a depository for the

Pushkin Museum. He and the others working on the project lived in former monks' cells in the monastery.

Baldin had also brought home some souvenirs: an eighteenth-century pistol, a ceremonial sword, and a collection of German military medals. He showed these objects to people freely and lent the medals to friends to use in amateur theatricals. In true Soviet fashion, someone informed on him to the MGB (predecessor of the KGB). The secret policemen who searched his room found the sword and the revolver but ignored the portfolio containing drawings and two little paintings. Baldin tried to explain to them that the weapons were only souvenirs while the drawings were the real treasure, but they snapped that they could not be tricked so easily. Baldin was in serious trouble for a while and lost his Party card, a catastrophe in those days. It meant the end of his career and might be followed by arrest, but letters of support written to the Central Committee and important Party officials by his friends and fellow officers saved him. His card was returned.

Frightened by these events, Baldin decided in 1947 to donate his collection to the Shchusev Museum of Architecture. At the same time he wrote an account of what had happened in Karnzow Castle to Marshal Kliment Voroshilov, who was then head of the Council of Ministers, proposing that an attempt be made to locate the other looted Bremen works. He never got an answer to his letter. The drawings remained in storage in the museum until many years later, when Baldin himself was appointed its director. At that moment, he began his unsuccessful campaign to return the drawings to Bremen.[5]

After listening to Baldin's story, Akinsha and Kozlov succeeded in locating two more caches of things from the Bremen collection. Both of them, it turned out, were in the secret depository of the Pushkin Museum. Another officer of Baldin's brigade, Vladimir Balabanov, had returned home after the war with thirty-four drawings taken from the cellar. He was an artist and he knew exactly what he had: drawings by Dürer, Rembrandt, and Van Dyck. Balabanov settled in Samarkand, and in the 1960s he decided to donate the drawings to the local museum. Museum officials immediately informed their supervisors in Tashkent of this extraordinary gift, and they promptly informed Moscow. A special courier from the Ministry of Culture was sent to Uzbekistan to seize the drawings, and they ended up in the Pushkin Museum depository. Exactly the same fate awaited another cache of fifty Bremen drawings that turned up in Siberia at the end of the 1960s and was deposited in the Novosibirsk museum. A third cache ended up in the Museum of Fine Arts in Baku. But there were still many drawings from Bremen in private hands.[6]

Kozlov got a lead. He was told by a friend at the Ministry of Culture about a 'crazy old man' who wanted to return to Germany a collection of Bremen Kunsthalle drawings he had stolen after the war. Ministry officials did not believe the story and were not interested in the old man. Kozlov could not discover his name but found out that he lived in the provincial city of N. It took him only a few weeks to track the man down and make contact with him. He told Kozlov that it was not he who had taken the drawings but an old friend, who was so afraid of publicity that he did not want even the name of the city he lived in made public.

A month later Kozlov and Akinsha set off for N. The Moscow underground was packed. A grey mass of people carrying heavy suitcases and rolling huge bags on wheels erupted from the train at Komsomolskaya, the gateway to three main railway stations. Manoeuvring through the mob, they moved slowly down the long corridors populated by beggars and newspaper sellers. The station's prize decoration is a heroic painting by the famous Socialist Realist artist Lansere of miners digging the tunnel for the metro, but these days the subway's grandeur is overlaid by a new culture. Part of the painted wall is covered with posters of Sylvester Stallone and of naked girls. The juxtapositions are confusing: Stallone fades into the background of half-naked muscular shock workers of socialist labour, and the impressive bosom of Samantha Fox appears in risky proximity to the toil-hardened hands of the metro builders.

They were lucky. Tickets for the night train to N. were available, and two hours later they were anxiously on their way. The train arrived at seven o'clock in the morning. It was grey and frosty, and the square in front of the railway station was filled with wooden kiosks selling American cigarettes, canned beer and sneakers with fake labels. It took them a long time to find the bus stop. They rode through the desolate outskirts of the city, then the bus crossed a bridge and they were in the old part of town, where lopsided wooden houses lined tiny winding streets and the bell towers of the few surviving churches thrust up above rusty corrugated iron roofs. The bus climbed a hill and stopped in the central square, beside the red brick wall of the local Kremlin. It was deserted except for the granite figure of Lenin pointing towards the future.

The house stood in a yard behind an old yellow building. It was a shabby five-storey structure erected in the days of Khrushchev. Dirty snow covered the yard and the heaps of decaying building materials left behind years ago. The apartment was on the first floor. The door was opened immediately when Kozlov rang the bell. They were expected.

The old man lived with two other people in a one-room flat that was modest even by Soviet standards. The wooden floor was painted dark red. Piles of disorderly papers covered an old desk, and the walls were lined with overflowing bookshelves. A shabby brown sofa was pushed against a wall. The old man proposed a cup of coffee. Sitting in the tiny kitchen he explained how his friend had come across the drawings. He had been in the army, and in May 1945, near the castle of Karnzow, he had found a package. When he opened it he discovered forty-five drawings and fifty-six prints marked with the Bremen Kunsthalle stamp. Somebody who had taken the drawings from the cellar had lost them or left them behind for some reason. His friend had only one wish: to return them to their legitimate owner. He wanted his anonymity preserved and he wanted no gestures of gratitude from the Germans. The old man was nervously smoking cheap Indian cigarettes, one after the other, and their acrid smell filled the flat. Kozlov and Akinsha were so on edge with suspense, they could hardly endure the delay. Finally the man noticed their impatience and interrupted the conversation. 'OK,' he said. 'Let's go and see them.'

He got down on his knees and fished under the sofa for a dusty brown portfolio. 'Russian Landscape Paintings of the 19th Century' was printed in fat black letters on the cover. It probably came from the 1950s, when sets of badly printed 'masterpieces of Russian realist paintings' filled the shelves of bookshops all over the country.

The old man put the portfolio on a table and slowly opened it. 'They're all here,' he said. 'I like this Watteau very much.' He handed Kozlov a small sheet of yellowed paper with a red chalk drawing of a female hand holding a crayfish. 'This Rembrandt isn't bad either,' he said, passing over a drawing of a seated woman. Soon the table and the shabby brown sofa were covered with drawings and etchings – by Baldung Grien, Jordaens, Rubens, Veronese, Tintoretto, Manet. 'This one is probably the best', the old man said finally. He picked up a superb watercolour by Dürer depicting a castle on a rock. Kozlov and Akinsha had imagined this moment. It was a dreary setting, this ugly flat in a grey provincial city, but there was no doubt that the drawings came from the Bremen Kunsthalle.

Like his friend who had found the drawings, the old man also wanted to remain anonymous. An art historian, he had gone to museums and discovered that official people were not interested in helping him, so he had decided to return the drawings directly to the Germans. Kozlov and Akinsha would contact the German Embassy in Moscow for him.

A few months later, early in March 1993, the old man stood with Akinsha and Kozlov on a Moscow street trying to flag down a taxi. He was clutching a shabby suitcase filled with the treasures from the Bremen Kunsthalle. Finally a car stopped and after negotiations agreed to take them to Mosfilmovskaya Street. They got out opposite the red brick building of the Germany Embassy, where the cultural attaché was waiting for them.

The attaché had agreed to receive the drawings, but he gave Akinsha the impression that he did not really believe it would happen. His doubts increased when the transaction, which was supposed to take place in February, was postponed. The art historian could not get a train ticket to Moscow because they were sold out. This was not an unusual situation in Russia, but it was hard to explain to the Germans.

In the cultural attaché's spacious office, two tables were pushed together. They were covered with drawings, watercolours, engravings, and etchings. To Akinsha's surprise, the usually cool diplomat was visibly nervous. Picking up the watercolour by Dürer, he confessed with awe that he had never held a great work of art in his hands before. They checked the works against a list compiled by the Bremen Kunsthalle. Then they signed some papers and solemnly drank a cup of coffee together. On the corner outside Akinsha bought a pack of American cigarettes in a kiosk. The three were exhausted and overwhelmed by the idea that they had just assisted in the transfer of several million dollars' worth of art.

The drawings are still in the embassy. The Russian government has made clear that it does not want them returned to Germany.

THE INVISIBLE BECOMES
VISIBLE

After the dissolution of the Soviet Union at the end of 1991, the newly sovereign Russian Republic declared its willingness to resolve the problem of the trophy works. In 1992, President Yeltsin and Chancellor Kohl signed the German-Russian Cultural Agreement, reaffirming the Good-Neighbourliness Treaty that Kohl and Soviet President Gorbachev had signed two years earlier. There was one important difference, however. In 1992, both sides knew that large quantities of works of art taken from Germany were hidden in Russian storerooms. A Joint Commission was set up to consider the restitution issue, with German and Russian co-chairmen and groups of experts on museums, libraries, archives, and law.

The commission met infrequently. At their June 1994 meeting, the Germans gave the Russians a list of the loot they believe is in Russia: about 200,000 art objects, two million books, and 'three kilometres' of archives, valued by them at more than ten billion Deutschmarks (£4 billion). The Russians gave the Germans a list of 39,588 lots (some containing multiple objects), of works of art that disappeared during the war from the museum in Orel and the Tsarskoe Selo and Pavlovsk palaces outside Leningrad.[1] But there were no agreements. There were some quiet, unofficial returns of books or archives by various agencies, but the Russian government officially returned only five books from the library of Gotha. The rest of the library remains in Russia.

The two countries are today farther apart than ever. At a conference on 'The Spoils of War' in New York in January 1995, sponsored by the Bard Graduate Center, German and Russian representatives confronted each other angrily in front of a large audience, with some of the Germans accusing the Russians of stalling and some of the Russians asserting that the Germans had no right to make any demands at all, considering how much devastation and suffering Germany had brought upon Russia in the war.

By their own admission, a major problem for the Russian experts is that they have almost no information about what happened to the displaced works of art on both sides; until recently they did not even know that information about Russian losses was available in open archives. Thus they do not know about the goods wagons filled with works of art taken by the Germans from the museums of Russia, Belorussia and Ukraine that were found in the Western occupation zones and returned to the Russians by the Americans in the late 1940s. By 1957, when the Soviet government was preparing the second return of works to the GDR, the documents concerning the earlier transaction were not available to the art experts, who never discovered that 534,120 objects from the museums of Kiev, Minsk, Smolensk, Pskov and Novgorod, and the palaces outside Leningrad, had been turned over by the Americans to the Department of Reparations, Supplies, and Restitution of the Soviet Military Administration in Germany, headed by Major General Leonid Zorin.[2] The fate of these objects is a mystery, but there is evidence that many of them never reached their former owners.

Without real information, a myth developed to the effect that hundreds of thousands of looted Soviet masterpieces had been hidden in Germany or dispersed to other Western countries and sold on the art market. It is widely believed in Moscow that many or most of them ended up in American private collections, although there is no evidence for this. Irina Antonova has declared that 'America is said to be saturated with objects from Russian museums.'[3]

The disagreement between the Germans and the Russians also has a legal aspect, revolving around their different interpretations of Article 16 of the 1990 Good-Neighbourliness Treaty. In Article 16, both sides agreed that 'lost or unlawfully transferred art treasures which are located in their territory will be returned to the owners or their successors'. But what exactly is meant by the phrase 'unlawfully removed'? The two sides understand it very differently. According to Dr Armin Hiller of the German Foreign Office, 'the Russian side argues that the cultural property stolen by the German occupiers in the USSR was "unlawfully removed" – an assertion which the German side has at no point in time disputed – while the cultural property taken from Germany by their own military and occupation authorities on a large scale was transferred to the Soviet Union "lawfully"'.

Invoking the Hague Convention of 1907, according to which 'works of art and science' and 'institutions dedicated to ... the arts and sciences' in occupied territory are protected against confiscation, and the two German-Russian treaties, the Germans claim that the Russians had no legal basis for taking works of art from Germany and are bound to return them by the treaties they signed.[4] The Russian government's position on the matter is based on a legal opinion prepared in 1994 by the Institute of State and Law of the Academy of Sciences. According to this document, the looting of Germany was legal because everybody did it. The Institute of State and Law experts said that the Allied Control Council, the body that ruled the defeated country, had recognized the 'compensation principle of restitution' – the right of countries looted by the Nazis to take German property as compensation. 'This list of measures taken by the Control Council and the High Command of the Soviet Military Administration in Germany connected with enemy property, including cultural valuables, proves that the Allied countries were guided by the same principle, which was one of the bases of the peace agreement.' They had the right 'to take, confiscate, or liquidate ... any enemy property'.[5]

The Allied leaders did agree, at the Teheran meeting in 1943 and the Yalta and Potsdam conferences in 1945, that countries occupied by the Germans could take reparations from Germany for their losses, including cultural losses. At the Potsdam conference, in July 1945, Stalin presented a letter to President Truman asking for the return of military and industrial equipment that the Soviets believed the Western Allies had removed from the Soviet occupation zone. Also on the list were the gold stock of the Reich and the collections of the Berlin museums, which the Americans had found in the Merkers salt mine.[6]

The Russian legal experts claim that the Allied Control Council gave the Soviets permission to remove whatever they wanted from their occupation zone. The Russians say that the Control Council adopted the principle of restitution in kind at a meeting on 17 April 1946, and decided to give its members permission to take the enemy's cultural property as compensation for 'objects of a unique character' destroyed or lost during the war.[7] But the final order was never made because the Soviets refused to give the Control Council a list of the art objects they had already removed to the USSR from their occupation zone. (It would have been very difficult for them to compile such a list, since by this time they had already secretly transported to Moscow, Leningrad and Kiev more than two million art objects belonging to German museums and private collections. Nor could they provide proof of their own losses to the Germans since museum inventories either did not exist or had been destroyed.) Because of their unwillingness to supply this information, the Control Council meeting ended without an agreement on restitution. The only agreement it reached allowed the confiscation of Nazi property.[8] The Russian lawyers, however, have now decided that all art objects looted by trophy brigades under orders from Moscow or the Soviet military administration were removed legally and can be kept.

The Russians also claim that if a peace treaty had been signed between Germany and the Allies, Germany would have been forced to accept the principle of restitution in kind – payment with cultural objects for the cultural losses resulting from the German occupation. The treaty would have stipulated that the Germans had no right to the restitution of their property, just as the treaty signed with Italy included such a stipulation.[9] But the Allies never signed a peace treaty with Germany, because the Western Allies and the Soviet Union never agreed on the status of the divided country.

A law based on this legal opinion is being drafted by the Russian Parliament. It would declare as property of the Russian Federation all works of art in Russian museums, no matter their provenance. Irina Antonova, a supporter of this law, believes that the world would accept it: 'If the law about federal property is adopted and the paintings and other art objects that are now in our possession are treated as the property of Russia, I hope that international approval of the decision will follow.' The law would make it impossible to return anything at all, because trophy works would become part of the national heritage.[10]

Antonova as a young staff member of the Pushkin Museum helped unload the art trophies arriving from Germany. Today she cites the example of Lord Elgin, who removed the marbles of the Parthenon to London, and of Napoleon, who looted Italy for the benefit of the Louvre. 'These are all examples of illegal export,' she says, 'but it was the will of history, and to begin a new redivision of artworks would be possible only by force, not by law.'[11]

This view is shared by the Russian nationalists, who have seized on the war loot issue with particular fervour. They regard the trophies as the last fruits of victory – the only ones the nation has not yet lost, and they believe that by refusing to return them, Russia demonstrates that it is still a great power that cannot be dictated to or humiliated by the West.[12]

On 26 October 1994, Klaus Goldmann and three other Berlin museum officials entered the Pushkin Museum through the staff entrance in the basement. Inside they turned over their passports and visas to Vladimir Tolstikov, the head of the department of archaeology. Tolstikov excused himself apologetically and disappeared for five minutes. Someone behind the scenes was checking their identity.

Antonova was waiting for the Germans in her conference room. They sat down around the table and put on the thin white cotton gloves museum people use to handle delicate objects. Then a curator brought out a tray of gold vessels. A cameraman filmed them for a few minutes as they admired the treasure of Troy for the benefit of Russian television. Tolstikov led them up a twisting staircase to a long, narrow room just below the roof, with cases lining the walls and running down the centre. They sat down again and put the gloves back on. Tolstikov and two other curators brought out the trays, one by one.

Goldmann had been looking for the Trojan gold for twenty-five years. He had always wondered why Professor Unverzagt had handed it over to the Russians in the Flakturm in violation of Hitler's order to remove cultural valuables from Berlin. There was another puzzle: Unverzagt claimed he had sent fifty crates of the museum's possessions to Grasleben, but the Americans returned only thirty in 1956. Could the three crates have been among the ones that had gone missing from Grasleben? Goldmann suspected that the gold might have disappeared into American hands. The museum did not even have photographs of most of the lost objects, because almost all of its photo documentation was destroyed in 1945.

Goldmann had considered other options. In the late 1950s, the Soviet Union returned 1.5 million art objects confiscated in the Soviet occupation zone to the German Democratic Republic. Since the Soviets said they had returned everything, and since at this time the Museum for Pre- and Early History had no counterpart in East Berlin, Goldmann thought it possible that the now homeless treasures had been sold for the hard currency the East German government so badly needed.

There were more sombre speculations. Could the gold have been diverted on its journey to Moscow by the people who were supposed to be guarding it? The priceless objects might have been hidden for future recovery or, even worse, melted down.

Even when he was convinced that the Trojan gold had been taken to Moscow, Goldmann worried. He knew that the Russians had made copies of the Sistine Madonna and many other pictures before returning them to Germany in the late 1950s, and he wondered if they might also have made copies of the gold pieces. One of the people with him was a restorer who would recognize in a moment whether the pieces were genuinely antique or not. And he had one last worry. He was afraid that the Soviets might have polished the gold, destroying its original patina. That would make it impossible to answer certain questions about the circumstances of the discovery: did Schliemann really find the objects at the site of Troy or did he buy them elsewhere, as his detractors had claimed? And did he make copies of his finds, as has been rumoured? If the gold was polished, such questions would be much harder to answer.

One look reassured Goldmann. The objects had been well cared for. They had not been polished. And they were as beautiful as he had imagined they would be. He could not help wanting them back in Berlin, although he knew that the Russians might never give them up. But he had been saying for years that it did not matter who owned the gold so long as it was, somewhere, on view again.[13]

On 9 February 1995, the theatre in the Hermitage was filled with an excited audience who had gathered for news about the upcoming April exhibition of Impressionist and Post-Impressionist masterpieces from German private collections. After the speeches came the moment the TV cameramen were awaiting with impatience. The heavy velvet curtain concealing the stage finally parted to reveal three easels. The one in the centre held Degas' *Place de la Concorde*, from the Gerstenberg Collection. On the left was Gauguin's *Two Sisters*, and on the right, van Gogh's last painting, *White House at Night*, both from the Krebs collection. The symbolism of the opening curtain was obvious: the pictures were visible again after being hidden in the museum's special depository for fifty years. What the museum director, Boris Piotrovsky, did not tell the audience was that two years earlier he had consented to a reunion – between the pictures in the Gerstenberg Collection and the heirs of the collector, Otto Gerstenberg.

Piotrovsky has stated repeatedly that Russia's crime was not to remove works of art from Germany – he believes that the Soviets had the right to compensation for their wartime losses – but to remove the works from world culture for such a long time. In 1993 he and Minister of Culture Yevgeny Sidorov made an agreement with Otto Gerstenberg's grandsons, Walther and Dieter Scharf, to divide the collection, with the prize – Degas' *Place de la Concorde*, worth at least £25 million at a conservative estimate – going back to the family. The first – and only – such agreement, it was brokered by Sotheby's international auction house, which is eager to have the pictures in its salesroom. But neither Piotrovsky nor anyone else has the power to carry out any agreement. As he recently remarked, even if President Yeltsin gave permission for the paintings to be returned to the Scharfs, they might be seized by the customs office. Until there is a legal framework for restitution, no agency in the country has the power to make decisions about the trophy works.[14]

Determined not to be outdone by the Hermitage, the Pushkin Museum very quickly organized an exhibition of sixty-three trophy paintings and drawings that opened in late February. The pictures were brought into the gallery and placed on the walls in an atmosphere of great secrecy. Staff members who worked on the show were issued special passes printed on yellow paper; no one else was allowed into the guarded galleries. The works that were installed in the second-floor colonnade, where it was impossible to limit access, went up on the walls at night and were covered with white paper so no one could see them.

Antonova dedicated the exhibition to the 'fiftieth anniversary of the great victory' and called it 'Twice Saved: Masterpieces of European Art of the 15th and 16th Centuries Removed to the Territory of the Soviet Union from Germany as a Consequence of the Second World War'. The name, which echoed the title of an article that had appeared in *Ogonyok* magazine in 1955 about the exhibition of Dresden Gallery paintings in this same museum, reflects Antonova's belief in the official story – that the trophy brigades performed a heroic deed by saving the masterpieces of Germany from destruction and robbery.[15] The phrase 'twice saved' refers to the salvation of the works of art first by the trophy brigades and then by museum officials and conservators. She also believes that Soviet museums did well to buy private trophies, saving them from the black market.

The grand marble staircase leading to the White Hall, where most of the paintings were hung, looks just as it did forty years ago, but the gigantic statue of Lenin that stood in front of the entrance to the White Hall is gone. In those days the entrance was blocked because the hall was packed with secret trophy works of art.

The paintings in the exhibition were familiar to Akinsha and Kozlov from tiny black-and-white photographs in old catalogues and from documents listing them as cargo or as inventory. In the gallery it was as if a crowd of ghosts had come to life in brilliant colour. The portrait of Lola Jimenez attributed to Goya, which had been flown to Moscow on the same plane as the Trojan gold, was almost shocking in the intensity of the sitter's red dress. Daumier's *Revolt*, from the Gerstenberg Collection, with its dominant brown tones enlivened by hot, bright strokes of Expressionist painting was, unexpectedly, a real masterpiece in the flesh, but *The Laundry Women* by the same artist was in bad condition and difficult to see under glass. The triptych by Hans von Marées of three nude boys was there – the picture found by Andrei Chegodayev in the cellar of a ruined bank in Magdeburg and dispatched to Moscow on a special plane because the military commandant of the city liked it so much. Renoir's small *Mme Chocquet at the Window*, stolen from the cellar of Karnzow Castle, glowed on one wall, and Manet's portrait of Rosita Mauri, from the Koehler Collection, which had arrived at the Pushkin Museum without any documents, surprised by its untypical yellowish cast.

A group of paintings from the collections of the great Hungarian Jewish families rounded out the show. The works by Corot, Manet, and Degas from the Hatvany Collection, and canvases that had belonged to the Herzogs, had been seen in public more recently than the other pictures because they had been put on exhibition by Adolf Eichmann. The head of the Gestapo's Jewish Office, who came to Budapest in 1944 to speed up the deportations of Jews, acquired a great deal of art in the course of his duties. In a notorious deal, he agreed to exchange the freedom of 1,200 Jewish families for gold, silver, cash, and paintings. Other works he simply confiscated. Eichmann was so proud of his loot he staged an exhibition in his residence, the Hotel Majestic. The paintings were later sent to Germany, where they were found by the Soviet trophy brigades. Finally these pathetic remnants of the Hungarian–Jewish culture the Nazis had destroyed came to Moscow as compensation for the losses the Nazis had inflicted on the Russians.[16]

As the Russian Parliament pondered a law that would decide the fate of these and hundreds of thousands of other works, as political and cultural figures debated the wisdom and morality of giving them back or keeping them in Russia, one high-ranking and influential cultural official made a simple suggestion. Valery Koulichov, head of the Department of Restitution of the Ministry of Culture, proposed that a new museum be constructed in Moscow for all the trophy works of art.[17] It would have to be a much humbler undertaking than the supermuseum envisioned by Sergei Merkurov and Igor Grabar in 1944, but then, as Karl Marx, a philosopher who was highly regarded in Russia until not many years ago, once wrote: 'History repeats itself twice, the first time as tragedy and the second time as farce.'

NOTES

The books referred to in shortened form in the notes will be found in the Bibliography. Documents in Russian archives are referred to by collection (*fond*), inventory (*opis*), file (*delo*), folio (*list*).

ABBREVIATIONS

AKA Private Archive of Konstantin Akinsha and Grigorii Kozlov
AMCR Archive of the Ministry of Culture of the Russian Federation
ANA *ARTnews* Archive
APM Archive of the Pushkin Museum
ARIC Archive of the Research Institute of Culturology
RCPSDMH Russian Centre for Preservation and Study of Documents of Modern History
RSALA Russian State Archive of Literature and Art
SARF State Archive of the Russian Federation
CAMD Central Archive of the Ministry of Defence
CC Central Committee
CCEO Committee on Cultural Educational Organizations of the Russian Federation
CPC Council of People's Commissars
CPSU Communist Party of the Soviet Union
MC Ministry of Culture of the USSR
PM State Pushkin Museum of Visual Arts
SH State Hermitage
SHM State Historical Museum

SCHLIEMANN'S TREASURE

1. A recent biography of Schliemann is Moorehead, *Lost Treasures*. See also *Troia: Kaleidoskop aus der Antiken Welt*.

2. Information about the Museum for Pre- and Early History came from the chief curator Klaus Goldmann.

THE AMBER ROOM

1. Voronov and Kuchumov, *Yantarnaya Komnata*; Kuchumov interview; Ovsyanov, 'Kak khranim', pp. 131–53.
2. Communication from Tete Böttger.
3. Birukov, *Yantarnaya Komnata*, p. 83.

MOSCOW: HOW MUCH IS A REMBRANDT WORTH?

1. The committee was organized on 2 November 1942 by a decree of the Supreme Soviet of the USSR. Its members included Politburo culture boss Andrei Zhdanov, the biologist Trofim Lysenko, the popular novelist Alexei Tolstoy, the well-known female pilot Valentina Grizodubova, Metropolitan Nikolai of Kiev and Galicia, and Nikolai Burdenko, who in 1943 was the head of a group sent by the committee to fabricate 'proofs' that the Polish officers massacred at Katyn by the NKVD had been killed by the Nazis. The committee was disbanded in 1946.
2. ARIC, inv. 1, file 299, Report on Museum Equivalents in German Museums the USSR Desires to Receive in Compensation for Damage Done to Soviet Museums, p. 77.
3. *Ibid.*, p. 94.
4. The artist Alexandre Benois (*My Memoirs*, Vols 4–5, Isskust, Moscow, 1989, p. 358) remembered Grabar's 'openly expressed will to play the main role', his boastfulness, and his tremendous energy.
5. SARF, coll. 7021, inv. 121, file 17, p. 144.
6. *Ibid.*
7. The Bureau of Experts was established by Decree No. 12 of the Extraordinary State Committee, 8 September 1943.
8. CAMD, coll. 353, inv. 5864, file 1, p. 27.
9. Kuchumov interview.
10. *Nurembergsky protsess* (Nuremberg Trials), Moscow, 1958, 3:584.
11. The lists of Soviet museum losses compiled in 1943–46 by the Extraordinary Committee were of very low quality and included much incorrect information. These lists were never seriously checked. According to the committee, the Nazis removed, damaged, or destroyed 564,723 museum objects, but an exact valuation of the losses is impossible today. SARF, coll. 7021, inv. 116, file 298.

12. The Commission on the Preservation and Registration of Monuments of Art of the Arts Committee of the CPC USSR was established on 28 May 1942 by a decree of the CPC. Its main tasks during the war were registration of architectural monuments destroyed or damaged by the occupiers, preservation of monuments in the liberated parts of the country, restoration planning, and publication of information about Nazi destruction of monuments.

13. SARF, coll. 7021, inv. 121, file 17, pp. 102–3.

14. *Ibid.*, p. 103.

15. *Ibid.*, p. 79.

16. *Ibid.*, p. 98.

17. *Ibid.*

18. Andreyeva, Ekaterina, 'Fashistskoe iskusstvo Italii i Natsional-sotsialisticheskoe iskusstvo Germanii v Sovetskoi khudozhestevennoi kritike, 1934–35 godov' ('Fascist art of Italy and National Socialist art of Germany in Soviet art criticism, 1934–35'), *Mesto Pechati* 3, 1993, p. 11.

19. SARF, coll. 7021, inv. 121, file 17, p. 86.

20. *Ibid.*, pp. 93–4.

21. *Ibid.*, p. 94.

22. *Ibid.*, p. 59.

23. All prices were given in so-called 'gold rubles' – Soviet rubles of 1927, when, as a result of the New Economic Policy, Soviet currency was convertible for a short time. The exchange rate in 1927 was 1 ruble = 5 US dollars. But during the discussion, members of the commission even proposed to value the losses of Soviet museums according to the rate of exchange of the Russian ruble in 1913.

24. SARF, coll. 7021, inv. 121, file 17, p. 59.

25. *Ibid.*, p. 64.

26. *Ibid.*, p. 68.

27. *Ibid.*, p. 69.

28. *Ibid.*, p. 74.

29. *Ibid.*, p. 75.

30. *Ibid.*

MOSCOW: PLANS FOR A SUPERMUSEUM

1. Romanuk, *Moskva-utrati*, p. 227.

2. SARF, coll. 7021, inv. 121, file 17, pp. 25–6.

3. *Ibid.*, p. 26.

4. *Ibid.*, p. 28.

5. *Ibid.*, p. 29.

6. *Ibid.*

7. ARIC, inv. 1, file 243. The meeting took place on 22 November 1943 in the State Historical Museum.

8. RSALA, coll. 962, inv. 6, file 1345, pp. 1–22.

9. *Ibid.*, p. 6.

10. *Ibid.*, p. 7.

11. *Ibid.*, pp. 15–20.

12. SARF, coll. 7021, inv. 121, file 17, p. 104.

13. *Ibid.*

14. RCPSDMH, coll. 17, inv. 125, file 308, pp. 2–8.

15. SARF, coll. 7021, inv. 121, file 17, p. 27.

16. ARIC, inv. 1, file 299, Report on Museum Equivalents in German Museums, p. 8.

17. *Ibid.*, p. 11.

18. *Ibid.*, p. 73.

19. Grabar, *Moya zhizn*, p. 110.

20. List of Equivalents, SARF, coll. 7021, inv. 116, file 292.

21. Grabar, *Moya zhizn*, p. 305.

22. SARF, coll. 7021, inv. 121, file 17, p. 25.

23. Grabar, *Moya zhizn*, p. 305.

24. ARIC, inv. 1, file 299, Report on Museum Equivalents in German Museums, p. 60.

25. SARF, coll. 7021, inv. 116, file 291, pp. 293–6.

26. *Ibid.*, file 291, pp. 1–2.

27. Williams, *Russian Art and American Money*, p. 187.

28. *Ibid.*, p. 185.

29. SARF, coll. 7021, inv. 116, file 291, pp. 293–6.

30. Roxan and Wanstall, *Rape of Art*, pp. 111, 157.

31. RSALA, coll. 962, inv. 6, file 1254.

32. *Ibid.*, file 1209.

33. *Ibid.*, file 1262.

34. Kogelfranz and Korte, *Quedlinburg-Texas und zuruck*.

THE TROPHY BRIGADES

1. RSALA, coll. 962, inv. 3, file 1350, pp. 4–8.

2. *Tegeran – Yalta – Potsdam*, Mezhdunarodnie Otnoshenia, Moscow, 1971, pp. 125–8; RCPSDMH, coll. 644, inv. 1, file 373, pp. 48–9.

3. RSALA, coll. 962, inv. 3, file 1350, pp. 1–3; file 1312, p. 151.

4. Sokolova memoir.
5. Filippov diary.
6. RSALA, coll. 962, inv. 6, file 1357, pp. 119–20.
7. *Ibid.*, file 1254, pp. 46–8.

BERLIN: THE DESTRUCTION OF THE MUSEUMS

1. *Verluste*, pp. 11–12.
2. Irving, *Hitler's War*, p. 496.
3. *Verluste*, pp. 11–12.
4. Howard memoir.
5. *Verluste*, pp. 12–13.
6. Howard memoir.
7. *Ibid.*
8. Vishnevsky, *Sobranie sochineni*, p. 275.
9. Zhukov, *Vospominania*, p. 668.
10. *Verluste*, pp. 13, 32.
11. Zhukov, *Vospominania*, p. 668; Bokov, *Vesna pobedi*, p. 237.
12. Bokov, *Vesna pobedi*, pp. 270–1.
13. RSALA, coll. 962, inv. 6, file 1357, pp. 75–6.
14. Bokov, *Vesna pobedi*, p. 282.
15. *Ibid.*, pp. 294–6.
16. *Ibid.*, pp. 302–5.
17. *Ibid.*, p. 325.
18. RSALA, coll. 962, inv. 6, file 1357, pp. 278–9; *Verluste*, pp. 17–44.

BERLIN: GOLD IN THE TOWER

1. Read and Fisher, *Fall of Berlin*, pp. 424–5.
2. Unverzagt, 'Materialien', pp. 321–43.
3. *Verluste*, pp. 17–44.
4. Read and Fisher, *Fall of Berlin*, pp. 77–9.
5. Speer, *Third Reich*, pp. 287–8.
6. Unverzagt, 'Materialien', pp. 343–5.
7. Andrew and Gordievsky, *KGB*, p. 342.
8. Belokopitov interview.
9. Bokov, *Vesna pobedi*, pp. 320–4.
10. Read and Fisher, *Fall of Berlin*, p. 445.
11. Bokov, *Vesna pobedi*, pp. 323–4; Trevor-Roper, *Last Days*, p. 224.
12. Belokopitov interview.

BERLIN: ALI BABA'S CAVE

1. Read and Fisher, *Fall of Berlin*, p. 157.
2. Unverzagt, 'Materialien', pp. 347–8.
3. Bokov, *Vesna pobedi*, pp. 343–5.
4. Unverzagt, 'Materialien', pp. 346–8.
5. RSALA, coll. 962, inv. 6, file 1357, pp. 7–9.
6. Druzhinin, 'V dni voini'.
7. RSALA, coll. 962, inv. 6, file 1357, pp. 7–9.
8. Belokopitov interview.
9. RSALA, coll. 962, inv. 6, file 1357, pp. 255–7.

BERLIN: FIRE IN FRIEDRICHSHAIN

1. *Verluste*, pp. 14–44.
2. Calvin Hathaway Papers.
3. Belokopitov interview.
4. Irving, *Hitler's War*, p. 822.
5. Bokov, *Vesna pobedi*, pp. 366–7.
6. RSALA, coll. 962, inv. 6, file 1254, pp. 54–9.
7. Druzhinin, 'V dni voini'.

BERLIN: THE GOLD DISAPPEARS

1. Unverzagt, 'Materialien', pp. 348–9; Akinsha and Koslov, 'Trophaen'.
2. Belokopitov interview.
3. Toland, *Last 100 Days*, pp. 442–3.
4. *Ibid.*, p. 657.
5. Andrew and Gordievsky, *KGB*, pp. 341–3.
6. Belokopitov interview.
7. Walter Andrae diary. Handschriften Abteilung Staat Bibliothek Preussischer Kulturbesitz.
8. Howard memoir.
9. Calvin Hathaway diary.
10. *Verluste*, pp. 17–44.
11. RSALA, coll. 962, inv. 3, file 1350, p. 12.
12. *Ibid.*, inv. 6, file 1357, p. 258.
13. *Ibid.*, file 1357, p. 23.
14. *Ibid.*, p. 260.

15. *Ibid.*, pp. 253–4.
16. *Ibid.*, pp. 23–4, 260.
17. *Ibid.*, p. 92.
18. *Ibid.*, p. 23.
19. ANA, Rothel Papers.
20. Smyth, *Repatriation*, p. 61.
21. Communication from Pavel Knishevsky.

BERLIN: THE FRIEDRICHSHAIN DISASTER

1. Howard memoir.
2. RSALA, coll. 962, inv. 6, file 1357, pp. 59–60.
3. *Ibid.*, pp. 25, 84–5.
4. *Ibid.*, p. 304.
5. *Ibid.*, p. 308.
6. *Ibid.*, inv. 3, file 1513, p. 196.
7. *Ibid.*, inv. 6, file 1333, p. 274.
8. *Ibid.*, file 1338, p. 30.
9. Calvin Hathaway Diary.
10. *Ibid.*
11. Howard memoir.
12. Letter from Captain Doda Conrad to Colonel Mason Hammond, Berlin, 6 August 1945. Hathaway Papers.
13. Letter to Hammond, 11 August 1945. Hathaway Papers.

BERLIN: CLEANING OUT THE CITY

1. RSALA, coll. 962, inv. 6, file 1357, pp. 75–6.
2. *Ibid.*, pp. 139–40; RCPSDMH, coll. 644, inv. 1, file 449, p. 714.
3. Letter to Colonel Mason Hammond, 11 August 1945. Hathaway Papers.
4. *Ibid.*
5. Belokopitov interview.
6. RSALA, coll. 962, inv. 3, file 1513, p. 30.
7. *Ibid.*, inv. 6, file 1357, p. 277.
8. *Ibid.*, pp. 141–3.
9. *Verluste*, pp. 17–19.
10. Howard memoir.
11. RSALA, coll. 962, inv. 6, file 1357, pp. 287–90; *Verluste*, pp. 17–44.
12. *Ibid.*, inv. 3, file 1513, p. 196.

13. Report to HQ US Group Control Council, RDER Division, MFAA Branch, 28 July 1945. Hathaway Papers.
14. *Ibid.*
15. Report of Norman T. Byrne, US Representative, Fine Arts Committee, Allied Kommandatura, Office of Military Government (US), Berlin District, 6 May 1946. Hathaway Papers.
16. Art and Archaeology, Restitution from Germany CDMP D-5/15, 18 May 1949. Klaus Goldmann Archive.
17. Report on the Fate of Art Treasures in the Soviet Zone of Occupation and in the Soviet Sector of Berlin, 30 August 1951. Hathaway Papers.

SILESIA: RADIOS AND VIOLINS

1. Konev, *Zapiski*, p. 338.
2. Filippov's unpublished diary is a major source of information for the brigade's activities in Silesia.
3. Chegodayev interview.
4. RSALA, coll. 962, inv. 6, file 1207, p. 24.
5. Sokolova memoir.

DRESDEN: MASTERPIECES IN A MINE

1. Konev, *Zapiski*, p. 498.
2. Sokolova memoir.
3. Volinsky [Rabinovich], *Sem dnei*, p. 65.
4. Sokolova memoir.
5. *Spasennie shedevri*, p. 51.
6. AKA, MC Record of the Questioning of Volodin, 3 May 1955.
7. *Spasennie shedevri*, p. 51.
8. AKA, Letter of Dresden Brigade members to Khrushchev, 5 May 1955.
9. AKA, MC Record of the Questioning of Volodin, 3 May 1955.
10. Seydweitz, *Drezdenskaya Galereya*, p. 69.
11. *Spasennie shedevri*, p. 37.
12. Sokolova memoir.
13. *Spasennie shedevri*, p. 52.
14. Sokolova memoir.
15. *Ibid.*
16. *Spasennie shedevri*, p. 37.
17. Sokolova memoir.

18. *Ibid.*
19. APM, Records of Volodin, 1955.
20. Sokolova memoir.
21. APM, Records of Volodin, 1955.
22. *Ibid.*
23. Sokolova memoir.

DRESDEN: 'THE CARGO IS OF STATE IMPORTANCE'

1. Dittrich, *Vermisste Zeichnungen.*
2. *Spasennie shedevri*, p. 38.
3. Sokolova memoir.
4. *Verluste*, p. 52.
5. *Spasennie shedevri*, p. 38.
6. Sokolova memoir.
7. *Spasennie shedevri*, p. 43.
8. *Ibid.*, p. 38.
9. Sokolova memoir.
10. *Ibid.*
11. Yurasov, *Vrag naroda*, p. 87.
12. AKA, Letter of Rototayev to deputy minister of culture, 29 April 1955; RCPSDMH, coll. 644, inv. 1, file 430, p. 177.
13. RSALA, coll. 962, inv. 6, file 1357, pp. 319–22.
14. AKA, Document on opening of crates sent by Commissariat of Finance, 16 March 1946.
15. AKA, Report of Alexeyev, Churakov, and Guber to deputy minister of culture, 1955.
16. AKA, Report of Varshavsky, 1 April 1955.
17. AKA, Report of Ovchinnikov to MC, 1955.

DANZIG: COUNTING COINS

1. RSALA, coll. 962, inv. 6, file 1326, pp. 166–9.
2. *Ibid.*, pp. 38–43.
3. *Ibid.*, pp. 38–46.
4. *Ibid.*, file 1357, p. 100.
5. *Ibid.*, file 1326, pp. 161, 165.
6. *Ibid.*, p. 158.
7. *Ibid.*, pp. 162–3.
8. *Ibid.*, pp. 38–43.

9. Yan Bialastocki and Mikhal Walicki, *Europeiskaya zhivopis v polskikh sobraniach* (European Paintings in Polish Collections), PIW, Warsaw, 1958, p. 474.

10. RSALA, coll. 962, inv. 6, file 1326, pp. 45–6.

11. *Ibid.*, file 1357, p. 66.

12. *Ibid.*, p. 97; Dariusz Kaczmarzyk, *Straty wojenne polski w dziedzinie vzezby* (Losses of Poland in Wartime), Ministerstwo Kultury, Warsaw, 1958, p. 16.

THURINGIA: IMPRESSIONIST MASTERPIECES IN A CELLAR

1. RSALA, coll. 962, inv. 6, file 1357, pp. 349–50, 352.
2. *Ibid.*, pp. 353–8.
3. *Ibid.*, p. 354.
4. *Ibid.*, p. 355.
5. *Ibid.*
6. *Ibid.*
7. *Ibid.*, p. 356.
8. *Ibid.*, p. 358.
9. *Ibid.*, pp. 263–8.
10. Nicholas, *Rape of Europa*, p. 339.
11. RSALA, coll. 962, inv. 6, file 1357, p. 261.
12. Wermusch, '5 Cezannes'.
13. Konchin, 'Tainik Villii Holzdorf'.
14. Henry-Künzel and Decker, 'Gift Horse', pp. 51–2.

LEIPZIG: TAKING ONLY THE BEST

1. RSALA, coll. 962, inv. 6, file 1357, p. 328.
2. *Ibid.*, p. 311.
3. AKA, List of Claims of the GDR.
4. RSALA, coll. 962, inv. 6, file 1291, p. 42.
5. *Ibid.*, file 1357, p. 315.
6. Yurasov, *Vrag naroda*, p. 69.
7. RSALA, coll. 962, inv. 6, file 1357, pp. 62–3, 330–1; file 1291, p. 54.
8. List of claims of the GDR.
9. RSALA, coll. 962, inv. 6, file 1291, p. 31; file 1357, pp. 27, 107, 138, 328; List of Claims of the GDR.
10. RSALA, coll. 962, inv. 6, file 1291, p. 23.
11. *Ibid.*, p. 32.

12. *Verluste*, pp. 65–6.
13. List of Claims of the GDR.
14. RSALA, coll. 962, inv. 6, file 1357, p. 54.
15. Akinsha and Kozlov, 'Soviets' war treasures', pp. 113, 117.
16. AKA, Letter of Alexeyev to MC USSR.
17. RSALA, coll. 962, inv. 6, file 1357, p. 116.
18. *Ibid.*, p. 336.
19. List of Claims of the GDR.
20. *Ibid.*
21. *Ibid.*; Domogala, *Rustkammer.*
22. List of Claims of the GDR.

FREIGHT TRAINS FULL OF TREASURES

1. Bokov, *Vesna pobedi*, p. 433.
2. RSALA, coll. 962, inv. 3, file 1513, p. 31.
3. *Ibid.*
4. *Ibid.*, inv. 6, file 1357, p. 69.
5. AKA, Order 177.
6. RSALA, coll. 962, inv. 6, file 1254, pp. 46–8.
7. Akinsha and Kozlov, 'Trophaen'.
8. RSALA, coll. 962, inv. 3, file 1513, p. 31.
9. *Ibid.*, inv. 6, file 1262, p. 35; file 1357, p. 43.
10. *Ibid.*, file 1357, pp. 62–3.
11. *Ibid.*, p. 145.
12. *Ibid.*, file 1325.
13. *Ibid.*, file 1292, p. 30.
14. *Ibid.*, file 1351.
15. AMCR, Report of Ignatieva to Zuyeva, chief of Cultural Educational Institutions Committee.

MOSCOW: TOO MUCH LOOT

1. RSALA, coll. 962, inv. 6, file 1292, p. 31.
2. *Ibid.*, file 1326, p. 43.
3. *Ibid.*
4. *Ibid.*, file 1209, p. 2.
5. *Ibid.*, file 1326, pp. 186–7.
6. *Ibid.*, file 1291, pp. 57–77.
7. *Ibid.*, file 1289, pp. 47, 54.

8. Akinsha and Kozlov, 'Trophaen'.
9. RSALA, coll. 962, inv. 6, file 1255, p. 214.
10. Torsuyev interview.
11. AKA, Letter of Ovchinnikova-Kharko to director of Pushkin Museum, 11 July 1969.
12. AKA, Report of Lapin to Konstantinov, 15 May 1945.
13. RSALA, coll. 962, inv. 6, files 1262, 1264.
14. *Ibid.*, file 1292.
15. *Ibid.*, file 1262, p. 48.
16. RSALA, coll. 962, inv. 6, file 1253, p. 121.
17. AKA, Letter on distribution of trophy artworks, 1945.
18. Chegodayev interview.
19. RCPSDMH, coll. 17, inv. 125, file 308, p. 20.
20. RSALA, coll. 962, inv. 6, file 1252, p. 17.
21. *Ibid.*, file 1255, p. 260.
22. AKA, Letter of Lebedev to Merkurov, 29 November 1945.
23. *Spasennie shedevri*, p. 71.
24. RSALA, coll. 962, inv. 3, file 1513, pp. 13–19.
25. Chegodayev interview; AKA, Letter of Butenko to director of Pushkin Museum, 12 July 1955; AKA, Letter of Zamoshkin and Guber to head, Department of Museums, Ministry of Culture, 21 July 1955.
26. AMCR, Report of Ignatieva to Zuyeva, chief of Cultural Educational Institutions Committee, 28 October 1946.
27. *Ibid.*
28. AMCR, Order of Cultural Educational Institutions Committee No. 69, 16 March 1946.
29. AMCR, Report of Ignatieva to Zuyeva, 20 October 1946.

LENINGRAD: THE HERMITAGE ADDS TO ITS COLLECTION

1. *Vecherny Leningrad*, 4 August 1956.
2. AKA, Document of the Central Depository of Museum Valuables of the Palaces on the Outskirts of Leningrad, 31 July 1945.
3. AKA, Letter of Leningrad City Council to Moskvin.
4. Rest and Varshavsky, *Podvig Ermitazha*, p. 181; RSALA, coll. 962, inv. 6, file 1262, pp. 5–34.
5. RSALA, coll. 962, inv. 6, file 1262, p. 4.
6. *Ibid.*, file 1357, p. 285.
7. Rest and Varshavsky, *Podvig Ermitazha*, p. 181.
8. RSALA, coll. 962, inv. 6, file 1262.

9. *Ibid.*, p. 133.
10. *Ibid.*
11. Bernard V. Bothmer, conversation with the authors.
12. RSALA, coll. 962, inv. 6, p. 11.
13. *Ibid.*, file 1325, p. 97.
14. *Ibid.*, p. 3.
15. *Ibid.*, file 1337, p. 14.
16. *Ibid.*, file 1349, pp. 210–19.
17. *Ibid.*, file 1316, p. 18.

MOSCOW: THE PLOT AGAINST ZHUKOV

1. Chegodayev interview.
2. RCPSDMH, coll. 17, inv. 125, file 305, pp. 22–3, 41–6, 49–51.
3. Chegodayev interview.
4. RSALA, coll. 962, inv. 6, file 1292, pp. 183–4.
5. *Ibid.*, inv. 3, file 1434, p. 5.
6. *Ibid.*, file 1427, p. 143.
7. SARF, coll. P–8300.
8. RSALA, file 1513, pp. 29–33.
9. Belokopitov interview.
10. *Voennie arkhivi Rossii*, pp. 184.
11. *Ibid.*, pp. 189–191.
12. *Ibid.*, p. 190.
13. *Ibid.*, p. 191.
14. *Ibid.*, pp. 192–5.
15. *Ibid.*, p. 244.
16. *Voenno-istorichesky zhurnal*, No. 6 (1989), p. 75.
17. *Voennie arkhivi Rossii*, pp. 196–207.
18. *Ibid.*, p. 210.
19. *Ibid.*, pp. 208–13.

THE RETURN TO SECRECY

1. Tikhanova interview.
2. Chegodayev interview.
3. Tikhanova interview.
4. RSALA, coll. 962, inv. 6, file 1316, pp. 20–1.
5. Sarabianov interview.
6. RSALA, coll. 962, inv. 6, file 1293, pp. 1–6.

7. *Ibid.*, file 1342, p. 27.
8. Chegodayev interview.
9. *Ibid.*
10. Yavorskaya interview.

MOSCOW: PRESENTS FOR STALIN

1. Chegodayev interview.
2. Chegodayev, Tikhanova and Belyaeva-Lorenz interviews.
3. Chegodayev and Tikhanova interviews.
4. Tikhanova, Belyaeva-Lorenz, interviews.
5. Demskaya interview.
6. AKA, Records of Hermitage curators' meetings, 1950.
7. Demskaya interview.
8. Chezodayev interview.

THE RETURN OF THE DRESDEN GALLERY

1. Mark Boguslavsky, 'Legal aspects of the Russian position in regard to the return of cultural property' (paper presented at symposium 'The Spoils of War. World War II and Its Aftermath: The Loss, Reappearance, and Recovery of Cultural Property', Bard Graduate Center for Studies in the Decorative Arts, New York, 19–21 January 1995).
2. *Ibid.*
3. *Literaturnaya Gazeta*, 31 March 1955. Only paintings from Moscow and Leningrad were mentioned in the Council of Ministers statement, which merely repeated the secret decision of the Secretariat of the Central Committee: AKA, Report of MC to CC CPSU, 1955.
4. *Kniga istoricheskikh sensatsii*, pp. 152–3.
5. AKA, Letter of Dresden Brigade members to Khrushchev, 5 May 1955.
6. *Pravda*, 3 May 1955.
7. *Spasennie shedevri*, p. 59.
8. *Ibid.*, pp. 60–1.
9. *Ogonyok*, 10 July 1955.
10. *Ogonyok*, 15 May 1955.
11. *Ogonyok*, 5 June 1955.
12. *Ogonyok*, 26 June 1955.
13. Demskaya interview.
14. *Ibid.*

15. AKA, Letter of Mikhailov to CC CPSU, May 1955.

16. Alfred Frankfurter, 'Return of the Dresden Paintings'. *ARTnews* 54, February 1956, pp. 20–5.

17. AKA, Letter of Mikhailov to Molotov, January 1956.

18. APM, Report of the Brigade to Save the Dresden Gallery, 1955.

19. Volinsky (Rabinovich), *Sem dnei*, p. 88.

20. AKA, USSR–GDR Protocol on the Beginning of the Return ..., 7 August 1958.

21. APM, Letter of Volodin and Churakov to Department of Propaganda, CC CPSU, 15 September 1976.

22. APM, Letter of Volodin and Churakov to head, State Committee of Radio and Television, 6 May 1984.

23. *Spasennie shedevri*, p. 50.

24. Chegodayev interview.

IS RECIPROCITY POSSIBLE?

1. *Pravda*, 8 January 1957.

2. Andrew and Gordievsky, *KGB*, pp. 430–1.

3. *Pravda*, 8 January 1957.

4. AKA, Letter of Petrov and Guber to MC USSR, 16 August 1955.

5. AKA, List of Claims of the GDR, 1957.

6. RCPSDMH, coll. 4, inv. 16, file 465, Report of the Commission to the Presidium of the CC CPSU, 30 July 1957; Decree of the Secretariat of the CC CPSU No. 41–29, 23 May 1957.

7. AKA, List of Claims of the GDR, 1957.

8. AKA, Pushkin Museum list of the Most Valuable Art Works in the Special Depository, 28 March 1957.

9. AKA, Information about Cultural Valuables from the GDR in the Pushkin Museum, 18 June 1957.

10. AKA, Information about Cultural Valuables from the GDR in the State Hermitage, 16 June 1957.

11. AKA, MC Information about Cultural Valuables of the GDR, Kept Temporarily in the USSR.

12. AKA, Report to head, Department of Museums, MC, 12 May 1957.

13. AKA, Report to Department of Visual Arts, MC, 12 May 1957.

14. AKA, List of Trophy Objects in the State Hermitage, 16 June 1957.

15. AKA, Information about Cultural Valuables in the Special Depository of the Pushkin Museum Which Are Impossible to Return Because of Bad Condition, 18 June 1957.

16. AKA, List of Objects in the Special Depository Which Must Be Liquidated Because of Bad Condition; List of Objects of Unknown Provenance in the Special Depository of the Historical Museum.

17. AKA, MC Information about the Return of Damaged Art Works.

18. AKA, MC List of Orders on Production of Needed Copies: List of MC to head, Directorate of Exhibitions and Panoramas, 10 October 1957.

19. AKA, Pushkin Museum List of Gold Objects of Trojan Treasure Which Must Be Copied, 30 January 1957.

20. AKA, MC Information, July 1957.

21. RCPSDMH, coll. 4, inv. 16, file 465, Report of the Commission to the Presidium of the CC CPSU, 30 July 1957.

22. AKA, Note of the Ministry of Foreign Affairs of the GDR, 19 October 1957.

23. Konchin, Evgraf, *Eti neispovedimie sudbi*, pp. 283–7.

24. National Archive, Ardelia Hall Collection, Rg. 260, Box 723.

25. AKA, Letter of Guber, Levinson-Lessing, and Vipper to Minister of Culture, 14 January 1958.

THE SECOND RETURN

1. RCPSDMH, coll. 4, inv. 16, file 465, Letter of Zorin to CC CPSU, 28 December 1957.

2. RCPSDMH, coll. 4, inv. 16, file 465, Decree of the Secretariat of the CC CPSU No. 59/99-GS, 'Concerning the Return to the GDR Government of German Cultural Valuables Temporarily Kept in the USSR', 4 March 1958; Protocol No. 143 of Presidium Meeting, 13 March 1958.

3. AKA, Letter of Mikhailov to CC CPSU.

4. AKA, MC Order No. 11, 24 May 1958.

5. AKA, USSR–GDR Protocol, 30 June 1958.

6. AKA, List of GDR Claims, 1957.

7. AKA, Message from Soviet Embassy in Berlin to Deputy Minister of Culture, 19 July 1958.

8. USSR–GDR Protocol, 7 August 1958.

9. AKA, Timing of Publications in the Soviet Press, 30 July 1958.

10. Belokopitov interview.

11. Tikhanova interview.

12. AKA, USSR–GDR Protocol, 29 July 1960.

13. RCPSDMH, coll. 4, inv. 16, file 7.

14. Akinsha and Kozlov, 'Soviets' war treasures', p. 118.
15. *Ibid.*
16. Akinsha and Kozlov, 'Bremen artwork's twisted tale'.

THE ART GULAG

1. Karlsen interview.
2. Demskaya interview.
3. Baldin interview.
4. Vertogradova interview.
5. Karlsen interview.
6. Goncharov interview.
7. AKA, Document on Return of Art Objects to the GDR, 6 December 1967.
8. AKA, Pushkin Museum Information about Trophy Art Objects, 20 April 1967.
9. Goncharov interview.
10. Mravik interview.
11. Goldmann interview.
12. AKA, Protocol on Transfer of Painting, 28 August 1986.

THE BREMEN DRAWINGS

1. Baldin interview.
2. *Ibid.*
3. Nadzharov, 'Yantarnaya Komnata naidena'; Kharitonsky, 'GRU: Mogu kopat'.
4. Kunstverein in Bremen. *Dokumentation.*
5. Baldin interview.
6. 'Rembrandt aus dem Keller'.

THE INVISIBLE BECOMES VISIBLE

1. Akinsha and Kozlov, 'To return or not to return', p. 156.
2. National Archive, Ardelia Hall Collection, Rg. 260, Box 723.
3. Antonova, 'Miy nikomu nichevo ne dolzhni'.
4. Armin Hiller, 'The German contents of the Russian repositories; the German–Russian negotiations' (paper presented at symposium 'The Spoils of War. World War II and Its Aftermath: The Loss, Reappearance,

and Recovery of Cultural Property', Bard Graduate Center for Studies in the Decorative Arts, New York, 19–21 January 1995).

5. AKA, E. Usenko, N. Ushakov, Y. Shulzhenko, Institute of State and Law of the Russian Academy of Sciences: Conclusion Regarding Legal Principles for Solution of Questions Connected with Cultural Valuables Removed to the USSR as a Result of the Second World War. No. 1420224–21154. 9 March 1994.

6. *Berlin (Potsdam) Conference*, p. 371.

7. Conclusion Regarding Legal Principles.

8. Kurtz, *Nazi Contraband*.

9. Conclusion Regarding Legal Principles.

10. Antonova, 'Miy nikomu nichevo ne dolzhni'.

11. *Ibid.*

12. Akinsha and Kozlov, 'To return or not to return', pp. 158–9.

13. Goldmann interview.

14. Hochfield, 'St Petersburg'; Gregory Ingleright, 'Jetzt kommt die Beute aus dem Depot', *ART* 4, March 1995, pp. 30–7.

15. Tolstoi, 'Dvazhdi spasennie shedevri'.

16. Mravik interview.

17. Valery Koulichov, BBC interview.

BIBLIOGRAPHY AND SOURCES

BOOKS

Andrew, Christopher, and Oleg Gordievsky, *KGB: The Inside Story*, HarperCollins, New York, 1990

Berlin, National-Galerie, *Gemälde der Dresdner Galerie: Übergeben von der Regierung der UdSSR an die Deutsche Demokratische Republik, Ausgestellt in der National-Gallerie 1955/56*

Bernhard, Marianne, *Verlorene Werke der Malerei, 1939–1945*, Henschelverlag Kunst und Gesellschaft, Berlin, 1965

Birukov, Valery, *Yantarnaya Komnata: Mifi i realnost* (The Amber Room: Myth and Reality), Planeta, Moscow, 1962

Bokov, Fyodor, *Vesna pobedi* (The Springtime of Victory), Voenizdat, Moscow, 1980

Dittrich, Christian, ed., *Vermisste Zeichnungen des Kupferstich-Kabinettes Dresden*, Staatliche Kunstsammlungen, Dresden, 1987 ·

Domogala, Rosemarie, *Die Rustkammer der Wartburg*, Wartburg-Stiftung, Eisenach, 1990

Elen, Albert J., *Missing Old Master Drawings from the Koenigs Collection*, Netherlands Office for Fine Arts, The Hague, 1989

Grabar, Igor, *Moya zhizn: Avtomonografiya* (My Life: Automonography), Iskusstvo, Moscow and Leningrad, 1937

———, *Pisma: 1941–1960* (Letters), Nauka, Moscow, 1983

Irving, David, *Hitler's War*, Hodder & Stoughton, London, 1977

Kniga istoricheskikh sensatsii (Book of Historical Sensations), Raritet, Moscow, 1993

Kogelfranz, Siegfried, and Willi Korte, *Quedlinburg-Texas und zuruck: Schwarzhandel mit geraubter Kunst*, Droemer Knaur, Munich, 1994

Konchin, Evgraf, *Eti neispovedimie sudbi* (These Strange Fates), Iskusstvo, Moscow, 1990

Konev, Ivan, *Zapiski komanduyushchevo frontom* (Notes of the Commander of the Front), Voenizdat, Moscow, 1991

Der Kunstverein in Bremen, *Dokumentation der durch Auslagerung im 2,*

Weltkrieg vermissten Kunstwerke der Kunsthalle Bremen, Kunstverein, Bremen, 1991

Kurtz, Michael, *Nazi Contraband: American Policy on European Cultural Treasures 1945–1955*, Garland, New York, 1985

Moorehead, Caroline, *The Lost Treasures of Troy*, Weidenfeld & Nicolson, London, 1994

Nicholas, Lynn H., *The Rape of Europa*, Knopf, New York, 1994

Read, Anthony, and David Fisher, *The Fall of Berlin*, W. W. Norton, New York, 1993

Rest, Yuli, and Sergei Varshavsky, *Podvig Ermitazha* (The Heroic Feat of the Hermitage), Sovetski Khudozhnik, Leningrad, 1969

Romanuk, Sergei, *Moskva-utrati* (Moscow Losses), Tsentr, Moscow, 1992

Roxan, David, and Ken Wanstall, *The Rape of Art: The Story of Hitler's Plunder of the Great Masterpieces of Europe*, Coward-McCann, New York, 1965

Seydwitz, Ruth and Max, *Drezdenskaya Galereya*, Iskusstvo, Moscow, 1965

Smyth, Craig Hugh, *Repatriation of Art from the Collecting Point in Munich after World War II*, Gerson Lecture, Schwartz/SDU Publishers, The Hague, 1988

Sovetsky Soyuz na mezdunarodnikh konferentsiyakh perioda velikoi otehestvennoi voini 1941–45: sbornik documentov (The Soviet Union on International Conferences During the Period of the Great Patriotic War 1941–45: Collected Documents), Vol. 6, *Berlin (Potsdam) Conference July 17–August 2, 1945*, Politizdat, Moscow, 1984

Spasennie shedevri (Saved Masterpieces), Sovetski Khudozhnik, Moscow, 1977

Speer, Albert, *Inside the Third Reich*, Macmillan, New York, 1970

Toland, John, *The Last 100 Days*, Bantam, New York, 1967

Trevor-Roper, H. R., *The Last Days of Hitler*, Macmillan, New York, 1947. Reprinted by Berkley, 1960

Die Verluste der Offentlichen Kunstsammlungen in Mittel- und Ostdeutschland, 1943–1946, Deutscher Bundes-verlag, Bonn, 1954

Vishnevsky, Vsevolod, *Sobranie sochineni* (Collected Works), Vol. 5, Khudlit, Moscow, 1960

Volinsky, Leonid [Leonid Rabinovich], *Sem dnei* (Seven Days), Detgiz, Moscow, 1958

Voronov, M., and A. Kuchumov, *Yantarnaya Komnata* (The Amber Room), Khudozhnik RSFSR, Moscow

Williams, Robert C., *Russian Art and American Money, 1900–1940*, Harvard University Press, Cambridge, Mass., 1980

Yurasov, Vladimir, *Vrag naroda* (Enemy of the People), Izdatelstvo imeni Chekhova, New York, 1952

Zhukov, Georgy, *Vospominania i razmishlenia* (Recollections and Thoughts), Vols 1–2, Voenizdat, Moscow, 1974

Zhukov, Yuri, *Operatsiya Ermitazh* (Operation Hermitage), Moscovityanin, Moscow, 1993

ARTICLES

Akinsha, Konstantin, 'Moscow: The secret depositories slowly open', *ARTnews* 91, April 1992

——, 'A Soviet–German exchange of war treasures?' *ARTnews* 90, May 1991

——, 'The Turmoil over Soviet war treasures', *ARTnews* 90, December 1991

Akinsha, Konstantin, and Grigorii Kozlov, 'Bremen artwork's twisted tale', *Christian Science Monitor*, 3 May 1993

——, 'Das Gold von Troja liegt in Moskau', *ART* No. 4, April 1993

——, 'The Soviets' war treasures: a growing controversy', *ARTnews* 90, September 1991

——, 'Spoils of war: the Soviet Union's hidden art treasures', *ARTnews* 90, April 1991

——, 'To return or not to return', *ARTnews* 93, October 1993

——, 'Trophaen der Roten Armee: Die Kostbarkeiten des Berliner Museums für Vor- und Fruhgeschichte', *Antike Welt*, 25 Jahrgang Sonderausgabe 1994

Antokolski, Pavel, 'Vechno zhivoe iskusstvo' (Eternal art), *Ogonyok*, 5 June 1955

Antonova, Irina, 'Miy nikomu nichevo ne dolzhni' ('We don't owe anybody anything'), *Nezavisimaya Gazeta*, 5 March 1995

'Art peril denied by East Germany', *New York Times*, 22 January 1956

Decker, Andrew, 'A worldwide treasure hunt', *ARTnews* 90, summer 1991

Druzhinin, Serafim, 'V dni voini i pobedi' ('In days of war and victory'), *Iskusstvo*, May 1980

Frankfurter, Alfred, 'Return of the Dresden paintings', *ARTnews* 54, February 1956

Henry-Künzel, Ginger, and Andrew Decker, 'Never look a gift horse in the mouth', *ARTnews* 93, April 1994

Hochfield, Sylvia, 'St Petersburg: Will the Hermitage return the Degas?', *ARTnews* 94, March 1995

——, 'Under a Russian sofa: 101 looted treasures', *ARTnews* 92, April 1993

Kharitonsky, Yevgeny, 'GRU: Mogu kopat a mogu ne kopat' (GRU [Military Intelligence]: 'We can dig or we can not dig'), *Kommersant*, 2–9 December 1991

Konchin, Evgraf, 'Tainik Villii Holzdorf' ('The hiding place in the Villa Holzdorf'), *Kultura* 30, July 1994

Kovalenkov, Alexander, 'Madonna', *Ogonyok*, 26 June 1955

Kretschmar, Bernhard, and Otto Nagel, 'Veliki akt druzhbi' ('The great act of friendship'), *Ogonyok*, 15 May 1955

Mikhailov, Nikolai, 'Zagovor protiv marshala' ('The plot against the marshal'), *Vechernii Klub*, 22 February 1994

Nadzharov, Alexander, 'Yantarnaya Komnata naidena' ('The Amber Room found'), *Rabochaya Tribuna*, 19 November 1991

Norris, Christopher, 'The disaster at Flakturm Friedrichshain: a chronicle and list of paintings', *Burlington Magazine* 94, No. 597, December 1952

'Otkritie v Moskve vistavki kartin Drezdenskoi Galerei' ('Opening in Moscow of the exhibition of paintings of the Dresden Gallery'), *Pravda*, 3 May 1955

Ovsyanov, Avenir, 'Kak khranim tak i ishchem' ('We preserve as we search'), *Zapad Rossii* 1, No. 5, 1993

'Rembrandt aus dem Keller', *Spiegel*, March 1993

'Sovmestnoe zayavlenie pravitelstvennikh delegatsii Sovetskovo Soyuza i Germanskoi Demokraticheskoi Respubliki' ('Joint statement of government delegations of the Soviet Union and German Democratic Republic'), *Pravda*, 8 January 1957

Svetlova, Natalia, 'U kartin Drezdenskoi Galerei' ('On the Dresden Gallery paintings'), *Ogonyok*, 15 May 1955

Tolstoi, Vladimir, 'Dvazhdi spasennie shedevri' ('Twice-saved masterpieces'), *Ogonyok*, 10 July 1955

Troia: Kaleidoskop aus der Antiken Welt, Ein Rückblick auf die aktuelle Berichterstattung über Troia aus den 25 Jährgangen der Antiken Welt, 1994

Unverzagt, Mechthilde, 'Materialien zur Geschichte des Staatlichen Museums für Vor- und Frühgeschichte zu Berlin während des Zweiten Weltkrieges – zu seinen Bergungsaktionen und seinen Verlusten', *Jahrbuch Preussischer Kulturbesitz* 25, 1989

'V sovete ministrov SSSR' ('In the Council of Ministers of the USSR'), *Literaturnaya Gazeta*, 31 March 1955

Voennie arkhivi Rossii (Military Archives of Russia), No. 1, 1993

Voenno-istorichesky zhurnal (Journal of Military History), No. 6, 1989

Volinsky, Leonid [Leonid Rabinovich], and Vladimir Perevozchikov, 'Kak eto bylo' ('How it was'), *Literaturnaya Gazeta*, 28 April 1955
Wermusch, Günter, '5 Cezannes, 4 Van Goghs, 2 Manets . . .' *Die Zeit*, 4 June 1993

UNPUBLISHED MEMOIRS AND DIARIES

Boris Filippov (RSALA)
Calvin Hathaway Papers, Columbia University, New York. Rare Book and Manuscript Library.
Richard Howard (ANA)
Hans Carl Rothel (ANA)
Natalia Sokolova, manuscript, never published in its entirety (AKA)
Mikhail Volodin (APM)

INTERVIEWS

Viktor Baldin
Andrei Belokopitov
Galina Belyaeva-Loreni
Andrei Chegodayev
Alexandra Demskaya
Klauss Goldmann
Nikolai Goncharov
Gleb Karlsen
Anatoly Kuchumov
László Mravik
Dmitri Sarabianov
Pyotr Sisoyev
Valentina Tikhanova
Yuri Torsuyev
Maria Vertogradova
Galina Yavorskaya

INDEX